3/97

ALFRED TENNYSON

Literary Lives
General Editor: Richard Dutton, Professor of English
Lancaster University

This series offers stimulating accounts of the literary careers ot the most widely read British and Irish authors. Volumes follow the outline of writers' working lives, not in the spirit of traditional biography, but aiming to trace the professional, publishing and social contexts which shaped their writing. The role and status of 'the author' as the creator of literary texts is a vexed issue in current critical theory, where a variety of social, linguistic and psychological approaches have challenged the old concentration on writers as specially-gifted individuals. Yet reports of 'the death of the author' in literary studies are (as Mark Twain said of a premature obituary) an exaggeration. This series aims to demonstrate how an understanding of writers' careers can promote, for students and general readers alike, a more informed historical reading of their works.

Published titles

Richard Dutton
WILLIAM SHAKESPEARE

Jan Fergus
JANE AUSTEN

Paul Hammond
JOHN DRYDEN

Joseph McMinn
JONATHAN SWIFT

Kerry McSweeney
GEORGE ELIOT
(Marian Evans)

John Mepham
VIRGINIA WOOLF

Michael O'Neill
PERCY BYSSHE SHELLEY

Leonée Ormond
ALFRED TENNYSON

George Parfitt
JOHN DONNE

Tony Sharpe
T. S. ELIOT

Cedric Watts
JOSEPH CONRAD

Tom Winnifrith and Edward
Chitham
CHARLOTTE AND EMILY
BRONTË

John Worthen
D. H. LAWRENCE

Forthcoming

Cedric Brown
JOHN MILTON

Peter Davison
GEORGE ORWELL

James Gibson
THOMAS HARDY

Kenneth Graham
HENRY JAMES

David Kay
BEN JONSON

Mary Lago
E. M. FORSTER

Alasdair MacRae
W. B. YEATS

Ira Nadel
EZRA POUND

David B. Pirie
JOHN KEATS

Gary Waller
EDMUND SPENSER

Barry Windeatt
GEOFFREY CHAUCER

Alfred Tennyson

A Literary Life

Leonée Ormond
Reader in English
King's College London

St. Martin's Press   New York

First published in the United States of America in 1993

Printed in Hong Kong

ISBN 0–312–09597–X

Library of Congress Cataloging-in-Publication Data
Ormond, Leonée.
Alfred Tennyson : a literary life / Leonée Ormond.
p.   cm. — (Literary lives)
Includes bibliographical references and index.
ISBN 0–312–09597–X
1. Tennyson, Alfred Tennyson, Baron, 1809–1892—Biography.
2. Poets, English—19th century—Biography.   I. Title.   II. Series:
Literary lives (New York, N. Y.)
PR5581.O76   1993
821'.8—dc20
[B]   93–2626
                                                              CIP

For Richard

'I thought to myself I would offer this book to you,
This, and my love together.'

Contents

Acknowledgements

Alfred Tennyson was a man who pursued many interests through a long and productive life. As a result, a biographical study of this kind has led me into several unfamiliar areas, and I have incurred numerous debts of gratitude, both to earlier writers and to individuals.

My first acknowledgement must go to Susan Gates of the Tennyson Research Centre in Lincoln. No words can adequately express my sense of her generosity and warmth over a period of several years. Thanks also go to the other members of the staff at the Lincoln City Library.

A number of Tennyson scholars have given me valuable support. Dr Aidan Day suggested this project to me and Professor Kathleen Tillotson, Professor Norman Page, Marion Shaw and Professor Robert Bernard Martin have all helped me in different ways. Professor Cecil Lang kindly sent me an early copy of the third volume of the edition of Tennyson's letters edited by himself and Edgar Shannon Jr. All three volumes have provided me with a source which has been invaluable, and I am grateful to Professor Lang for permission to quote material published there. The only comparable debt is to Professor Christopher Ricks's exemplary edition of Tennyson's poems, and I am grateful for his permission to print a number of passages.

I have, as always, to thank the London Library, and I have also received help from a number of institutions with Tennyson manuscripts and material, including Trinity College, Cambridge, the Bodleian Library, Newport Record Office, Jersey Record Office and the Theatre Museum. I am grateful to Lord Tennyson for permission to quote from letters and other documents written by members of the Tennyson family, and to the Jowett Copyright Trustees for permission to quote from a letter written by Benjamin Jowett.

Friends have answered a wide variety of questions. Among them are Michael Archer, Professor Isobel Armstrong, Sir Nicholas Baring, Dr Christopher Brown, Henry Brownrigg, Professor Morton Cohen, Janet Cowen, Gillian Cumiskey, Oliver Davies, Dr Sophie Forgan, Dr John Harvey, Dr Elaine Jordan, Terence Leach, Catherine Norman, Professor Richard Proudfoot, Dr Margaret Reynolds, Dr Andrew Sanders, Rika Satoh, Gillian Stoker, Virginia Surtees, the

ix

late Lord Tennyson, Rachel Wrench, Angus Wrenn and John Woolford. My head of department at King's College, London, Professor Janet Bately, has been a source of encouragement to me in completing this project, and Dr Richard Dutton has been a remarkably good natured and helpful editor.

My husband and sons have accompanied me on a number of 'Tennyson walks', in the Pyrenees, in the Alps, in Ireland, in the Lake District, on the Isle of Wight and in the Channel Isles. On occasion, they have guessed, with groans, that 'he' had been there before them. Thanks go to them all, but, most particularly, to my husband, Richard, who has helped me to find the time and opportunity to write this book, and whose comments on my drafts have always been pertinent and illuminating.

Leonée Ormond
Highgate

List of Abbreviations

ET Journal   *Lady Tennyson's Journal*, ed. James O. Hoge, Charlottesville, 1981.
Letters   *The Letters of Alfred Lord Tennyson*, ed. C. Y. Lang and Edgar J. Shannon Jr, 3 vols, Oxford, 1981–90.
Memoir   Hallam Tennyson, *Tennyson: A Memoir*, 2 vols, London, 1897.
Ricks   Christopher Ricks (ed.) *The Poems of Tennyson*, 2nd edition, 3 vols, 1987.
TRC   Tennyson Research Centre, Lincoln.

Unless otherwise indicated, all references in the text to Tennyson's poetry and plays, as well as to the annotations, come from the Eversley Edition of 1908–13, edited by Hallam Tennyson.

1

A Lincolnshire Boyhood

Lecturing in 1983, Philip Collins choose, with some hesitation, the title 'Tennyson, Poet of Lincolnshire', while astutely noting that the alternative, 'Tennyson, Poet, of Lincolnshire', would provide less room for argument.

Alfred Tennyson certainly came from Lincolnshire. He was born at Somersby Rectory on 6 December 1809, of parents both of whom were natives of the county (although the Tennysons derive originally from the Yorkshire side of the Humber). The poet's father, George Clayton Tennyson, was the son of a lawyer who practised in Market Rasen, sixteen miles from Lincoln; his mother, Elizabeth Fytche, was the daughter of a former rector of Louth, a market-town which stands between the spine of the Lincolnshire wolds and the North Sea.

Lying to the east of the old Roman road north, now the A1, Lincolnshire retains an air of remoteness. Pre-eminently an agricultural county, it is marked by a pattern of squared fields, arable land interspersed with green pastures.

In the early part of the nineteenth-century the county, with its wild-looking villagers, struck outsiders as primitive. There were few signs of civilisation. Agricultural development was inhibited by the nature of the terrain. The fen-lands to the south were largely undrained, and the ploughing-up of the wolds was a long-drawn-out process. Transport was unreliable and slow, particularly in the eastern district, Lindsey. Even Louth, with a population of 5000, could not boast a single comfortable inn, and only on the coast, at the newly established bathing resorts of Mablethorpe and Freiston Shore, were there signs of significant change.

On the edge of the wolds, between the towns of Horncastle and Spilsby, Somersby was, in Alfred Tennyson's own words, 'secluded in a pretty pastoral district of softly sloping hills and large ash trees'. (Letters, I, 255) A small village, its one distinguishing feature is a house with four towers, attributed to Sir John Vanbrugh. The low-lying rectory is next door, with a long garden running down to a brook which joins the River Lymn.

1

The setting is peaceful, but there was little harmony in the rectory during the poet's childhood. His father, George Clayton Tennyson, was a deeply disappointed man, whose deteriorating mental state and alcoholism cast a blight on his family. Much of the problem stemmed from his relationship with his father. George Tennyson the elder, coming from comparative obscurity, had made his way as a lawyer, using his earnings to finance a small property empire. He and his wife, Mary Turner, had four children: two daughters, Elizabeth and Mary, and two sons, the elder by six years being Alfred Tennyson's father, George, and the younger, Charles.

It is not unusual for a father to prefer one son to another, nor for brothers to be locked in bitter rivalry for parental affection and estate. In this story, George Clayton Tennyson was destined to be the loser. Charles was the beloved son who came to be regarded as his father's heir. George was packed off to Cambridge to study for the church, a profession for which he felt himself unsuited. His desperate efforts to win his father's affection and respect only alienated the older George, who treated his son quite callously.

In different circumstances, the cultivated Dr George Clayton Tennyson who played the harp and collected old masters and antiquarian books, and took a DCL in 1813, might have rubbed along as a scholarly and secular clergyman. If his learned sermons were incomprehensible to his humbler parishioners, such a drawback was far from exceptional. What rankled, and finally drove him to the verge of insanity, was a bitter sense of injustice. Both he and his children claimed that old George Tennyson had disinherited him, denying his elder son both the money and the position which rightly belonged to the first born. In simplified terms, old George did give his elder son the family inheritance, but he reserved for his younger son the fortune he had earned himself. Charles became a member of Parliament, and local grandee, while his brother's family slid down the social tree. When Charles changed his name to Tennyson d'Eyncourt, one of his sons noted with relish that this would distinguish them from the 'hogs', his epithet for George Clayton Tennyson's family.

In 1806, the year after their marriage, George and Elizabeth Tennyson set up home at Somersby, the parish being held with that of the next village, Bag Enderby. Dr Tennyson subsequently acquired two more livings, both in Grimsby. A comparison between Somersby rectory and Bayons Manor, the massive gothic mansion which Charles built, will help to account for the Doctor's violent feelings. His two married sisters also lived in far greater style than he; the Calvinistic Mary Bourne in the substantial Dalby Manor, a few miles away, and Elizabeth Russell in Brancepeth Castle, County Durham, the stately home of her wealthy manufacturer husband.

Eleven of the George Tennysons' twelve children survived into adulthood, and, as the family grew, Somersby Rectory could scarcely house them all, together with the household staff. With the help of the coachman, Horlins, Dr Tennyson added to the house by building on a dining-room in the gothic style. As a child, Alfred slept in the attic with his elder brothers, Frederick and Charles. Here he hooted to the young owl which became a household pet, and the subject of two early poems.

Elizabeth Tennyson was by all accounts a gentle, affectionate and loving soul. Her children found her room a 'kind of Heaven',[1] but she was ill-equipped to protect them from their father's violent swings of mood. She must have been attractive when young, claiming to have had 25 offers of marriage. Nor was she without humour, or a certain flirtatiousness in her attitude to her sons. She loved poetry, and would read aloud to her children Beattie's *Minstrel*, Thomson's *Seasons* or the work of Felicia Hemans. These lively moments, together with a passion for animal rights, give body to what would otherwise be a stereotyped image of piety and endurance. Her eldest son, Frederick, described her as 'tender-hearted and loveable', but not 'imaginative'.[2]

Alfred's 'Isabel' stresses Elizabeth Tennyson's loyalty, and her madonna-like calm:

> The stately flower of female fortitude,
>   Of perfect wifehood and pure lowlihead.
>   . . .
> A clear stream flowing with a muddy one,
>   Till in its onward current it absorbs
>   With swifter movements and in purer light
>   The vexed eddies of its wayward brother.

(11–12; 30–33)

The image of pure water retaining its separate identity in a wider sea is repeated several times in Tennyson's earliest poetry. Here it refers to the union of his parents, but its recurrence must also reflect a deep-seated need to retain identity in a disturbing environment. In old age, he recalled his early impulsion to withdraw himself from the world around him: 'on a stormy day . . . spreading my arms to the wind, and crying out "I hear a voice that's speaking in the wind", and the words "far, far away" had always a strange charm for me'. (*Memoir*, I, 11)

Tennyson told his wife that he had more than once run into Somersby churchyard longing to share the peace of the dead. The alternative to such disintegration and melding was the more painful assertion of his identity. In a sonnet, published when he was twenty-one, Alfred Tennyson proclaimed his determination to express the force of his own spirit, using once again the image of separate streams which join and yet remain distinct:

> Mine be the strength of spirit, full and free,
> Like some broad river rushing down alone,
> With the selfsame impulse wherewith he was thrown
> From his loud fount upon the echoing lea:-
> Which with increasing might doth forward flee
> By town, and tower, and hill, and cape and isle,
> And in the middle of the green salt sea
> Keeps his blue waters fresh from many a mile.

> (1–8)

For Tennyson, water was the governing element. As a child, he found the words 'and there was no more sea' from *Revelation* deeply disturbing. His earliest experience of flowing water came from playing in the brook at the bottom of the Rectory garden. This, the scene of castle-building and mock-tournaments, becomes in *In Memoriam* CI, a source of 'memory' and 'association', like William Wordsworth's River Derwent in *The Prelude*. Tennyson, characteristically, knew that 'memory fades', and that something is always lost. Referring to the family's departure from Somersby in 1837, he sought to transcend the self, and to understand that 'association' is renewed, like the brook, from generation to generation. When the Tennysons leave, the brook will create new memories in the minds of other children.

Every summer, the young Tennysons were taken to the seaside village of Mablethorpe, where they stayed in rented cottages. Even today, when the hinterland is crowded with shops, bungalows and caravans, the great beach of Mablethorpe offers an expansive vision, stretching far into the distance under a cool, open sky. In Tennyson's day, the sense of space and scale must have been far greater. In his 'Ode to Memory' a word-picture from the past conjures up the sand dunes along the coast, and the marshland behind them. Another, shorter, poem recalls his feelings for the desolate North Sea, particularly in an unpublished second stanza:

> I love the place that I have loved before,
> I love the rolling cloud, the flying rain,
> The brown sea lapsing back with sullen roar
> To travel leagues before he comes again,
> The misty desert of the houseless shore,
> The phantom-circle of the moaning main.

Ricks, I, 542[3]

As often happens in large families, the Tennyson children formed themselves into clans within the whole. Alfred was closest to his two elder brothers, Frederick, born in 1807, and Charles, born in 1808. These three shared broadly similar experiences, but Frederick stands slightly apart from the other two; fair where they were dark, educated at Eton, privileged by, but in conflict with, his father. The four younger sons (Edward, Arthur, Septimus and Horatio) were more malleable and more prone than their elders to the prevailing family vice of lethargy. The four daughters (Mary, Emilia, Matilda and Cecilia), by contrast, were vital and characterful. Matilda was somewhat eccentric, perhaps as a result of an early accident, but the other three were exceptionally well educated for girls of their day. Temperamentally, all four were to find it difficult to adapt to the world's expectations of young women.

Tall, carelessly dressed, carrying and often reading books, the young Tennysons were an object of fascination to outsiders. Alfred, it is said, often declaimed to himself as he walked along, seeming not to know whether it was night or day. 'To the aggravation of the neighbouring gamekeepers he would spring all their traps, and more than one of them threatened that, if they caught "that there young gentleman who was for ever springing the gins," they would duck him in the pond'. (*Memoir*, I, 19)

The three eldest boys went first to the village school, and from there to the Grammar School in Louth, Alfred in 1816. Asked whether he wanted to go to sea or to school, 'School seeming a sort of Paradise to him, he said to school'. (*ET Journal*, 311) He lived in

Harvey's Alley with his grandmother, whose meanness was notorious. The headmaster, Revd J. Waite, and his staff brutally thrashed the boys, and Alfred remembered being beaten for failing to remember the Lord's Prayer. Another time, he was hit on the head by a fellow-pupil and sat crying on the steps. He told his son that the only boy who was kind to him was later transported as a criminal. As a grown man, he could not suppress his horror of Louth School and avoided going down the street where it stood. Nor was the education any compensation. The lines '*Sonus desilientis aquae*' (a misquotation from Ovid), two snatches of Homer, and the memory of a wall covered with weeds, were the only good things which he carried away.

Alfred Tennyson left Louth Grammar School in 1820, at the age of eleven, and from then until 1827 he lived at home in Somersby. During these years, George Tennyson's mental state deteriorated. He may have begun to suffer from epileptic fits, and his despair drove him to alcohol. Prescriptions of laudanum and calomel compounded the problem, and the determination with which he set about teaching his children was a further aggravation. They were to be the 'phoenix' rising from his own ashes.

Dr Tennyson's skill lay in teaching classical languages. He gave the boys an edition of the *Iliad* edited by Christian Gottlieb Heyne, a pioneer in the critical study of Greek texts. In later years, Alfred Tennyson wrote on the flyleaf of a volume of his copy: 'My father who taught us Greek made us – me & my brother Charles – write the substance of Heyne's notes on the margin to show that we had read them, & we followed the same command of his, writing in our Horaces, Virgils & Juvenals etc etc the criticisms of their several commentators'.[4]

Alfred's translation of the first part of Claudian's *Rape of Proserpine*, apparently written before he was fourteen, has been described as of 'amazing poetic power', if showing 'grave faults' in translation.[5] The story that he recited four *Odes* of Horace from memory before going to school in Louth is apocryphal, but his surviving translations from the *Odes* and *Epodes* reveal his precocity. In Mablethorpe he projected himself into the world of the *Iliad*:

> Here often when a child I lay reclined:
>   I took delight in this fair strand and free;
> Here stood the infant Ilion of the mind,
>   And here the Grecian ships all seem'd to be.[6]

At ten or eleven, excited by Pope's translation of the *Iliad*, Tennyson wrote 'hundreds and hundreds of lines in the regular Popeian metre, nay even could improvise them, so could my two elder brothers, for my father was a poet and could write regular metre very skilfully' (*Memoir*, I, 11).

Dr Tennyson made little attempt to teach his family mathematics, for which visiting tutors may have been found. When the boys reached Cambridge, they found themselves in consequence at a considerable disadvantage. Alfred, who hated the subject, made little effort to master it. The sciences, on the other hand, caught his imagination. There is a detailed comparison of the eyes of different farm animals in one of his early notebooks, and his lifelong interest in flowers and plants must also date from his Somersby days. From his father's encyclopedias and reference works comes much of the material for the wide geographical knowledge displayed in *Poems by Two Brothers*. He was devoted to the books of Thomas Bewick, and entranced by their woodcuts of birds, animals and pastoral scenes. Dr Tennyson had inherited a passion for astronomy from his grandfather, and he passed this on to his children.

Art history was also on the boys' curriculum. Dr Tennyson wrote out a list of the major painters, with brief explanatory notes, and built up his own collection of Italian renaissance and Flemish works. Among them were a copy of Titian's *Death of St Peter Martyr* (known in the family as *Cain and Abel*) and a *Feast of the Gods*, by Hendrick Van Balen and Jan Breughel the elder, a subject associated with the Trojan War, which inspired an episode in Tennyson's early poem 'Oenone'.[7] Both Charles and Alfred were enthralled by another of their father's paintings, *Armida and Rinaldo with the Decoying Nymph*, illustrating a scene from Tasso's *Gerusalemme Liberata*. According to Tennyson's niece, Agnes Weld, 'Both my uncles . . . have often told me of the influence exerted upon their minds by the poetic dreams that were suggested to them by the beautiful picture'.[8] Charles Tennyson's sonnet, 'Dear is that picture' describes the scene, with the witch Armida prevented by Cupid from striking the sleeping Christian Knight, Rinaldo.

Dr Tennyson's library was another potent source of inspiration for the boys. At the age of eight or so Alfred covered 'two sides of a slate with Thomsonian blank verse in praise of flowers'. Later, he wrote a 6000-word epic in the style of Sir Walter Scott 'full of battles, dealing too with sea and mountain scenery' (*Memoir*, I, 11–12). Tennyson's 'Recollections of the Arabian Nights', published in 1830, pays tribute to the imaginative life conjured up by the book's abundant wealth of exotic names and fantastic events.

The foundations of Tennyson's immense knowledge of English poetry and mastery of metre were laid in his boyhood. He read, and often learnt by heart, any poetry he could lay his hands upon. John Milton was probably the most important influence upon him, together with three eighteenth-century poets, James Thomson, William Collins and Thomas Gray, from whom he derived some of his early techniques in writing poetry of landscape. Thomas Campbell was one popular poet of the day whom Tennyson admired. Another was Sir Walter Scott, whose versions of traditional ballads, 'Clark Saunders', 'Helen of Kirconnell' and 'May Margaret', Tennyson later declaimed to friends at Cambridge. He freely admitted having worshipped Lord Byron as a boy, and graphically recollected his sense of shock on hearing of the poet's death in 1824.

Writing poems and stories came naturally to the Tennyson children. They slid their work under the vegetable dishes to be read aloud later, one form popular with them being epistolary fiction. It was their mother who encouraged them to write. For their father, proud as he became of Alfred's poetry, creative writing was no more than a diversion from classical study. Alfred's gift for story-telling was a useful means of amusing the younger children. His sister, Cecilia, recalled him in 'the winter evenings by the firelight . . . how he would fascinate this group of young hero-worshippers, who listened open-eared and open-mouthed to legends of knights and heroes'. (*Memoir*, I, 5) From an early age, he had determined to become a 'popular' poet, roaming the fields around Somersby declaiming his own couplets.

The two major poems of his early youth are the poetic play, 'The Devil and the Lady', and the Miltonic epic, 'Armageddon', written when he was fourteen and fifteen respectively. Neither was completed, but both are astonishing achievements for an adolescent. 'The Devil and the Lady' is in the style of the English renaissance dramas which 'the brothers and sisters would sometimes act' at Somersby. (*Memoir*, I, 5) It is uncharacteristically full-blooded. Magus, a necromancer, is so worried about leaving his young wife, Amoret, on her own while he goes on a journey that he persuades the devil to protect her virtue.

The solemn 'Armageddon' is very different, an account of the last days of the world:

In the East
Broad rose the moon, first like a beacon-flame
Seen on the far horizon's utmost verge,
Or red eruption from the fissured cone
Of Cotopaxi's cloud-capt altitude;
Then with dilated orb and marked with lines
Of mazy red athwart her shadowy face,
Sickly, as though her secret eyes beheld
Witchcraft's abominations, and the spells
Of sorcerers, what time they summon up
From out the stilly chambers of the earth
Obscene, inutterable phantasies.

(Ricks, I, 78–9)

A young angel appears to the poet, who feels his soul becoming 'godlike', and ascends to a lofty viewpoint. From here he sees, with visionary power, the whole surface of the earth. When the poem breaks off, the watcher is still awaiting the outcome:

As if the great soul of the Universe
Heaved with tumultuous throbbings on the vast
Suspense of some grand issue.

(Ricks, I, 85)

Many of the books from Dr Tennyson's library survive in the Tennyson Research Centre in Lincoln, but by no means all. The young Tennysons were avid readers of contemporary fiction, and Alfred remembered reading novels as he ate the fruit among the gooseberry bushes. In 1831, when Arthur Hallam mentioned to him that he was reading Charlotte Smith's *The Old Manor House* (1793), the poet replied, 'We were all brought up on that book!'[9] The novel, with its secret, threatened world of love, its rescuing hero and its isolated maiden, has distant affinities with 'The Lady of Shalott'. Tennyson's taste for novel-reading was lifelong. His particular favourite being Jane Austen, whose characters he believed came closer to those of Shakespeare in 'realism and life-likeness' than those of any other writer. (*Memoir*, II, 372)

That the Tennysons knew the work of Ann Radcliffe is clear from

references in *Poems by Two Brothers*, the volume published by Charles
and Alfred in 1827. At this period, Alfred was passing through a
fashionable gothic phase. A brother remembered him forming 'with
clay a Gothic archway in the bole of an old tree'. (*Memoir*, I, 17) The
quotations from Ann Radcliffe with which Tennyson annotated his
early poems are full of exaggerated emotion. He introduced 'The
Passions' with a passage from *The Mysteries of Udolpho*,: 'You have
passions in your heart – scorpions; they sleep now – beware how
you awaken them! they will sting you even to death'. (Ricks, I, 150)
A pompous note to another poem, 'On Sublimity', quotes from
Radcliffe's *The Romance of the Forest* (1791).

'On Sublimity' clearly reflects Tennyson's reading of Edmund
Burke's famous essay, 'A Philosophical Inquiry into the Sublime and
the Beautiful' of 1756, which he misquotes in another 'learned' footnote: 'According to Burke, a low tremulous intermitted sound is
conducive to the sublime'. (Ricks, I, 130) Burke's essay distinguishes
between the sublime, which is the object of terror, fear and wonder,
and the beautiful, which is, by contrast, smooth and pleasing. His
assertion that aesthetic reactions are the product of sensation and
therefore empirically observable and predictable was scorned by the
romantic poets, but his concept of the sublime deeply influenced the
taste of the period.

Tennyson, true to his time, often consciously affects sublimity.
Not having travelled further than Cambridge before 1827, he must
have derived his ideas of savage scenery from earlier writers or from
travel works. The same sources presumably lie behind his doom-
laden references to fallen cities and civilisations, and to devastating
military defeats.

Poems by Two Brothers, of 1827, is a less original work than either
'The Devil and the Lady' or 'Armageddon'. It contains over forty
poems by Alfred, rather more by Charles and a handful by Frederick.
The publishers were Jacksons of Louth, who reputedly gave the
authors £20, half in books. The gesture was a generous one. Although the volume received two polite notices, it did not sell out
until Alfred became famous. Delighted with their first publication,
the authors hired a cab to drive them to Mablethorpe, and 'shared
their triumph with the winds and waves'. (*Memoir*, I, 23)

Two months later, Alfred and Charles travelled with their mother
to London, where, according to their aunt, only Westminster Abbey
'particularly charmed' Alfred: 'it suited the *pensive* habit of his soul'.[10]
Forty-five years later Tennyson told James Mangles that he 'had

gone up St Paul's as a boy, had a clear recollection of sitting outside the Ball'.[11] St Paul's and Westminster Abbey remained favourite places.

The visit to London probably reflects the worsening circumstances at home. During the autumn Dr Tennyson's violence became a subject of anxiety on both sides of the family, and, in November, he was sent off to France to visit friends. In the same month, Alfred joined Charles at Cambridge.

2

Cambridge

Tennyson arrived in Cambridge on 9 September 1827. On the first evening he was so appalled by 'the noise, the lights and the lines of strange faces'[1] in Trinity hall that he fled from the scene. William Hepworth Thompson, who noticed his departure, at once decided that he must be a poet. In his undergraduate days, Tennyson's rough dress, often far from clean, long untidy hair, and strong Lincolnshire accent, singled him out as an oddity at one of the smartest of Cambridge colleges.

Tennyson was fortunate to have two brothers already in residence. He began by sharing lodgings with both of them, and then moved to Trumpington Street with Charles. Alfred kept a snake which one night disappeared through a hole in the floorboards. 'He laid hold of its tail – heard two of its ribs crack, then left hold. The landlady of his lodgings said she would have up the boards'.[2]

A letter written in Tennyson's second term, for all its consciously affected melancholy, tells the reader a good deal about his attitude to the university and sense of solitude:

> I am sitting Owl-like and solitary in my rooms (nothing between me and the stars but a stratum of tiles) the hoof of the steed, the roll of the wheel the shouts of a drunken Gown and drunken Town come up from below with a sea-like murmur . . . I know not how it is but I feel isolated here in the midst of society. The country is so disgustingly level, the revelry of the place so monotonous, the studies of the University so uninteresting, so much matter of fact.
>
> (*Letters*, I, 22–3)

Educationally, Cambridge had little to offer Tennyson. Woefully ignorant of mathematics, he made no effort to improve, and his tutor, William Whewell, turned a blind eye when he read a volume of Virgil under his desk. There had been a classical tripos since 1824,

12

but the examination could be undertaken only after achieving the mathematical qualification. Old George Tennyson had recommended a clerical career for Alfred and his brothers, and a degree would have been an essential qualification for this. As it was, he went down without one.

There is little evidence in Tennyson's poetry that the city of Cambridge made much impression on him. The undergraduate sonnet, 'Lines on Cambridge of 1830', succinctly conjures up the ancient buildings and traditions of Cambridge, but only as a means of denigrating irresponsible academics, whose ideas are as antiquated as their surroundings.

Tennyson was not alone in his criticism of the manner and matter of education in Cambridge. It was generally accepted among the livelier students that parts of the syllabus were out-of-date. Religious teaching centred on William Paley's *Evidences of Christianity*, a work of natural theology, which found evidence for the existence of a designer (God) in the contemplation of the external world. Although Paley's observations were remarkably accurate, the book's dry and rational style was redolent of the studied attitudes of the unreformed Church of England. By the late 1820s, at least a quarter of a century had passed since the great evangelical revival, and even longer since John Wesley had brought enthusiasm back to the religious life. If 1833, faith was on the march once more, among the High Church zealots who founded the Oxford movement. Attitudes hardened, and the churches were riven by dissension for the rest of the century.

Cambridge, by contrast with Oxford, was something of an evangelical stronghold. Arthur Hallam commented with surprise upon the strength of anti-Catholic feeling in the University. The Low-Church movement centred on Holy Trinity Church, where a fellow of King's College, Charles Simeon, was vicar. Tennyson's dramatic monologue, 'St Simeon Stylites', written in 1833, may contain a covert satire on the excesses of the Simeonites or Sims. If so, the poem rises above the limitations of its subject. The saint, rejoicing in the self-inflicted pain which attracts the reverence of others, speaks with a fervour which can almost convince the reader:

> O Lord, thou knowest what a man I am;
> A sinful man, conceived and born in sin:
> 'Tis their own doing; this is none of mine;

> Lay it not to me. Am I to blame for this,
> That here come those that worship me?

(119–23)

Frustration with establishment dryness was one stimulus behind the foundation of the Cambridge Conversazione Society, the debating group whose members were known familiarly as 'The Apostles'. The Society was formed in 1820 and Tennyson was elected to membership in 1829. Such debating groups were a feature of early nineteenth-century life. By challenging accepted judgements and beliefs, the Apostles came to be associated with intellectual excellence. To hostile outsiders, they represented a mutual admiration society, self-righteous and exclusive, but, among themselves, the members were as boisterous and high-spirited as other undergraduates.

Among the first generation of Apostles Frederick Denison Maurice had been a dominant voice. Brought up in a household divided by religious differences, Maurice had a personal need to create synthesis and harmony. His lifelong search for religious unity eventually made him a radical figure within the Church of England. For all his denials, he is often described as the leader of the 'Broad Church' movement, a group within the Church whose ideas derived in part from the teachings of Samuel Taylor Coleridge.

Long past his great period as a poet, Coleridge influenced the Apostles through his philosophical and religious writings. He advocated a broad response to religious problems, cutting through the textual arguments which dominated the thinking of biblical scholars, and refusing to be drawn into narrow sectarianism. Growth must come from within: 'Christianity is not a theory, or a speculation; but a life; – not a philosophy of life, but a life and a living process'.[3]

Like other romantic writers, Coleridge emphatically rejected the rationalism and empiricism of eighteenth-century philosophy. For him, the mind was not a blank to be filled by the evidence of the senses, but subject to influences from outside the limits of objective experience. During his studies in Germany Coleridge had absorbed some of the ideas of Immanuel Kant, and it was in part through Coleridge's influence that German idealist philosophy had such a marked impact on progressive thinking in Cambridge.[4]

Tennyson was no intellectual. He rarely entered into debate with the Apostles, but listened by the hour. In 1874, he told a questioner:

'I have but a gleam of Kant, and have hardly turned a page of Hegel, almost all that I know of him having come to me "obiter" and obscurely thro' the talk of others; and I have never delivered myself to dialectics' (*Memoir*, II, 158). Tennyson read Hegel's *Philosophy of History* with his wife in 1858, and, twelve years later, she records that he read to her sections of Kant's *Prolegomena*, the work, originally published in 1783, in which Kant summarised the central arguments of his *Critique of Pure Reason* of 1781.

Kant's philosophy found ready acceptance in the religious climate of the 1820s, because it allowed concepts of morality and free will to co-exist with metaphysical and religious beliefs. A practising Christian himself, Kant argued that if questions cannot be decided by objective proof, then it is not improper to decide them by faith. Some kinds of reality lie outside the world of human experience, and by contrast with this reality the material world can seem ephemeral or illusory. This, together with Kant's assertion that space and time are dimensions imposed upon us by our own sensibility, which do not exist in and for themselves, bears some relation to Tennyson's thinking.

Such divisions between the material and the 'real' (often interpreted within a Platonic framework), are a commonplace in the poems of Percy Bysshe Shelley, which Tennyson came to know well in Cambridge. Shelley's 'Adonais' sets up a clear counterpoint between the knowable, and so incomplete, world of the senses, and the 'real' world beyond:

> The One remains, the many change and pass;
> Heaven's light forever shines, Earth's shadows fly;
> Life, like a dome of many-coloured glass,
> Stains the white radiance of Eternity,
> Until Death tramples it to fragments.[5]

From first to last, Tennyson was drawn, like the romantics, to the idea of a 'reality' beyond the concrete world. It could be argued that he did not need the theories of Kant and Shelley, or of his Apostolic friends, to supplement his own mystical impulses.

The term 'Cambridge network' has been applied to the men who upheld the thinking of Coleridge and Maurice. Among them were Julius Charles Hare and Connop Thirlwall, both fellows of Trinity. In the next generation, the members of an inner group among the Apostles were nicknamed 'the mystics'. These were followers of

Maurice and of John Sterling, generally recognised as the most brilliant Apostle of the 1820s. The progressive King Edward's Grammar School at Bury St Edmunds provided one cell of mystics, among them John Mitchell Kemble (a member of the famous acting family), William Bodham Donne, James Spedding and Joseph Williams Blakesley. All four joined the circle of Tennyson's close friends.

Though many of the Apostles came from noncomformist backgrounds, religious doubt was endemic among them. Tennyson's friend, Richard Chenevix Trench, for example, was to suffer a severe loss of faith before entering the church in 1832 and rising to become Archbishop of Dublin. Arthur Hallam, another victim of this crisis of faith, explored his feelings of spiritual depression in a series of poems written just before he met Tennyson in 1829. Tennyson's 'Supposed Confessions of a Second-Rate Sensitive Mind not in unity with itself', was his first major contribution to the literature of doubt.

Tennyson attempted to distance himself from his poem by using the word 'supposed', and by attributing mediocrity to his hypothetical narrator. The wish to believe, coupled with an inability to do so, creates a mood of deep insecurity very characteristic of Tennyson and his friends:

> too forlorn,
> Too shaken: my own weakness fools
> My judgment, and my spirit whirls,
> Moved from beneath with doubt and fear.

(135–8)

In comparison with the controlled arguments of Tennyson's later religious dialogues in 'The Two Voices', or *In Memoriam*, 'Supposed Confessions' is a stilted presentation of a number of dramatised attitudes. For this reason perhaps, its most telling lines are those in which the poet puts himself in the place of a lamb bred for the slaughter, living in ignorance of its destined end. It is not the fate of 'vacillating' man, but the sensuously evoked image of an innocent animal which moves the reader:

> In a time,
> Of which he wots not, run short pains
> Through his warm heart; and then, from whence
> He knows not, on his light there falls

A shadow; and his native slope,
Where he was wont to leap and climb,
Floats from his sick and filmed eyes,
And something in the darkness draws
His forehead earthward, and he dies.

(160–8)

Tennyson was elected to the Apostles on the strength of his victory in the Chancellor's poetry competition of 1829. As a member, he was required to deliver a Saturday evening address to the society. After struggling with a paper on ghosts, which he failed to finish, he resigned from the society after only four months. Though his career as an Apostle appeared to have ended dismally, his loyal friends rallied round, and adopted him as the unofficial poet to the society.

Dr Tennyson's insistence that Alfred enter the Chancellor's poetry competition proved to be one of the few sensible acts of his last years. Frederick Tennyson was rusticated from Cambridge in late 1828 for non-attendance at chapel. The rector's fury and disappointment soon involved the whole family. Terrified that he might attack or murder them, Mrs Tennyson and her children left home in March 1829. It was during this turbulent period that Alfred agreed to enter the competition. Not wishing to write a new poem, he sent home for the manuscript of 'Armageddon', and then adapted it to the prescribed subject, 'Timbuctoo'. He even retained the blank verse of the original poem, when the heroic couplet was the expected, if not prescribed, form for entries to the competition.

The African city of Timbuctoo was in the news in 1829. A number of attempts to enter the Moslem stronghold had ended in failure. In 1826, a Scotsman, Alexander Laing, managed to gain admittance, only to be murdered. Two years later, a Frenchman, René Caillié, spent fifteen days in Timbuctoo, disguised as a Mohammedan. Caillié's account, which some believed to be a fake, pricked the myth: 'The legendary aspects of Timbuctoo which had been built up and magnified over the centuries were shattered by the discovery that this fabled city of "minarets, obelisks, and towers" was in reality a settlement of low-built, mud-walled huts'.[6]

In his poem, Tennyson was concerned with this conflict between imagination and reality, seeing the Timbuctoo of fable and legend as threatened by the cold light of reason. He reflects this directly in the lines:

the time is well-nigh come
When I must render up this glorious home
To keen Discovery: soon yon brilliant towers
Shall darken with the waving of her wand;
Darken, and shrink and shiver into huts,
Black specks amid a waste of dreary sand,
Low-built, mud-wall'd, barbarian settlements.

(238–44)

Tennyson discussed his poem with another competitor, Arthur Henry Hallam, who had entered Trinity almost a year after himself. Their two 'Timbuctoo' poems provide a revealing comparison. Hallam also regrets the fading of the imaginative vision, but he remains enclosed within a romantic framework, quoting both directly and indirectly from Wordsworth, Coleridge and Shelley. Like Wordsworth in the 'Immortality' ode, although with less conviction, Hallam rounds off his poem without total loss of hope, as the mythic concept of Timbuctoo continues to inspire the source of poetic power, the imagination.

In Tennyson's poem, the imaginative force of the mythic is also celebrated, but the outcome is different. The city is overwhelmed by an earthquake, and the arrival of 'keen Discovery' signals the failure of the imagination in an alien world.

Tennyson won the prize. He believed Hallam's to be the better poem, but Hallam himself accepted Tennyson's superiority: 'The splendid imaginative power that pervades it will be seen through all hindrances. I consider Tennyson as promising fair to be the greatest poet of our generation, perhaps of our century'.[7] Tennyson, too shy to read his poem aloud, asked a friend, Charles Merivale, to take his place at the official ceremony.

In the notes which Hallam added to his 'Timbuctoo', in response to accusations of 'obscurity', he refers his reader to 'that magnificent passage in Mr Shelley's "Alastor", where he describes "the spirit of sweet human love" descending in vision on the slumbers of the wandering poet'.[8] Many years later, Tennyson told a friend that 'Alastor', which describes a poet's hopeless search for an ideal of beauty only seen in dreams, had been the first Shelley poem he encountered. 'I said "This is what I want!" – and I still like it the best, though one can't tell how much these first loves are to be trusted'.[9]

'Alastor's pride of place in Tennyson's affections probably had much to do with Arthur Hallam. If Tennyson's election to the Apostles was one result of his victory in the poetry competition, his friendship with Hallam was another. Hallam had come up to Cambridge determined to hold out against the Shelleyan tide: 'I cannot bring myself to think *Percy Bysshe* a fine poet', he insisted.[10] By mid-February 1829, when his 'Timbuctoo' was completed, he had capitulated, and in November he was unsuccessfully supporting the Oxford poet, Shelley, against the Cambridge poet, Byron, in a debate at the Oxford Union. In the same month, at a meeting of the Apostles, Tennyson and Hallam both voted against a motion 'that the poems of Shelley have an immoral tendency'. This was the year when Hallam and a group of friends organised the first English publication of Shelley's 'Adonais' – only a few years before Hallam himself became the subject of another great nineteenth-century elegy, *In Memoriam*.

Arthur Henry Hallam was the son of a famous historian, Henry Hallam, and of Julia Elton, daughter of a Somerset squire. The Hallams, like the Tennysons, were a Lincolnshire family, but they had left the county earlier. Arthur's great-grandfather, a surgeon of Boston, was twice mayor of the town. Rising socially, he had sent his son to Eton and Cambridge.

Living in Wimpole Street, in the West End of London, the Henry Hallams were part of a successful upper-class world. Unlike the Tennysons', their burgeoning young were dogged by mortality. At Henry Hallam's death, only one daughter survived him. The appeal and intellectual brilliance of the elder son, Arthur, were evident even in childhood. At Eton, his friends vied with each other for his attention. Two of his intimates, William Ewart Gladstone and James Milnes Gaskell, moved from Eton to Oxford, but, at the insistence of his father, Arthur went to Cambridge. Henry Hallam declared that his son needed the rigorous discipline of mathematics, but there is some evidence that the historian had fallen out with his own alma mater.

As a constitutional historian of Whiggish sympathies, Henry Hallam was inclined to base his conclusions on demonstrable fact, not on idealism or metaphysics. His most recent biographer says that he 'had the reputation of being a martinet to his family',[11] an opinion which his correspondence with his son abundantly confirms. In late 1828, for example, he expressed anxiety that Arthur was becoming too engrossed by the ideas of Coleridge. Arthur's reaction was to try to work out his own 'metaphysical creed', if necessary in defiance of his father.[12] In the following year, he was being warned against the dangers of reading too much Wordsworth and Shelley, an admonition which he ignored.

In the preface to his son's *Remains*, Henry Hallam discusses the tensions between them. He remained convinced that Arthur would have outgrown his passion for poetry and philosophy. Henry Hallam's passionate concern to ensure a successful career for his son mirrored a sense of disappointment with his own. Such interference bred a spirit of resistance if not of outright rebellion. Arthur Hallam's pleasure in the society of the bohemian Tennysons was a natural reaction to the strains and restraints of home life. His early death brought his father's programme of education to an abrupt end, but its results were equivocal, not least for the father who was left behind to contemplate them.

Like Tennyson, Arthur Hallam began by disliking Cambridge, 'this odious place'. 'There is nothing in this college-studded marsh, which it could give you pleasure to know', he wrote to his favourite sister, Ellen.[13] For all his brilliant and sanguine temperament, Hallam was often depressed. Haunted by religious doubts and indifferent health, he longed to escape to the peace of Italy: 'it is a hot atmosphere I am breathing. I dislike, as far as regards myself, the interchange of opinions I have described. I long for repose – I long for leisure to exert my mind in calmness'.[14]

A common love for poetry brought Hallam and Tennyson together, but the friendship which sprang up during 1829 soon reached far beyond the bounds of Shelley and the poetry competition. The bond between them became deep and powerful. Each was able to offer the other consolation through periods of trial and tribulation. Hallam's friendship was an antidote to the family ructions at Somersby, while Tennyson in turn was able to support Hallam through a dark period of religious doubt. Hallam's poetry pays high tribute to the personal and poetical gifts of his friend, his sound judgement and bright future. In a poem addressed to Robert John Tennant, Hallam recommends him to value Tennyson:

> Thou hast a friend – a rare one –
> A noble being, full of clearest insight –
> A man whom we're beforehand with the time
> In loving and revering; but whose fame
> Is couching now with panther eyes intent,
> As who would say, "I'll spring to him anon,
> And have him for my own!"[15]

Jack Kolb is surely right in detecting in Hallam a fear of intimacy. A magnet to others, he feared the dependency which attraction brought. With Tennyson, Hallam stood on equal terms. This friend did not make demands to which he felt unable to respond.

Intense friendships between young men are today construed as homosexual. Emotional support in this case lacked any overt sexual expression. In later life, however, Tennyson felt some need to defend *In Memoriam* and the memory of his friend from such an imputation. He vigorously denied that he had ever addressed Hallam with endearments. Whether sexually attracted or not, the two men were bound by a love that was deep, generous and remarkably unpossessive. They were, like their friends, Robert Monteith and Francis Garden, or Jack Kemble and William Donne, an acknowledged 'couple' among the Cambridge group.

A vivid recollection of them is given by Tennyson's brother-in-law, Edmund Lushington, in a note written just before his death in 1893. He recalled the occasion: 'when Arthur Hallam read in the College Chapel his essay which gained the first declamation prize. The place where the reader stood was slightly raised above the aisle of the chapel; A. T. sat on the bench just below, listening intently to the spoken words'. (*Memoir*, I, 201) Long after Hallam's death, Tennyson predicted that, had his friend lived, he would have been renowned as an orator rather than a poet. It was his power of thought and expression, combined with personal radiance, which Tennyson sought to enshrine in *In Memoriam* LXXXVII. Returning to Cambridge after Hallam's death, the poet stands outside his friend's old rooms, from which comes the sound of noisy entertainment. He recalls the atmosphere of a different time:

> Where once we held debate, a band
>   Of youthful friends, on mind and art,
>   And labour, and the changing mart,
> And all the framework of the land;
>
> When one would aim an arrow fair,
>   But send it slackly from the string;
>   And one would pierce an outer ring,
> And one an inner, here and there.

>   (21–8)

The debate ends with Hallam's decisive intervention.

> And last the master-bowman, he,
>   Would cleave the mark. A willing ear
>   We lent him. Who, but hung to hear
> The rapt oration flowing free
>
> From point to point, with power and grace
>   And music in the bounds of law,
>   To those conclusions when he saw
> The God within him light his face,
>
> And seem to lift the form, and glow
>   In azure orbits heavenly-wise;
>   And over those ethereal eyes
> The bar of Michael Angelo.[16]

(29–40)

By December 1829, Hallam could admit that 'this odious place has been less odious to me this term than before'.[17] He invited Charles and Alfred Tennyson home to Wimpole Street for the first days of the Christmas vacation. The saw Jack Kemble's sister, Fanny, whom Hallam admired, play Juliet at Covent Garden with her father as Mercutio. It was her first great role. The effect of the city on Tennyson was not entirely beneficial, however. It may have been on this visit that he experienced one of his 'moods of misery unutterable', as he realised that 'in a few years all its inhabitants would be lying horizontal, stark and stiff in their coffins' (*Memoir*, I, 40).

The Tennysons reciprocated with an invitation to Hallam to visit Somersby. Two years later, Frederick Tennyson expressed anxiety that their friends, Robert Monteith and Francis Garden, might prove 'rather too magnificent for a little Parsonage in a remote corner of Lincolnshire'.[18] Arthur Hallam fell happily into rectory life. With the absence of Dr Tennyson, family tensions were not apparent, and Hallam found the atmosphere of the household pleasantly relaxing after the strains of Cambridge and the high-mindedness of Wimpole Street. The beauty of the countryside, the company of the Tennyson brothers and their attractive sisters, mild socialising with the local gentry, all proved highly conducive. He paints such a delightful picture of the rectory and its inhabitants that it is hard to believe it the same place as the family battleground so often endured by the young Tennyson.

During the years of their friendship, Hallam took upon himself the role of manager to the genius of his wayward friend. For Tennyson, composition took place in the head, not on the page, and he admitted that he puffed away hundreds of lines in pipe smoke. Hallam was foremost among the poet's friends in encouraging him to recite and circulate his poems, and in offering advice and criticism. Though he could memorise poems verbatim, Tennyson was casual about manuscripts. He mislaid one whole volume, and Hallam copied down an early version of 'The Lotus Eaters' for fear that would disappear as well.

It was Hallam who laid plans for getting his friend's work into print. In October 1829, he developed a project for a joint volume of poems by himself and Tennyson, as a means of furthering his friend's career. Proffered contributions from others were declined. Then Hallam himself withdrew, largely at the insistence of his father, who took exception to the love poems addressed to Anna Wintour, whom Hallam had met in Italy. Hallam put a brave face on it, explaining his decision to Elizabeth Tennyson on literary grounds:

To this joint publication, as a sort of seal of our friendship, I had long looked forward with a delight which, I believe, was noway selfish. But there are reasons which have obliged me to change my intention, and withdrew my own share of the work from the press. One of these was the growing conviction of the exceeding crudeness of style, and in parts morbidness of feeling, which characterised all my earlier efforts.[19]

'Morbidness of feeling' was surely Henry Hallam's expression, not his son's.

The projected volume, now reduced to 56 poems by Tennyson alone, and entitled *Poems, Chiefly Lyrical*, was published in June 1830 by the London bookseller Effingham Wilson in an edition of 600. Publisher and poet took half shares in the book, which was a comparative financial failure. In 1833, Wilson billed Tennyson for £11 as his share in the loss, a sum which Hallam, in his role as manager, assured Tennyson that he need not pay.

Poems, Chiefly Lyrical includes a handful of outstanding pieces: 'Supposed Confessions of a Second-Rate Sensitive Mind'; 'The Kraken'; 'Recollections of the Arabian Nights', 'A spirit haunts the year's last hours', and, finest of all, 'Mariana'. As a whole, the volume seems to express a melancholy, even death-dominated, vision of life. The Kraken is forced out of 'his ancient, dreamless, uninvaded sleep' of dark unconsciousness by the blazing fires of the day of judgement. Rising to the surface, the great beast roars. (l. 3) 'The Dying Swan' mingles pain and pleasure as the bird sings for the first, but also for the last, time. Creativity, these poems imply, is associated with extinction; the song, the poetic utterance, becomes an act of suicide.

Mariana lives in a world of stagnation, and her dreary refrain 'He cometh not', is far from the 'awful', 'jubilant' song of the swan. In Shakespeare's *Measure for Measure*, Mariana, deserted by her lover, Angelo, lives in the 'moated grange'. The relief of marriage comes in the final act. It is hard to suppose that Tennyson's hopeless Mariana will ever be rescued from her solitude. Ian Kennedy's suggestion that Tennyson took the imagery of the moated grange from Shakespeare, but that he had in mind the desolation of Goethe's Mariana, abandoned by Wilhelm Meister, gives a further, convincing, meaning to the poem.[20]

With its images of unused, neglected and rusted objects, 'Mariana' becomes a metaphor for sexual frustration and despair:

> With blackest moss the flower-plots
>   Were thickly crusted, one and all:
> The rusted nails fell from the knots
>   That held the pear to the gable-wall.
> The broken sheds look'd sad and strange:
>   Unlifted was the clinking latch;
>   Weeded and worn the ancient thatch
> Upon the lonely moated grange.

>   (1–8)

The woman Mariana is evoked through her surroundings, and Tennyson's ability to create atmosphere and mood by sound, particularly vowel sound, is marvellously effective. As in much of his finest early work, the poet expresses his own feelings by dramatising the emotions of a woman, and the suggestion that 'Mariana' dates from his first, lonely, months in Cambridge is a tempting one.

Tennyson's friends were convinced that he was the 'coming poet' of their generation. In the early 1830s, there was an obvious place and market for a talented young writer. William Wordsworth and S. T. Coleridge were still alive, but past their best. Walter Scott, whom Tennyson had admired as a boy, had turned to fiction. His most immediate rivals were the woman poets, Felicia Hemans and Letitia Landon ('L.E.L.'), both several years his senior. Tennyson's preoccupation with death, desolation and frustration is characteristic of women writing at this period. He not only adapted their female persona, but in time appropriated most of their public. The immediate problem for him, however, was how to make a mark and be noticed by the reviewers.

Well educated and well read, reviewers of the 1830s were not specialists. There was little analysis of poetic technique and style, certainly not the refined apparatus of literary criticism which has evolved today. It was taken for granted that discussion could range over a wide area, including history and morality. One reviewer of Tennyson's 1830 volume, W. J. Fox, opened his critique with a statement that a poem was 'not less susceptible of improvement than the machinery of a cotton-mill'.[21] What mattered was the content.

We now take for granted the pre-eminence of the romantic poets, but in 1830 this was not so. The heavy-weight critic of *Blackwood's*, John Wilson (alias Christopher North), attacked Tennyson for the same fault which *Blackwood's* had earlier detected in John Keats, a lack of sympathy for the ordinary feelings of mankind. Though Keats's work was to fall into relative obscurity, it exercised a decisive influence over the young Tennyson in its sensuous imagery and rich language, and it was to these qualities that Wilson reacted:

At present he has small power over the common feelings and thoughts of men. His feebleness is distressing at all times when he makes an appeal to their ordinary sympathies. And the reason is, that he fears to look such sympathies boldly in the face, – and will be – metaphysical. What all the human race see and feel, he seems to think cannot be poetical; he is not aware of the transcendant and eternal grandeur of commonplace and all-time truths, which are the staple of all poetry.[22]

Wilson's ideal poet was William Wordsworth, whom he praises for drawing upon the truth of the objective world, 'the great poets put it into language which rather records than reveals, spiritualizing while it embodies'.[23] Tennyson was to face the challenge posed by his great predecessor many times. He reacted privately by describing Wordsworth, 'old Wordey',[24] as barren, prosaic and 'thick ankled'.[25] He valued the older man as a composer of sonnets and of blank verse, 'on the whole the finest since Milton' (*Memoir*, II, 70), but was otherwise ambivalent about his work, mingling general admiration and respect with pointed criticism of individual poems. He had, however, formed his impressions of Wordsworth without knowing *The Prelude*, published posthumously in 1850.

Wilson's review appeared in May 1832, nearly two years after the book's publication. He was provoked to write it by Arthur Hallam's praise of *Poems, Chiefly Lyrical* in the *Englishman's Magazine* of August 1831. This remains one of the best critiques of Tennyson's early work. Following the prophetic line of S. T. Coleridge, Hallam sees the poet as a being apart, for whom popular taste is an irrelevance: 'Whenever the mind of the artist suffers itself to be occupied, during its periods of creation, by any other predominant motive than the desire of beauty, the result is false in art'.[26] Hallam accepted Wilson's counter-attack with equanimity, assuring Tennyson, who was deeply upset, that the *Blackwood's* review would serve to publicise the book. Wilson was not, in any case, entirely hostile to Tennyson's poetry, 'we may have exaggerated Mr Tennyson's not unfrequent silliness,' he wrote, 'but we feel assured that . . . we have not exaggerated his strength – that we have done no more than justice to his fine faculties – and that the millions who delight in Maga will, with one voice, confirm our judgement – that Alfred Tennyson is a poet'.[27]

Romantic poetry was the major literary discovery of Tennyson's Cambridge years. Greater access to books inevitably expanded the frame of reference of his own poetry. A substantial proportion of the work in *Poems, Chiefly Lyrical* is influenced by boyhood reading at Somersby. The *Arabian Nights*, the poems of Byron and Scott, the account of the Kraken by the Norwegian bishop, Erik Pontoppidan, these were among sources either for subject-matter or for verbal constructions. In Cambridge, Tennyson moved into worlds unexplored by his father. Like many of his contemporaries, he was caught up in the enthusiasm for German literature. Goethe's possible influence upon 'Mariana' has been noted, and Tennyson also encountered the German historian Barthold Georg Niebuhr, whose work had been translated into English by Connop Thirlwall. Niebuhr's sociological approach to history, with his scientific method, appealed to the Apostles: 'Niebühr for them was a god, who for a lengthy period formed all their sentiments'.[28]

The more formal studies of Cambridge extended and deepened Tennyson's understanding of classical literature. He was affected by the revival of interest in the *Idylls* of Theocritus, poems where shepherds meet to talk and sing together. It was a passion which lasted. Francis Palgrave recalled how, in about 1857, Tennyson read

Theocritus's 'Hylas' to him, ending 'with that involuntary half-sigh of delight which breaks forth when a sympathetic spirit closes, or turns from, some masterpiece of perfect art' (*Memoir*, II, 495).

At Cambridge, Tennyson was obsessed with a classical theme which had fascinated him since childhood, the story of the city of Troy whose destruction was contained within its creation. According to legend, Neptune and Apollo helped King Laomedon to build Troy, Apollo creating walls through the power of music. When the king refused to pay the two gods, they cursed his city. Various punishments fell upon him, and the city was eventually sacked by the Greeks during the reign of his son, Priam.

The idea of building city walls through the power of Apollo's music suggested to Tennyson a parallel between the lyrical creation of a dream city, and the act of creating a poem. 'Ilion, Ilion', begun in Cambridge and never completed, is such a harmonic work, an onomatopoeic mood-piece with virtually no narrative, no apparent personal expression, and no description:

> Ilion, Ilion, dreamy Ilion, pillared Ilion, holy Ilion,
> City of Ilion when wilt thou be melody born?
> Blue Scamander, yellowing Simois from the heart of piny Ida
> Everwhirling from the molten snows upon the mountainthrone,
> Roll Scamander, ripple Simois, ever onward to a melody
> Manycircled, overflowing thorough and thorough the flowery
>   level of unbuilt Ilion,
> City of Ilion, pillared Ilion, shadowy Ilion, holy Ilion,
>   To a music merrily flowing, merrily echoing
>   When wilt thou be melody born?
>
> (Ricks, I, 282)

'Oenone' reiterates this myth of conception and inevitable death, implicit in the Trojan story. The legend kept its hold over Tennyson's mind for several years longer. In one of the great dramatic monologues of 1833, Tithon, another son of Laomedon, hears the song of the goddess Aurora:

> In wild and airy whisperings more sweet
> Than that strange song I heard Apollo sing,
> While Ilion like a mist rose into towers.
>
> (Ricks, I, 622)

3

Arthur Hallam

Tennyson's undergraduate years were passed at a time of social and political unrest, both at home and abroad. The end of the Napoleonic wars brought about a collapse in the price of corn, caused by the return of cheap imports from Europe, and this in turn created hardship among the agricultural community. At the same time, industrial expansion was drawing workers from the land into the overcrowded, insanitary and disease-ridden towns. Efforts by groups of workers to gain improved wages and conditions through collective bargaining (the start of the trade union movement) were declared illegal. It seemed impossible to redress the social and political inequalities of the time through a system of government that favoured the landowning élite. Reaction to the French Revolution, followed by the war with France, had temporarily stifled the movement for reform. With the end of the war, the movement gathered force once more, and became the dominating issue of the 1820s. Whigs and radicals joined in an alliance that steadily gained ground and threats of revolution added to the mood of change and crisis.

Low agricultural wages in the south of England inspired a wave of arson attacks, with widespread burning of ricks, machinery and farm property. In 1830, rickburners, both from within and from outside the district, attacked a number of villages around Cambridge. Students prepared themselves to defend the university from an assault which never materialised. Among them was the young Tennyson. 'I remember seeing thirty ricks burning,' he wrote, 'and I helped to pass the bucket from the well to help to quench the fire.' The double memory, of fire and smoke and the passion of the rickburners, supplied him with a remarkable image for the wrath of Ida in *The Princess*.

> over brow
> And cheek and bosom brake the wrathful bloom
> As of some fire against a stormy cloud,

When the wild peasant rights himself, the rick
Flames, and his anger reddens in the heavens.

(IV, 263–7)

'Rights' suggests a broad sympathy with the plight of the labourers. Tennyson's divided loyalties were readily explicable, for he had been brought up in an agricultural community, and had experienced the distress suffered by the gangs of unemployed itinerant labourers in the wold country. His own father had expressed instinctive sympathy with the oppressed urban poor, declaring in 1819 that the Manchester magistrates responsible for the Peterloo massacre should be indicted for murder. If found guilty and hanged, their example would serve as a useful reminder to the clergy and magistracy not to exceed their powers.

Liberalism was not Jacobinism, however. Tennyson was horrified by the idea of violent revolution. An early poem, 'Come hither, canst thou tell me if this skull', expressed a feeling of revulsion from mob rule in its account of the sacking of the royal tombs at St Denis in 1793:

(Oh! souls without a thought

Save the blind impulse of the brutal zeal
Which urges the mad populace to vent
Upon the breathless dead that cannot feel,
The fury of their senseless chastisement).

(Ricks, I, 166)

The revolution of 1830, which resulted in the replacement of the Bourbon Charles X by the Orleanist Louis Philippe, intensified English interest in French political life. Radical ideas about the ownership of property, the position of women, and the replacement of organised Christian worship by a new religion of man, had been put forward by Charles Fourier and Claude-Henri Saint Simon. In Britain, their nearest counterpart was the progressive mill-owner and socialist, Robert Owen. Tennyson himself was well aware that inequalities in society were fermenting dissatisfaction, and he understood and feared the 'rapid spread' of Saint Simonism. He told his aunt in March 1832: 'Reform (not the measure, the passing of which is unavoidable) but the instigating spirit of reform which is likely to subsist among the people long after the measure has past into a law, will bring on the confiscation of church property and maybe the downfall of the church altogether: but the existence of the Sect of the St. Simonistes is at once a proof of the immense mass of evil that is existent in the 19th century and a focus which gathers all its rays' (Letters, I, 69).

The first reform bill passed into law on 4 June 1832. On hearing the news, the Tennysons rang the bells of Somersby Church, to the annoyance of the new rector, Mr Robinson. Tennyson's use of the word 'unavoidable' in his letter to his aunt, however, is an indication of his own anxiety. The political poems of the early 1830s, like 'I loving freedom for herself', put forward a case for organic growth, not abrupt disjunction.

Alan Sinfield has shown the ambiguous spirit in which Tennyson exalted his idea of freedom in these poems of the 1830s: 'Tennyson tried to redefine the Shelleyan watchword "freedom", and it drove him into a commitment to the dominant middle-class order. He managed to reconstruct the Reform Bill combination of reaction, self-interest, progress and coercion in terms of a Whig view of history, even as it was happening.'[1] Like his fellow Apostles, Tennyson could admire Shelley's poetry without appropriating his radical political views.

The reform bill proved to have limited scope. The more chronic abuses of the old electoral system were swept away, representation passed from the rotten boroughs (those with seats but few voters) to the new manufacturing centres, but universal suffrage remained only a distant ideal. In the years which followed, groups of radicals, including the Chartists, demanded more sweeping changes. In the House of Commons itself there were still the same faces, and MPs, whether Tory, Whig or Radical, continued to be drawn largely from the ranks of the aristocracy and the professions.

Political events at home and abroad were the subject of keen discussion and analysis in Cambridge. Arthur Hallam took a jaundiced view of the Belgian insurrection, which he was far from regarding as heroic. The abortive Polish rising (1830–31), on the other hand, fired Tennyson's imagination, a magnificent doomed outburst against Russian tyranny which he would recall until the end of his days. He published two sonnets on the subject, apart from some hundreds of lines of a poem inadvertently destroyed by a maid. The

second sonnet, 'Poland', echoes an earlier poem on the theme of
political outrage, Milton's 'On the late massacre in Piedmont':

> How long, O God, shall men be ridden down,
> And trampled under by the last and least
> Of men? The heart of Poland hath not ceased
> To quiver, tho' her sacred blood doth drown
> The fields, and out of every smouldering town
> Cries to Thee.

(1–6)

The cruel and despotic rule of Ferdinand VII in Spain prompted
Tennyson's only foray into revolutionary politics. A liberal insurrection against him in the early 1820s ended with the invasion of a
French army. Tennyson and his friends became involved in a new
insurrection in 1830. Three of them joined an expeditionary force in
Gibraltar, while Tennyson and Hallam agreed to carry money and
messages to a group of rebels in the Pyrenees. It was a risky and
foolhardy adventure by idealists who understood nothing of the
true situation in Spain. They set out in holiday mood (apparently
with Frederick Tennyson) in July 1830. The only evidence for their
stay in Paris is a later comment on Titian's *Allegory of Vanity* in the
Louvre, a picture which inspired a memorable passage in 'The
Gardener's Daughter'.

The friends left Paris shortly before the three day 'July Revolution'
which brought Louis Philippe to the throne, an event which stimu-
lates no comment in their surviving letters. From Paris, they travelled south by coach, through Poitiers, and then across the high
ground of central France to reach Montpellier, near the Mediterranean coast, where they were delayed by illness. After Montpellier
came Narbonne and Perpignan, before they branched off inland
towards the Pyrenees.

Tennyson's response to the southern scenery he now experienced
for the first time is to be found in his poem, 'Mariana in the South'.
This was an oblique companion piece to the earlier 'Mariana', which
'came into my head between Narbonne and Perpignan'. The sterile,
rusted imagery of the first 'Mariana' here becomes that of a parched
landscape, seemingly dead under an overpowering sun. 'When we
were journeying together this summer through the South of France,'
wrote Hallam later, 'we came upon a range of country just corres-

ponding to his preconceived thought of a barrenness, so as in the South, and the portraiture of the scenery in this poem is most faithful.'[2]

When the poem, originally published in 1832, was revised for the 1842 edition, some of the 'faithfulness' to the scene was lost, including the precise description of the landscape south of Narbonne. Formerly a thriving port, Narbonne has been stranded by the retreating sea, in a wide area of stony wastes and salt lakes, bounded to the west by the line of the Pyrenees:

> Down in the dry salt-marshes stood
>   That house darklatticed. Not a breath
>   Swayed the sick vineyard underneath,
> Or moved the dusty southernwood.

> (Ricks, I, 397)

The desperation of the first Mariana is expressed through claustrophobic and obsessive surroundings. Her southern successor is overwhelmed by heat and exhaustion. Her dreams of a lost home, with the familiar sounds of running stream and wind among the leaves, are contrasted to the 'sick' trees and the dried up river outside the house where she is living. 'Mariana in the South' lacks the exceptional concentration of language and image of the earlier poem. As Arthur Hallam put it: 'the second . . . paints the forlorn feeling as it would exist under the influence of different impressions of sense', it required 'a greater lingering on the outward circumstances, and a less palpable transition of the poet into Mariana's feelings, than was the case in the former poem'.[2]

Hallam and Tennyson had arranged to meet the Spanish rebel Ojeda at Pont d'Espagne, four or five miles above the mountain village of Cauterets, in the centre of the main Pyrenean range. Today, Pont d'Espagne is a famous beauty spot crowded with buses, tourists and souvenir-sellers, but in 1830 it was just remote enough for a secret assignation. Seeing the Lusig Pass in 1833, Hallam told Tennyson that it was 'something like the *Pont d'Espagna* . . . a savage chasm, where from narrow wooden bridges slung at great heights from rock to rock, one may gaze at the foaming torrent working its way far beneath'.[3]

Ojeda duly appeared at the rendezvous and the two friends handed over to him the money and messages they were carrying. They were, however, shocked by the rebel leader's announcement that he would like to cut the throat of every priest in Spain. Unconvinced by Ojeda's hasty correction: 'mais vous connaissez mon coeur', Tennyson thought: 'and a pretty black one it is'. (*Memoir*, I, 54)

Their assignation completed, Hallam and Tennyson returned to Bagnères de Bigorre, where they had arranged to meet Frederick Tennyson. In place of Frederick was a message asking them to join him in Paris. As Hallam later told Charles Tennyson:

> we remained at Cauterets, and recruited our strength with precipitous defiles, jagged mountain tops, forests of solemn pine, travelled by dewy clouds, and encircling lawns of greenest freshness, waters, in all shapes, and all powers, from the clear runnel bubbling down over our mountain paths at intervals, to the blue little lake whose deep, cold waters are fed eternally from neighbouring glaciers.[4]

There was no road in 1830, and the travellers had to pass once more through the narrow defile of the Gave de Cauterets, on both sides of which rise steep slabs of slate, some of them with trees and brushwood, others bare. About half way along is the Butte de Limaçon, where a series of waterfalls throw up a cloud of white foam. This was the 'cataract formed by the sunshine on the foam of the torrent of Cauteretz'[5] from which Tennyson drew an image for Paris's smile in 'Oenone':

> And his cheek brighten'd as the foam-bow brightens
> When the wind blows the foam.
>
> (60–1)

Further down the defile, the Vignemale mountain appears, with the village of Cauterets couched below it.

In *In Memoriam* LXXI, Tennyson writes of the conversations they held as they walked along, talking 'of men and minds, the dust of change' (l. 10). This was probably Tennyson's most precious memory of Arthur Hallam, and the valley of Cauterets gave the word 'valley' a special significance in his work. 'For Love,' as he wrote in *The Princess*, 'is of the valley'. (VII, 184)

Cauterets was already a popular thermal resort, recommended for respiratory complaints. Alfred de Vigny, Chateaubriand and Victor

Hugo are among French writers known to have stayed there. Then, as now, energetic visitors walked up past Pont d'Espagne to the Lac de Gaube, a walk recalled in *The Princess*, where Ida is described

> standing like a stately Pine
> Set in a cataract on an island-crag.

(V, 336–7)

Higher up is Hallam's 'blue little lake', the Lac Bleu.

A more extended expedition took the two men to the Cirque de Gavarnie. With its vast platforms of snow, this immense glacial corrie is surrounded by some of the highest peaks in the Pyrenees. The waterfalls are spectacular, and one of them falls, almost without a break, down a rock wall of 1266 feet. Tennyson, who tried to capture the effect in 'The Lotus Eaters', said that he revolved the lines in his mind as he lay and looked up at the falling water:[6]

> And like a downward smoke, the slender stream
> Along the cliff to fall and pause and fall did seem.

(II, 8–9)

The journey to the Pyrenees proved a formative experience in the development of the young poet. It opened his eyes to a new landscape, and quickened his imagination. The first results are to be found in his poem about Oenone, the nymph whom Paris abandoned for Helen. For this he drew extensively upon impressions of the Pyrenean landscape:

> There lies a vale in Ida, lovelier
> Than all the valleys of Ionian hills.
> The swimming vapour slopes athwart the glen,
> Puts forth an arm, and creeps from pine to pine,
> And loiters, slowly drawn. On either hand
> The lawns and meadow-ledges midway down
> Hang rich in flowers, and far below them roars
> The long brook falling through the clov'n ravine
> In cataract after cataract to the sea.

(1–9)

Tennyson and Hallam were not alone in Cauterets for long. They were joined there by friends, and the party returned home by sea, on board the *Leeds*, which sailed from Bordeaux to Dublin on 8 September. The double sea-passage avoided repeating the long and exhausting road journey through France and kept them away from the disturbances in Paris. They were fortunate to find sympathetic companions on the *Leeds*. An amateur artist, John Harden, was travelling with his wife and two daughters, Jane and Jessie. With them the young men 'sang songs, played games, & talked & acted with that more relaxed and more pleasant freedom of society, which is usual in seavoyages'.[7] John Harden's drawings of the group on deck, together with written recollections by Jessie Harden, bring alive this brief episode:

> Mr. Hallam was a very interesting, delicate-looking young man, and we saw nothing of him the first day; he was in the saloon. The second day was warm, and he came on deck, and kindly read to us some of Scott's novels . . . In my father's original pencil sketch Mr. Tennyson had a large cape, a tall hat, and a very decided nose.[8]

The hat and cloak, copied from Spanish exiles in London, were to become the poet's habitual dress, a legacy from the Spanish adventure.

From Dublin, Tennyson and Hallam crossed to Liverpool, and on 20 September they caught the first train to run from Liverpool to Manchester. The myopic Tennyson misread the rails as grooves, recalling the error vividly in a line from 'Locksley Hall', 'Let the great world spin for ever down the ringing grooves of change' (I, 182).

Tennyson returned to Lincolnshire, Hallam to his family's country house in Essex. Both found it difficult to adjust to home life after the excitements of the summer. Henry Hallam was not impressed by his son's adventure: 'he does not seem quite to comprehend that after helping to revolutionize kingdoms, one is still less inclined than before to trouble one's head about scholarships, degree, and such gear'.[9] Tennyson, finding his father at home after more than a year's absence, promptly fell ill. He recovered more quickly than expected, and was back at Trinity in November. Meanwhile, in Spain the situation went from bad to worse. Attacks and risings miscarried, two of Tennyson's friends, Richard Trench and Jack Kemble managed to escape from the south, but one of their party, Robert Boyd, was captured and executed at Malaga in December 1831.

A second journey to Europe in July 1832 took Tennyson and Hallam to the Low Countries and Germany. The journey began badly with six days in cholera quarantine on an island off Rotterdam. Tennyson told Jack Kemble: 'I am bugbitten, flybitten, fleabitten, gnatbitten, and hungerbitten. I have had no sleep for the last three nights and have serious thoughts of returning to England though it were in an open boat' (Letters, I, 77). On their release, they spent several days at the Hotel des Pays in Rotterdam, feeling the joy of liberation in what was then a picturesque old town. From Rotterdam, they back-tracked to Delft, known for the tomb of William the Silent, and to The Hague, with the famous collection of pictures at the Mauritshuis. Here, and in Brussels and Cologne, Tennyson developed his taste for the fine arts, singling out the work of Van Dyck as exceptional.

The countryside of Holland and Northern Germany struck both travellers as 'ugly and flat', but Cologne delighted them, especially the still unfinished medieval cathedral. 'The part completed is very beautiful Gothic. Alfred was in great raptures, only complaining he had so little time to study the place'.[10] Returning in 1846, Tennyson described the Cathedral as 'A fragment, but the wonder of the world' (Ricks, III, 626).

Cologne's churches are renowned, not only for their beautiful stained glass, which ravished the two travellers, but also for their medieval and early renaissance statues, among them an outstanding group of 'beautiful madonnas'. The Gothic paintings of the Cologne School, and of Stefan Lochner in particular, appealed to the taste of Arthur Hallam. He describes a 'gallery of pictures quite after my own heart, rich glorious old German pictures, which Alfred accuses me of preferring to Titian & Raffael'.[10] Hallam's 'Sonnet on an old German Picture of the Three Kings of Cologne', published in February 1833, takes Lochner's *Altar of the Patron Saints* in the Cathedral as its subject. The gallery of 'old German pictures' was either the Archepiscopal Museum, with its collection of medieval art, or the Wallraf-Richartz Museum which housed an important collection of early German paintings.

After Cologne came the quiet university town of Bonn, which reminded them of Cambridge, and then the picturesque splendours of the Rhine. They climbed the Drachenfels, where Siegfried is said to have killed the dragon, 'looked round at the mild vine-spread hillocks . . . ate cherries under the old castle wall at the top of the crag, then descended to a village below, & were carried over in a boat to the place from which I am writing'. This was Nonnenwerth, an island which Tennyson conjectured was a little larger than that occupied by the lady of Shalott, '& the stream is rather more rapid than our old acquaintance that ran down to Camelot'. From their 'cell like' room in the former convent, rebuilt in the eighteenth-century, a prospect opened of the peaks of the Drachenfels and Rolandseck, 'with the hills about Bingen glooming in the distance'.[11]

The second stanza of Tennyson's 'O Darling Room', a poem which brought down much scorn on his head, touches on some of the details of their journey:

> For I the Nonnenwerth have seen,
> And Oberwinter's vineyards green,
> Musical Lurlei; and between
> The hills to Bingen have I been,
> Bingen in Darmstadt, where the Rhene
> Curves toward Mentz, a woody scene.

(Ricks, I, 500)

Nights were spent at Andernach and Boppard, and they must have visited Koblentz, a place for which Tennyson formed an inveterate dislike. At some point in their journey they escaped injury when their rowing-boat nearly collided with a larger vessel. At Bingen, they climbed to another celebrated viewpoint, the Niederwald, before returning north on a steamboat described by Hallam as 'unquestionably one of the damnedest ships I am acquainted with'.[12] They passed through Aix-la-Chapelle [now Aachen], with its medieval treasures, and Brussels, established as an independent capital two years before. At Ath in Hainault, the postillion driving them 'observed upon our having *Virgil* in the carriage'.[13] This was probably not the man who overturned the coach and flung them into a wet ditch. The sprightly Hallam recovered first and gave the decisive directions for righting the coach, to the amazement of a group of local Belgians who had come to help.

The Rhine journey did not inspire Tennyson in the same way that the earlier trip to the Pyrenees had done. Hallam summed it up in an analogy with the gastronomy of the country: 'enough to kill twenty men of robust constitution, much more one who suffers paralysis of

Alfred Tennyson

the brain like Alfred. He has written no jot of poetry'.[14] The climate and country reminded the poet too much of home. It was not foreign or exotic: 'Alfred swears that the Rhine is no more South than England, & he could make a better river himself!'.[14]

James Spedding said of Tennyson that he 'was a man always discontented with the Present till it has become the Past, and then he yearns towards it, and worships it, and not only worships it, but is discontented because it is past'.[15] This characteristic helps to explain the warmth with which Tennyson writes of the Rhine in *In Memoriam* XCVIII:

> You leave us: you will see the Rhine,
>   And those fair hills I sailed below,
>   When I was there with him; and go
> By summer belts of wheat and vine. . . .

(1–4)

After their German journey, Hallam returned to Somersby with Tennyson. He had regarded himself as engaged to Emily Tennyson since the spring of 1830, but parental opposition on both sides had been expressed in a ban on meetings between the betrothed pair until Arthur came of age in March 1832. If the ban was intended to include correspondence, it failed, for Arthur continued to rally Emily with long and affectionate letters of encouragement. Often ill, she was a victim of patriarchal intransigence. Even when the engagement was finally authorised by Arthur's father, her own grandfather refused the dowry the Hallams were insisting upon, and no date for the marriage was ever fixed.

Alfred Tennyson's feelings about the engagement are difficult to guess. Robert Martin ingeniously argues that the powerfully charged passage in 'Oenone' describing the choice of Paris may express the poet's own feeling of rejection, now that Hallam's choice had fallen on another. If this is true, Tennyson was casting himself either as the loyal and deserted Oenone, or as the goddess Pallas Athene, whose offering to Paris is wisdom.

Whatever disquiet the engagement may have aroused in Tennyson's subconscious, he was the natural go-between and confidant between the couple, and must have felt sympathy for them during their protracted engagement. A visit to Somersby in August 1832 only deepened Hallam's melancholy about the future: 'yet, when

I look into Emily's eyes, I sometimes think there is happiness reserved for me'.[16] By the end of August, he was back in Surrey, surrounded by text books and studying for the law. Efforts to persuade old George Tennyson to increase his grand-daughter's dowry were unavailing, and the prospect of marriage seemed as distant as ever.

Tennyson's own situation was as dismal as Hallam's. Chaotic family life at Somersby had taken a new turn in February 1831, when Dr Tennyson became so ill that Charles and Alfred were summoned home from Cambridge to his bedside. Their father's complaint was officially described as typhus, but it was almost certainly a stroke provoked by chronic alcoholism. On 15 March, Alfred wrote to his Uncle Charles: 'All shadow of hope with respect to my poor Father's ultimate recovery has vanished. Yesterday he lost the use of one side. It is evident that he cannot last many hours longer' (Letters, I, 53). Dr Tennyson died on the following day and was buried at a modest ceremony notable for the absence both of his father and his brother.

In a poem written eighteen months later, on the death of James Spedding's brother, Edward, Tennyson recalls his father, the man 'without whose life I had not been'. This is a curious passage, dominated by negatives and statements of absence, but positive in its recollection of Dr Tennyson as a man who smiled and talked with his son:

> One went, who never hath return'd.

> He will not smile – not speak to me
> Once more. Two years his chair is seen
> Empty before us.

(24; 20–3)

Dr Tennyson's death left Alfred, at twenty-one, effective head of the family. He was the only one on whom the others could rely; in his brother, Arthur's, words: 'notable among his brothers for strength and independence of character'. (*Memoir*, I, 17) The impractical Frederick, often away from home, settled in Italy in 1835. The second son, Charles, took orders in 1832 and moved, first to Tealby, near Market Rasen, and then, in 1835, to Grasby, further north, where he had inherited the estate of his uncle, Sam Turner. Charles, the sweetest-natured of the Tennyson children, was a gifted poet. Coleridge, who had criticised the younger brother's work, was full of praise for Charles's volume of sonnets, published in 1830. Unhappily, Charles became addicted to opium, probably during his father's last years. Though he broke the habit at the time of his marriage, he gradually relapsed.

Visits to Charles, his favourite brother, were one of Alfred's pleasures in the unhappy years following Dr Tennyson's death. An unusual glimpse of them together, dating from the early 1830s, comes from one of the reminiscences in W. H. Barrett's *Tales from the Fens*:

> This chap and his brother had been at Cambridge . . . Father used to go miles with them into the Fen, but they didn't do much fishing, he said, because they were always writing verses. One day when they'd called at a pub and drunk a pint that had been in the barrel a bit longer than it should have been, Alfred wrote on the mantleshelf in the taproom –

> > The beer you've sold us here to drink
> > Would rot the inside of any sink

> > Signed C. and A. T.[17]

The younger brothers were a serious problem. Efforts to establish them in useful careers failed, and one by one they slipped back into the safety of Somersby. In 1832, Edward, the most nervous and depressed, was placed in an asylum. He remained a mental patient for the rest of his life. There were fears, fortunately never fulfilled, that Septimus would follow him. Somersby Rectory itself was only a temporary sanctuary, it was destined for the new incumbent, and an alternative family home would have to be found.

Financially the family was at the mercy of old George Tennyson. Dr Tennyson had left 'almost enough cash and easily disposable personalty to cover his debts',[18] but his three eldest sons had all run up sizeable bills in Cambridge, Frederick's the largest, Alfred's the least. Their grandfather decided to cover this by taking bonds from the three young men and their mother, subtracting the interest from their mother's income, and eventually bequeathing the bonds to the younger children. This was intended to compensate those who had had few advantages for the selfish improvidence of their elders.

In May 1831, Alfred informed his uncle that he wished to go back to Cambridge to take his degree. The reply, as reported by Charles Tennyson d'Eyncourt, was unhelpful: 'I told him it was a useless expense unless he meant to go into the Church. He said he would. I did not think he seemed much to like it. I then suggested Physic or some other Profession. He seemed to think the Church the best and has I think finally made up his mind to it' (Letters, I, 59). A degree was of little importance to Alfred, who had no intention of becoming a clergyman. Before the summons home, he had so little hope of passing the examinations that he wondered whether his poor eyesight might allow him to apply for an aegrotat. Abruptly taken away from his friends, however, and thrust back into the constricting world of the rectory, a return to the University offered the means of escape.

The year following his father's death was a gloomy and unsettling one. Tennyson sank into a state of lethargy and despair, intensified by fears about his eyesight. Some insight into his feelings is to be found in the letters of Arthur Hallam. In October 1831 Alfred accompanied Emily to Cheltenham for treatment to a pain in her side. Visiting them there, Hallam reported 'Alfred in such precarious health that I cannot altogether repress my fears about him'.[19] By January, Hallam had decided that Tennyson's real ailment was 'extreme nervous irritation . . . It is most melancholy that he should have so completely cut himself off from those light mental pleasures, which may seem insignificant in themselves, but in their general operation serve to make a man less unhappy, by making him more sociable, and more disposed therefore to receive satisfaction from the numberless springs of enjoyment which the mechanism of society affords'.[20]

Tennyson did not heed the advice, but did leave Somersby when he could, staying with friends in Cambridge or London. In June 1832 James Spedding told W. H. Thompson: 'The great Alfred is here . . . smoking all the day, and we went . . . on a pilgrimage to see him; to wit, Two Heaths, my brother and myself, and meeting Allen on the way, we took him along with us, and when we arrived at the place appointed we found A. T. and A. H. H. and J. M. K. [Kemble]. So we made a goodly company, and did as we do at Cambridge' (Letters, I, 74).

During visits to London, Tennyson and Hallam worked together in Wimpole Street, or walked about, deep in conversation. Hallam was writing amazingly mature reviews and essays which left their mark on Tennyson's own thinking. The two men were often at the theatre, or in the art galleries. The new National Gallery had recently opened in three rooms at 100 Pall Mall, the former home of John Julius Angerstein, whose paintings formed the nucleus of the national collection. Two further groups of paintings, a gift from Sir George Beaumont, and a bequest from the Revd Holwell Carr had been added in 1826 and 1828. The foundation of the National Gallery, together with the purchase of the Elgin Marbles for the British Museum in 1816, marked important developments in the history of the arts in England.

In the early 1830s, the National Gallery boasted a small and unrepresentative collection. Its strengths in particular areas, however, were already remarkable. There were fine examples of Rembrandt, Rubens and Van Dyck, and, among the great Italians, Titian and Correggio. Two of Tennyson's favourite pictures were Titian's *Bacchus and Ariadne* acquired in 1826 and Angerstein's Sebastiano del Piombo, *The Raising of Lazarus*.

Tennyson was a poet of landscape from the beginning. In his work he pictured both the details and broad effects of the countryside. The experience of the National Gallery, with its great holding of works by Claude Lorraine, deepened his awareness of the technical structures through which the painter can present the world. His understanding of these skills is apparent in 'The Palace of Art', on which he was working in 1832, during a period when he was an *habitué* of 100 Pall Mall.

Up to the publication of 'The Palace of Art', in December 1832, Tennyson continued to insert and remove stanzas of the poem. Many of these changes were made in an extended passage describing the pictures on the walls of the palace of beauty. (With its 'great rooms and small' and 'long-sounding corridors', the palace sounds a little like the Louvre.) He conceived of the imaginary paintings in two series, the first landscapes and the second subject pictures. The word 'devise' was used to describe each of these four-line word paintings.

Tennyson's 'devised' landscapes are of different kinds, reflecting his awareness of both old and modern masters. Several touch in the details of the foreground, before lifting the mind's eye to a background of hills and sky.

> And one a foreground black with stones and slags,
>   Beyond, a line of heights, and higher

All barr'd with long white cloud the scornful crags,
And highest, snow and fire.

(81–4)

Each landscape is a small Tennyson poem, where the language
evokes an emotional response associated with the pictured scene.
Crags are 'scornful', the coast is 'iron', the waves 'angry' and 'rock-
thwarted' (69; 71).

Tennyson's myopia played a part in the structure of his verbal
landscapes. They have a sharply realised foreground, and an indis-
tinct, often shadowy, background. Titian was among the old masters
who made striking use of this effect, and Tennyson saw the Ellesmere
collection, which included a number of famous Titians from the
Orleans sale, at Stafford House in London. He was attracted to the
idyllic early pastoral, *The Ages of Man*, rather than by the dramatic
late works (National Gallery of Scotland). Certain lines from 'The
Gardener's Daughter', a poem which also draws upon Tennyson's
experience of Titian's *Allegory of Vanity* in Paris, were omitted because Edward Fitzgerald recognised them as 'taken from' *The Ages of
Man* (*Memoir*, I, 198). 'Then there was a touch of *Titian landscape*,'
wrote Fitzgerald,' (I guessed it, and was right) in the "Gardener",
"Autumn touching the fallows," etc., which I thought and think
threw the living figures better into relief than the Daughters of the
Year, who now pass thro' the Garden.' (*Memoir*, II, 161)

The lines which Tennyson, always anxious about any suggestion
of 'borrowing', removed were:

> Her beauty grew: *till drawn in narrowing arcs*
> *The southing Autumn touch'd with sallower gleams*
> *The granges on the fallows.*

(*Memoir*, I, 198)

The poem describes a young painter's first sight of Rose, the model
for his finest portrait and later his wife. The painter and his friend,
Eustace (a figure usually associated with Arthur Hallam), enter the
garden, and find the gardener's daughter binding up a rose thrown
down in the night's gale. Tennyson undoubtedly set out to emulate
Titian here, saying later: 'The centre of the poem, that passage describing the girl, must be full and rich. The poem is so, to a fault,

especially the descriptions of nature, for the lover is an artist, but, this being so, the central picture must hold its place' (*Memoir*, I, 197).

In London, Tennyson avidly sought the cultural pleasures unobtainable in rural Lincolnshire. At the theatre, the young Fanny Kemble was the talk of the town, and, through their connection with her brother, Jack, Tennyson and Hallam were welcomed into the Kemble family circle. On 20 June 1832, they saw Fanny play one of her great roles, Julia in Sheridan Knowles's *The Hunchback*. Hallam reported that Tennyson 'was in great delight at it: Fanny Kemble acted better than ever, &, I think, *because she knew Alfred was there*. She has lent him her unpublished play, the Star of Seville, which he admires extremely; & so do I.'[21] A week later, Tennyson and Hallam were among a group who spent the evening with the Kembles. They heard Fanny sing her setting of the traditional ballad 'The Twa Sisters of Binnorie'. Tennyson's own version, 'The Sisters', was apparently written soon after.

Social pleasures apart, Hallam's recommended cure for his friend's depression was hard work, 'steady purposes' and 'more regular' habits.[22] He was keen that Tennyson should concentrate his energies on the production of a new volume, instead of publishing stray poems here and there in literary annuals. Hallam took upon himself the task of finding a publisher and of establishing the terms. In May, Christopher North's hostile review reinforced Tennyson's hesitations about further volumes, making Hallam's task all the harder.

The publisher whom Hallam had chosen was Edward Moxon, a self-made man and amateur poet. He owned *The Englishman's Magazine*, in which Hallam's review of *Poems, Chiefly Lyrical* had appeared. The conjunction of Hallam and Moxon proved a fortunate one. Moxon, convinced of the quality of Tennyson's poetry, was determined to add his name to a list which included all the major poets of the first half of the century. He remained Tennyson's publisher until his own death in 1858.

Tennyson was by no means an easy author to handle. There were lengthy delays at the proof stage, while the poet altered lines, and, for all Hallam's remonstrances, removed 'The Lover's Tale'. *Poems* was finally published in December 1832. As with *Poems, Chiefly Lyrical*, the edition was not a best-seller. Of the 450 copies printed, only 300 had been sold two years later.

The contents of the new volume were well known to Tennyson's friends, who had heard them declaimed. 'The Palace of Art' was evidently inspired by discussions among them about the value of poetry in general. At a late stage in the poem's development, Tennyson further revised it in response to their criticism. As Dwight Culler neatly phrases it: 'Since it is notorious that poems cannot be written by a committee, it is very probable that *The Palace of Art* would have been a better poem had it been written by Tennyson alone.'[23]

The palace, built by the 'soul' of the poem, is abundantly rich and beautiful, and dedicated to aesthetic values. Its sumptuousness becomes overwhelming, however, and its creator eventually flees, oppressed by the emptiness of her existence. In one way, 'The Palace of Art' reflects the Apostles' belief in the importance of the poet, but the effect of the poem is ambivalent. The most memorable passages describe the palace itself, high on a crag, with streams gushing out beneath, and incense floating above. This stunning beauty is, however, flawed and life-denying, a source of melancholia and madness. The 'soul' becomes entirely selfish, not caring

> what the sects may brawl.
> I sit as God holding no form of creed,
> But contemplating all.

> (210–12)

Such hubris and lack of concern for the fate of others eventually drives the 'soul' away from the palace into the purgation of retreat.

The dialogue of 'The Palace of Art' takes place in the mind of a woman, and a surprisingly high proportion of the poems in the 1832 volume adopt a female viewpoint; 'The Lady of Shalott', 'Oenone', 'Mariana in the South', 'The May Queen' and 'Fatima' amongst them. Most of these women are isolated figures, tormented by unsatisfied longings. Their creation reveals a remarkable empathy with the feminine psyche, which stands in odd juxtaposition to the claims of Jane Carlyle that the young Tennyson was ill at ease with women, and seemed even to despise them.

'The Lady of Shalott' is said to derive from an Italian novelette, 'Donna di Scalotta', not from the story of Elaine in Malory's *Morte Darthur*. Tennyson's account of a woman alone in a tower, weaving a web, and under a mysterious curse forbidding her to look directly on the world below, is on one level an allegory of the divisions in the poet. Isolated, the lady can create her solipsistic work of art. Once she admits her own sexuality by looking at Sir Lancelot, she is condemned to descend from her tower and die. More controlled than the two Marianas, or the 'soul' of 'The Palace of Art', the Lady of Shalott's doom is more certain. Yet her acceptance of the fate of love releases her from one kind of creativity into another. Like the 'Dying Swan', she sings only in death, but not with the swan's power and force:

> a carol, mournful, holy,
> Chanted loudly, chanted lowly,
> Till her blood was frozen slowly,
> And her eyes were darken'd wholly.

(145–8)

The note of finality struck by the death of the Lady of Shalott is unusual in Tennyson's early poems. Sometimes the well-informed reader can supply an ending. Those who know Homer will understand that Troy will burn, that the Lotus Eaters will be dragged away from the seductions of drugged inactivity. The world of action, which the sailors emphatically reject, is about to claim them again, and their very emphasis upon ease is denied by the rhythmic vigour with which they profess its alternative.

The volume enjoyed a reasonably positive reception. Looking back in the 1890s, Aubrey de Vere, who had been an undergraduate in 1832, recalled his first sensation of disappointment on finding the poems less spontaneous than those in the earlier volume. Slowly, however, he recognised Tennyson's advance in technical accomplishment and seriousness. Edward Fitzgerald praised those poems which he already knew from manuscript versions, but thought most of the others not worth reading, and quoted 'To Christopher North' to prove his point. Hallam was 'so glad it is out. I could have wished many things corrected, & some inserted; but I am thankful for it & delighted with it, as it is. The faults are human; the genius divine.'[24]

Of the reviewers, W. J. Fox praised the volume in the *Monthly Repository* (as he had *Poems Chiefly Lyrical* in the *Westminster*). The critic of *The True Sun* (presumed to be John Forster) ended with this prayer: 'May his youthful spirit never grow old – while it ripens with coming years. His faculty is a great and happy one – and planted in a fertile soil. It will assuredly produce a most rich and abundant harvest'.[25]

To the end of his life, Tennyson took little notice of favourable reviews, brooding on every word of hostile comment. The balance of criticism was not unfavourable to the book, but he seized upon every negative response, suffering acutely from each. That in *The New Monthly* is thought to have been written by Edward Bulwer (later Bulwer Lytton), who accused Tennyson of pretentiousness, and affectation of style. Knowing that Bulwer was a friend of Charles Tennyson d'Eyncourt, Tennyson was outraged.

A more savage review, the most distressing Tennyson ever received, came from John Wilson Croker in *The Quarterly* of April 1833. Croker was proud of his earlier attack on Keats, published in the same journal in 1818, which many believed had contributed to the poet's early death. Croker, like Wilson before him, seized upon Tennyson as a follower of 'the lamented Keats',[26] and meted out similar treatment. Although there is nothing in the review which bears directly upon political matters, Croker, a staunch Tory and a vehement opponent of the Reform Bill, had clearly decided that Tennyson must be a radical. This added fuel to his dislike of the poems themselves.

It has been suggested that Croker's violent reaction stemmed from anger at one particular poem, 'To Christopher North'. Croker, however, had not needed such a pretext. Instinctively, he detected a suppressed eroticism or even erotic evasion in the volume. Quoting 'Oenone', for example, he introduced a pause after the arrival of Juno, Pallas Athene and Venus, at 'Naked they came', and then referred to the lush description of flowers and plants which follows:

> It would be unjust to the *ingenuus pudor* of the author not to observe the art with which he has veiled this ticklish interview behind such luxuriant trellis-work, and it is obvious that it is for our special sakes he has entered into these local details, because if there was one thing which 'mother Ida' knew better than another, it must have been her own bushes and brakes.[27]

Tennyson never forgot the attack. Though he passed it off lightly in later life, telling his son that he had come to regard it 'with some amusement', this was probably untrue. More to the point were his feelings at the time: 'he confessed that he had been almost crushed by it' . . . he 'half resolved to live abroad in Jersey or the south of France, out of reach of these barbed and poisoned arrows'.[28]

An intelligent reply to Croker's critique came from John Stuart Mill, in *The London Review* for July 1835. Mill saw Tennyson as a poet with 'the power of *creating* scenery, in keeping with some state of human feeling; so fitted to it as to be the embodied symbol of it, and to summon up the state of feeling itself, with a force not to be surpassed by anything but reality'.[29] In Mill's view, as Tennyson progressed from a luxuriance of 'sensuous imagery', with the subject sometimes 'buried in a heap of it',[30] towards an advance in 'general spiritual culture . . . higher aims will become more and more predominant in his writings'.[31]

By the time of Mill's review in 1835, however, Arthur Hallam was dead. Tennyson had reached such a point of despondency that he tried to stop Mill from publishing at all, fearing that any reference to the book would arouse fresh attacks. 'He was so far persuaded that the English people would never care for his poetry, that, had it not been for the intervention of his friends, he declared it not unlikely that after the death of Hallam he would not have continued to write.' (*Memoir*, I, 97) Even in 1848, when he was on the verge of great success, Tennyson told a young poet: 'Do not publish too early, you cannot retract' (*Memoir*, I, 278).

Late in March 1833, Tennyson took his eldest sister, Mary, to London to spend three weeks with the Hallams. She went in place of Emily who was ill. Tennyson and Hallam took her to the time-honoured sights: the zoo, the Tower, Westminster Abbey, Kensington Gardens and Hyde Park. Less conventional were the visits to the new Pantechnicon in Belgrave Square and to the Adelaide Gallery of Practical Science in Agar Street, off the Strand. There they say 'wonderful Magnets', a 'Steam Gun' which fired cannon balls and Carey's Oxy-hydrogen Microscope which projected huge images of 'all the horrible lions & tigers which lie "perdus" in a drop of spring water'.[32] Looking into a microscope on another occasion, Tennyson commented: 'Strange that these wonders should draw some men to God and repel others. No more reason in the one than in the other' (*Memoir*, I, 102).

Tennyson had come to London bent upon seeing the Elgin Marbles from the Parthenon, bought for the nation in 1816, and on display in the British Museum. Astonishing as it now seems, the proposal to purchase the sculptures was a controversial one. While a group of artists, led by Benjamin Robert Haydon and Sir Thomas Lawrence, argued passionately in favour of the acquisition, others found little to admire. The connoisseur, Richard Payne Knight, for instance, regarded the damaged marbles as primitive, lacking in those sublime qualities exemplified by the Apollo Belvedere in the

Vatican. That the Elgin Marbles made a great impression on Tennyson is clear from later evidence:

> Sculpture is particularly good for the mind: there is a height and divine stillness about it which preaches peace to our stormy passions. Methinks that, in looking at a great status like the Theseus (maim'd and deface as it is), one becomes as it were Godlike, to feel things in the Idea. (*Memoir*, I, 172)

Throughout the nineteenth-century, Roman copies were invariably preferred to Greek sculptures, indeed they were often mistaken for Greek originals. Tennyson fell into both camps. He continued to admire the Elgin Marbles, taking his sons to see them in later years, but he also liked Roman portrait heads. In his study at High Beech stood a cast of one of the most famous, the so-called *Clytie*, possibly a portrait of Mark Antony's daughter, Antonia. This beguiling female image, once dismissed as an eighteenth-century forgery, is now thought to be a much-restored original work.

Clytie belongs to the important group of statues bequeathed to the British Museum by Charles Townley in 1805. Another is the head of *Antinous*, the lover of the Emperor Hadrian, which Edmund Gosse saw Tennyson contemplating in 1871. 'Tennyson bent forward a little, and said, in his deep slow voice, "Ah! this is the inscrutable Bithynian!" There was a pause, and then he added, gazing into the eyes of the bust: "If we knew what he knew, we should understand the ancient world"'.[33] Sculpture interested Tennyson. He wanted to add a group of vignettes of sculpture to 'The Palace of Art', but found it even more difficult than 'devising' paintings, and only completed drafts of Elijah and Olympias.

After the London visit, Tennyson took his sister home to Somersby. He returned to London in June 1833, after spending the last week of term in Cambridge. Travelling up to town with his friends, he lost 'a portmanteau "full of Dantes and dressing gowns"'.[34] Tennyson was teaching himself Italian (a language which Hallam knew well) with the intention of reading Dante in the original. He bought a French–Italian grammar, and Italian words and phrases were written onto the chimney breast of his Somersby bedroom, only to be washed away by an over-zealous maid.

Tennyson's time in London was spent in what his friend Stephen Spring-Rice called 'a regular Camb debauchery style'.[34] At the end of July he travelled north to Robert Monteith's home in Lanarkshire,

Carstairs, for what proved to be a short, and dismally wet, holiday. Hallam spent part of July in Somersby with Emily Tennyson. On 31 July, he wrote to Tennyson from London: 'I feel tonight what I own has been too uncommon with me of late, a strong desire to write to you. I do own I feel the want of you at some times more than at others; a sort of yearning for dear old Alfred comes upon me and that without any particularly apparent reason. I missed you at Somersby, not for want of additional excitement; I was very happy. I had never been at Somersby before without you.'[35]

Either now, or before leaving for Scotland, Tennyson gave a supper in his lodgings, when he recited passages from 'The Gardener's Daughter' to Hallam, Robert Tennant, Edward Moxon and Leigh Hunt. On what was probably the following day, Tennyson and Hallam were part of a group invited to the home of the poet, Samuel Rogers, in St James's. Rogers's collection of old masters was celebrated, his rooms full of treasures purchased on his Italian travels. On this occasion, almost certainly their last meeting, Tennyson and Hallam again stood before a fine painting by Titian, the early *Noli Me Tangere* (National Gallery, London). Set against a pastoral landscape, the risen Christ appears to the kneeling Mary Magdalen. Tennyson can never have forgotten the occasion, nor the picture.

The mystical imagery of certain passages of *In Memoriam* is close to that of *Noli Me Tangere*, where the emphasis falls upon the impassable division between living and dead. Mary Magdalen's hand is held a few inches from Christ, but his stance and gestures signify the barrier between them. In another of Rogers's paintings, an *Ecce Homo* (by or after Guido Reni, National Gallery, London), Christ's anguished head is crowned with thorns, as the poet imagines his own to be in *In Memoriam* LXIX:

> I met with scoffs, I met with scorns
>   From youth and babe and hoary hairs:
>   They call'd me in the public squares
> The fool that wears a crown of thorns.

> (9–12)

Hallam was to spend the summer in Central Europe with his father, while Tennyson returned to Somersby. Letters arrived, some reminding Tennyson of ground over which they had travelled together the year before. Hallam's last letter to Tennyson, written from

Vienna on 6 September, is full of his delight in the glorious Venetian paintings in the Imperial Gallery: 'such Giorgiones, Palmas, Bordones, Paul Veroneses! and oh Alfred such Titians! by Heaven, that man could paint! I wish you could see his Danaë. Do you just write as perfect a Danaë'.[36]

In the first week of October, Matilda Tennyson picked up the family's letters in Spilsby. One, addressed to Alfred, came from Hallam's uncle, Henry Elton. She gave it to him 'when he was seated at the dinner-table' and 'poor Aunt Emily was summoned to have the news broken to her'.[37] The 'news' was that of Arthur Hallam's death, after a few days' illness in Vienna. Hallam's constitution had never been robust, and his poor circulation had already given cause for alarm. Even with these warnings, his death came as a terrible shock, first for his father and family, and then, two or three weeks later, for the Tennysons. Frederick Tennyson's words, in a letter to his cousin George Tennyson d'Eyncourt, show how profound were the hopes for the future invested in Arthur Hallam:

> We all looked forward to his society and support through life in sorrow and in joy, with the fondest hopes, for never was there a human being better calculated to sympathize with and make allowance for those peculiarities of temperament and those failings to which we are liable, – His loss therefore is a blow from which you may well suppose, we shall not easily recover.
>
> (Letters, I, 104)

Emily secluded herself for a long period; it was more than a year before she regained even her usual precarious state of health. The younger children mourned a man whose exceptional kindness they never forgot. Nearly forty years later, Matilda told James Mangles of the 'amiable' Hallam, '[He] was always anxious to take on expedition her & her sisters'.[38]

Alfred's grief was less dramatic than Emily's, but longer lasting. He had lost his closest friend, the man who had encouraged and organised the publication of his early work. Each of Hallam's friends was deeply shocked by the pointless waste, but Tennyson, as *In Memoriam* makes clear, was shaken into questioning the whole meaning of human existence.

R. W. Rader has pieced together the fragmentary details of Tennyson's movements during the months immediately after Hallam's death.[39] In October, he travelled south to see Henry Hallam

and his London friends. Edward Fitzgerald reported: 'Tennyson has
been in town for some time: he has been making fresh poems, which
are finer, they say, than any he has done'.[40] One account of Tennyson's
mood at this time is given in a letter written to him in late November
by Robert Tennant, who hoped that he could: 'look back upon the
mournful past without that bitterness of spirit which you felt when
I saw you' (*Memoir*, I, 498). Tennyson's spirits were sufficiently
depressed for him to refuse an invitation from Mrs Rawnsley in
these terms: 'It would be of no use to come among you with an
uncheerful mind – and old remembrances sometimes come most
powerfully upon me in the midst of society' (Letters, I, 105). Yet, a
little later, he was attending local Christmas parties, at one of which
Mary and he demolished more than their fair share of a barrel of
oysters.

Tennyson's anxiety that his friend should be buried in England is
the subject of one of the earliest written sections of *In Memoriam*:

> So draw him home to those that mourn
> In vain; a favourable speed
> Ruffle thy mirror'd mast, and lead
> Thro' prosperous floods his holy urn.

> (IX, 5–8)

The body was returned to England by sea in December, and Henry
Hallam wrote to Somersby with details of the funeral, held on
3 January 1834, at Clevedon Church, overlooking the Bristol Channel. For whatever reason, Tennyson had already decided not to
attend. A volume of Hallam's writings was projected, to which his
father hoped that Tennyson would contribute a memoir. Always ill
at ease in prose, Tennyson apparently attempted the task, but soon
acknowledged failure. When Arthur Hallam's *Remains* were published in 1834, the memoir was by Henry Hallam himself. Tennyson
slowly constructed his own memorial, circulating the elegy poems
which he had been writing among their mutual friends.

It would be possible to read *In Memoriam* as an autobiography of
Tennyson's life between 1833 and the late 1840s. However, Tennyson's
own uncertainty about the arrangement of the parts is a warning
against assuming that the overall pattern of dark despair slowly
yielding to the light of faith represents the poet's actual state of
mind.

The elegy poems were not the only ones to be written in response to the news from Vienna. Within weeks, or even days, of hearing of Hallam's death, Tennyson had begun 'The Dogs Howl', 'Break, Break, Break', 'Morte d'Arthur', 'Tiresias', 'Ulysses' and 'Tithon'[41]. He continued to work on 'Thoughts of a Suicide', begun earlier, and later given the title 'The Two Voices'. 'When I wrote "The Two Voices"', Tennyson said later, 'I was so utterly miserable, a burden to myself and to my family' (*Memoir*, I, 193). This was long thought to refer to the period after Arthur Hallam's death, but it is now apparent that Tennyson was already writing this poem of despair during Hallam's lifetime. The dialogue between a voice counselling annihilation and a speaker desperate to find some reason for living, prefigures the arguments of *In Memoriam*, as the voice of despair insists upon man's insignificance in a vast and uncaring universe:

> 'Tho' thou wert scatter'd to the wind,
> Yet is there plenty of the kind.'
> . . .
> 'Or will one beam be less intense,
> When thy peculiar difference
> Is cancell'd in the world of sense?'

> (32–3; 40–2)

Hallam's death accentuated, rather than created, Tennyson's fear of vacancy, his terror that all might be transient and without meaning, and man born merely to be swept away into nothingness. He continued work on 'The Two Voices' with fresh grounds for his desperation. Many have found the consoling ending to the poem, in which a second voice puts forward a case for life, unconvincing.

With less attempt at distancing himself from the poem than 'The Two Voices', *In Memoriam* projects the inner dialogue of the poet. For each of the other four major poems begun at this time, Tennyson adopts a different persona or mode. In three of the four he turned to dramatic monologue for his form and to the classical world for his setting, but in the fourth, 'Morte d'Arthur', he reverted to the objective mode of the narrative poem, and returned to the Arthurian subject matter of 'The Lady of Shalott' and 'Sir Launcelot and Queen Guinevere'. For the informed reader, the meaning of the title 'Morte d'Arthur' is straightforward enough, and the questions which Arthur raises in bidding farewell to his last knight,

Sir Bedivere, are apparently those which were preoccupying
the poet:

> Comfort thyself: what comfort is in me?
> I have lived my life, and that which I have done
> May He within Himself make pure! but thou,
> If thou shouldst never see my face again,
> Pray for my soul. More things are wrought by prayer
> Than this world dreams of.
>   . . .
>   I am going a long way
> With these thou seëst – if indeed I go –
> (For all my mind is clouded with a doubt)
> To the island-valley of Avilion.

(243–8; 256–9)

The dying man, Arthur, can find a way of expressing doubt and
uncertainty. Bedivere, left behind, can only revolve 'memories':

>   till the hull
> Look'd one black dot against the verge of dawn,
> And on the mere the wailing died away.

(270–2)

When Bedivere disobeys Arthur's instruction to throw the sword,
Excalibur, back into the water, it is the beauty of 'memories' he
cannot release. Tennyson renders the hilt of Excalibur with an extraordinary, flashing actuality, expressed through hard consonants.
Bedivere's final act of love, when he can bring himself to perform it,
is to accept, as Arthur does, than an end has come to fellowship, to
walking in the gardens and halls of Camelot, or, as it may be, of
Cambridge:

>   I think that we
> Shall never more, at any future time,
> Delight our souls with talk of knightly deeds,
> Walking about the gardens and the halls
> Of Camelot, as in the days that were.

(17–21)

The fall of Excalibur, 'like a streamer of the northern morn', releases King Arthur from one cycle of existence (l. 139). The arm of the Lady of the Lake, rising from the water, takes back her gift. In 'Tithon', begun at much the same time, the goddess Aurora has granted the gift of immortality, but not of eternal youth, to her lover, Tithon or Tithonus. Now, withered by old age, he begs her to cancel it:

> Release me: let me go: take back thy gift.

> (Ricks, I, 621)

There is much to distance 'Tithon' from the poet, the great age of the speaker, the nature of his relationship to Aurora, but, as with 'Morte d'Arthur', the language, and the mood of acute distress mirrors that of Tennyson himself:

> what everlasting pain,
> Being immortal with a mortal heart,
> To live confronted with eternal youth:
> To look on what is beautiful nor know
> Enjoyment save through memory.

> (Ricks, I, 621)

'Tiresias', begun in late 1833, but not published until 1885, speaks with another voice from classical tradition, that of the seer of Thebes, who has been blinded as a punishment for witnessing Diana at her bath. As in 'Tithon', the speaker is overwhelmed by a sense of the powerlessness and worthlessness of his present existence. The poem opens with the line: 'I wish I were as in the years of old' (l. 1).

Unlike Robert Browning, Tennyson never implies that the listeners in his dramatic monologues are about to reply. Tiresias is talking to Menoeceus, son of Creon, King of Thebes, whom he is urging to kill himself in order to preserve the city from destruction. When the young man leaves to carry out the sacrifice, he acts rather than speaks, dropping 'one warm tear' upon the 'useless' hand of the unseeing Tiresias (l. 159), just as Aurora, having heard Tithonus's monologue, drops her tears upon his cheek, and leaves to bring daylight to the world. In a passage recalling the discussions of the 'Palace of Art', Tiresias tells Menoeceus that virtue lies in action:

> Virtue must shape itself in deed, and those
> Whom weakness or necessity have cramp'd
> Within themselves, immerging, each, his urn
> In his own well, draw solace as he may.

(84–8)

'Ulysses', according to Tennyson himself, represents his most immediate response to the loss of his friend. Like 'Tiresias', it argues for action, even when action means death. Bored by the domestic and public life of Ithaca, Ulysses decides to return to the sea, leaving his son, Telemachus, to rule in his place. 'Ulysses' is perhaps Tennyson's most controversial poem. It has been criticised for the father's dismissive attitude to his son: 'He works his work, I mine' (l. 43). Is this a reversal of the conclusion of 'The Palace of Art', as Ulysses abandons duty for a private spiritual salvation?

> To follow knowledge like a sinking star,
> Beyond the utmost bound of human thought.

(31–2)

There is no evidence that Tennyson intended to put forward a case for such irresponsibility, although successive readers of the poem have detected one.

Each of these poems introduces a survivor, a figure forced to continue with a weary existence. Of the four, 'Ulysses' is the most positive in its argument for movement, for continuing to struggle, and for taking control of the 'lees' of the survivor's life. Its deepest relevance to Tennyson's own predicament lies in the final lines where Ulysses exhorts his men to dare to undertake another hazardous voyage:

> that which we are, we are;
> One equal temper of heroic hearts,
> Made weak by time and fate, but strong in will
> To strive, to seek, to find, and not to yield.

(67–70)

4

The Unsettled Years

In the dark days after Hallam's death, Tennyson continued with a programme of self-education. He bought a number of dictionaries and grammars, with the intention of studying German, Italian and Greek. Robert Tennant reported that 'although much broken in spirits [he] is yet able to divert his thoughts from gloomy brooding, and keep his mind in activity' (*Memoir*, I, 109). Tennyson's plan was to devote the mornings to subjects such as history, chemistry, botany, electricity, animal physiology and mechanics, and the afternoons to languages. Sunday was dedicated to the study of theology, and the evenings set aside for poetry.

Like all such schemes, this was more rigorous in intention than in practice. Some French books were read, among them works by Racine, *Molière* and Victor Hugo, but it was the study of recent scientific texts that seems to have proceeded with most momentum. In the 1830s, science, like politics, had entered a particularly challenging phase. An educated man could keep up with the broad outlines of research, and Tennyson was able to contemplate the dominant issues of the day, in a way quite impossible for a layman today. For the rest of his life he continued to read scientific journals and books, and to translate their lessons into his poetry. Tennyson's scientific references are rarely extended in length, and he does not use technical language to express them. In introducing scientific themes he may have been responding to a demand for more relevance in contemporary poetry, but there is no sense that he is self-consciously parading his knowledge.

Science was no stranger to poetry. Milton and Donne used discoveries in the natural world as a source of imagery, a fact of which Tennyson was well aware. Nearer to his own time, and greatly respected by Tennyson, was Goethe. Allusions to scientific theory abound in Goethe's oeuvre, and the German writer also produced a notable piece of original research, *The Theory of Colours* (Tennyson owned Charles Eastlake's English translation of 1840).

In the 1850 *Preface* to *Lyrical Ballads*, Wordsworth declares that, should science ever become 'familiarized to men . . . ready to put on, as it were, a form of flesh and blood, the Poet will lend his divine spirit to aid the transformation, and will welcome the Being thus produced, as a dear and genuine inmate of the household of man'.[1] For Wordsworth, that day had yet to dawn, and, for many of Tennyson's contemporaries, the advances of science represented a threat: science and art were inimical. The recurrent fear that science would undermine religion also persisted.

Tennyson's rejection of Paley's belief that the existence of God can be proved by the perfection of the natural world is implicit in the negatives of *In Memoriam* CXXIV:

> I found Him not in world or sun,
> Or eagle's wing, or insect's eye.

(5–6)

At Cambridge, Tennyson had been stimulated by more challenging ideas. He was fascinated by theories about the development of the human foetal brain, which suggested that it passed through stages analogous to a progress from lower to higher forms of animal life. A stanza, later deleted, for 'The Palace of Art', summarised these ideas:

> 'From change to change four times within the womb
> 　The brain is moulded,' she began,
> 'So through all phases of all thought I come
> 　Into the perfect man.'

(Ricks, I, 446)

This theory of foetal development implied that human beings were too close to animal life for comfort. In the early nineteenth-century, many leading British scientists were involved in analysing questions of 'origin'. Unlike their counterparts in France, they tried to reconcile their theories with conventional religious and biblical learning. Two sciences were felt to be particularly threatening, geology and astronomy. In a late poem, which looked back to this period, Tennyson called them the 'terrible Muses!' ('Parnassus', 16), and it is these scientific disciplines that he invokes in his poems of the 1830s and 1840s.

Tennyson's growing interest in astronomical research led him into spheres where new discourses were overturning received truths.

Despite myopia, he was remarkably familiar with the aspect of the heavens, looking upon the stars as 'my friends of old' (Ricks, I, 181). Poems from all periods of his work are scattered with references to the constellations, bright stars and planets. Like many Victorians, he was at home with the movements of the night sky, rarely making an extended reference without indicating time and season. In 'Locksley Hall', for example, he writes precisely of a late evening in spring:

> Many a night from yonder ivied casement, ere I went to rest,
> Did I look on great Orion sloping slowly to the West.
>
> Many a night I saw the Pleiads, rising thro' the mellow shade,
> Glitter like a swarm of fire-flies tangled in a silver braid.
>
> (7–10)

In 1796, a Frenchman, Pierre Simon de Laplace, put forward what became known as the 'nebular hypothesis', stating that the sun and the planets were made up of fiery gases still in process of creating further astral bodies. The earth and the planets had spun off from the sun, and, being smaller, had cooled more quickly. As the process continued, earth and sun would eventually cool altogether, and human life be extinguished. It is not clear when Tennyson first encountered the ideas of Laplace, but Arthur Hallam knew them by 1828, and, in 1832, was writing of Laplace and Kant as two men leading the way to 'the altars of true Science'.[2]

Laplace's seminal work, *La Mécanique Céleste*, was made accessible in English through Mary Somerville's translation, published in 1831 in a popular version, *The Mechanism of the Heavens*. She was a correspondent, and probably an acquaintance, of Henry Hallam, and Tennyson may have approached Laplace through her book. His copy of her best-known work, *The Connexion of the Physical Sciences*, which includes a compressed version of Laplace's theories, is dated 'Xmas 1838'. Tennyson's attitude to the nebular hypothesis has been extensively discussed, but without reference to Mary Somerville. As a pioneering woman scientist, she seems a likely prototype for his Lady Psyche, the lecturer who expounds the hypothesis theory in *The Princess*:

> 'This world has once a fluid haze of light,
> Till toward the centre set the starry tides,

And eddied into suns, that wheeling cast
The planets; then the monster, then the man'.

(101–4)

Temperamentally, Alfred Tennyson was attuned to the gloomier
prognostications of modern scientific research. 'Terrible' as Urania,
the muse of astronomy, may be, she holds an exalted position in *In
Memoriam*, and had a deep attraction for the poet. She appealed to
that side of Tennyson's nature which was always drawing him away
from the everyday world into a state beyond the actual, into abstraction. The vast expanses of the heavens provided a metaphor for
infinity. When astronomers suggested that the universe was without
end, stretching far beyond the solar system, Tennyson was divided
between an agonising awareness of the littleness and vulnerability
of man, and an immense creative excitement at the possibilities of
infinite space. In *In Memoriam* III, he uses the words of a personified
Sorrow to describe a universe out of control, and passing towards
extinction:

'The stars,' she whispers, 'blindly run;
A web is wov'n across the sky;
From out waste places comes a cry,
And murmurs from the dying sun.'

(5–8)

New developments in geology presented Tennyson with a more
earthly and, ultimately, a more disturbing spiritual challenge. The
evidence of fossilised remains and of geological strata was less productive of transcendental imagery than astronomy, and it frequently
emerges in Tennyson's poetry in constructed dialogue as hard-edged
as the stones themselves. The issues involved in the geological controversies were similar to those in astronomy. If new developments
in astronomy eventually led to a rejection of the assertions of Genesis about the creation of the sun, the stars and the earth, fossil
evidence seemed to invalidate the Mosaic belief that the creation of
the earth occurred in 4004 BC. It established that the earth was many
millions of years old. Fossils also provided evidence of vanished
species, suggesting that 'nature' or God was capable of misdirection
and waste, and that man himself might ultimately become extinct. In

a famous passage from *In Memoriam*, Tennyson faces his reader with these issues:

> Are God and Nature then at strife,
>   That Nature lends such evil dreams?
>   So careful of the type, she seems,
> So careless of the single life;
>
> That I, considering everywhere
>   Her secret meaning in her deeds,
>   And finding that of fifty seeds
> She often brings but one to bear.
>
> (LV, 5–12)
>
> 'So careful of the type?' but no.
>   From scarped cliff and quarried stone
>   She cries, 'A thousand types are gone:
> I care for nothing, all shall go.'
>
> (LVI, 1–4)

Many scientists of the period, including Tennyson's tutors, Whewell and Adam Sedgwick, were also clergymen, which helps to explain their obstinate determination to resist the conclusions of these new discoveries. Scientific research in Britain tended to be descriptive rather than speculative. The progressive theory, emphasising 'the continuity of progress and the undisturbed length of geological periods'[3] was put forward by Sedgwick and William Buckland. It has even been suggested that Sedgwick's lectures were a direct source for the geological passages in Tennyson's poem.[4]

The theory against which progressivism argued was that of uniformitarianism, slow evolution over a period of ages. Evolutionary ideas are customarily associated with Charles Darwin and his *Origin of Species*, but the theory predates him by many years. By 1836, Tennyson had read Charles Lyell's *Principles of Geology*, first published from 1830 to 1833. To conventional thinkers, Lyell's book was deeply disturbing, and it has been assumed that it influenced *In Memoriam*. More recently, however, it has been convincingly argued that Tennyson was not a Lyellian at this early date, and that his geological references are consistent with the theories of the English, progressivist, school.[5]

Tennyson's poem 'Youth' describes the passage of a river as it flows through different landscapes and changing seasons. Like the image of the path which recurs in *In Memoriam*, the river of 'Youth' gives the poet a metaphor for life's movement from the past into a projected future. Following in the tradition of Wordsworth and of Keats, he outlines a progression from a careless early life, rejoicing in sensation, to a more thoughtful, and more disturbing, state of maturity. Past and future call out to him in conflicting voices, one telling him to look back; the second 'Cried in the future "Come along"'. 'Confused' by their calls, the river 'stays', meandering in the plain. In personal terms, the poet goes back to his home and deliberately cuts himself off from wider experience:

> Now idly in my natal bowers,
>   Unvext by doubts I cannot solve,
> I sit among the scentless flowers
>   And see and hear the world revolve:
>
> Yet well I know that nothing stays,
>   And I must traverse yonder plain:
> Sooner or later from the haze
>   The second voice will peal again.

> (*Memoir*, I, 113)

In a rejected draft of the poem's opening, Tennyson speaks more directly, seeming to relate Hallam to the sun:

> Though what I sought I knew not well,
> I was not made to live alone,
> My heart was never meant to dwell
> Housed like the caddisworm in stone.
>
> I had one true friend, to whose light
> My soul her early tendrils curled,
> For whom my love was infinite
> Who is the mother of the world.

> (Ricks, I, 633)

From Hallam, Tennyson had learnt a capacity to give and inspire love. As *In Memoriam* predicts, his life was a long one, and Hallam proved irreplaceable. Later friends shared some of his characteristics, older ones were valued because they had known Hallam, but none could compensate for his loss.

Tennyson never ceased to enjoy male friendship. After his marriage, he continued to escape to London periodically for hours of relaxed talk. But, from 1833 onwards, women became more important in his emotional life. 'Not made to live alone', he fell in love twice in the following years, first with Rosa Baring, and then with a quite different woman, Emily Sellwood.

Tennyson probably met Charlotte-Rosa Baring around 1832. The daughter of Frances Eden by her first husband, William Baring, she lived at the seventeenth-century Harrington Hall, two miles from Somersby. Her step-father, Arthur Eden, had leased it in 1825. Little biographical material about this period has survived, but in 1962 Ralph Rader published a series of articles illuminating a once concealed area of Tennyson's early life.[6]

Rosa Baring and Tennyson formed part of a group of local young people, including Drummond and Sophy Rawnsley, Francis Charles Massingberd and a local clergyman, John Rashdall. This was a Jane Austen world of picnics, expeditions and dances. Alfred Tennyson loved dancing, particularly waltzing, which must have helped to release some of his inhibitions and inner tensions. The young Sophy Rawnsley, said to be the original of his 'airy fairy Lilian', was a regular partner. Yet even dancing could suddenly leave him with a feeling of emptiness: 'I remember that sometimes in the midst of the dance, a great and sudden sadness would come over me, and I would leave the dance and wander away beneath the stars, or sit on gloomily and abstractedly below stairs. I used to wonder then, what strange demon it was, that drove me forth and took all the pleasure from my blood, and made me such a churlish curmudgeon'.[7]

Within this circle of friends, there were subtle social distinctions. All were gentry, but their manner of life differed considerably, with the Edens and Tennysons probably representing the outer ends of the scale. The Tennysons were perplexed by financial difficulties, they were unconventional and eccentric. The wealthy Edens passed the season in London and Rosa was herself a considerable heiress through her father's banking connections.

If this picture of financial and social disparity recalls Tennyson's early relation to Arthur Hallam, there were few other similarities. Rosa, like Hallam, was the centre of a group of admirers, but she lacked the capacity to recognise Tennyson's quality. Her outstanding characteristic was her beauty. In the portrait by the fashionable artist, Richard Buckner, Rosa is presented as dark haired, confident and poised. With her full figure and broad mouth, she is like one of those Titian women whom Tennyson admired. Rosa is associated with 'Locksley Hall', a story of the betrayal of love, which ends with the arranged marriage of the wavering heroine. Her own arranged marriage, to the wealthy Robert Duncombe Shafto, took place in 1838.

Biographers of Tennyson are divided in their estimate of Rosa Baring's significance in his life. Sir Charles Tennyson was the first to suggest that H. D. Rawnsley's account of a light-hearted friendship in *Memories of the Tennysons* might not tell the whole story. After the publication of Ralph Rader's book, Christopher Ricks wrote of 'a brief and frustrated love, . . . never to fade from his memory'.[8] But Tennyson's latest biographer, Robert Martin, counters some of Rader's claims: 'We can only conjecture about Tennyson's relations with Rosa Baring, but his love appears to have been more imaginary than actual, more dutiful than driving. What finally seems most persuasive is that in later years Rosa was quite unaware that Tennyson had ever entertained any particularly deep feelings for her'.[9]

In fact, it appears that Rosa did recognise herself as the 'heroine' of 'Locksley Hall', and spoke to others about it. As early as 1847, Mary Russell Mitford told Elizabeth Barrett about a conversation with William Harness who had met the heroine of Locksley Hall and her husband. The recently married Elizabeth Barrett Browning nursed a romantic interest in Tennyson, whom she had yet to meet. She replied tartly: 'Well! I dont [sic] agree with Mr Harness in admiring the lady of Locksley Hall. I MUST either pity or despise a woman who could have married Tennyson & chose a common man. If happy in her choice, I despise her. That's a matter of opinion, of course'.[10] This might refer to another woman in Tennyson's life, as yet undiscovered, but Rosa Baring is the obvious candidate.

Robert Martin describes the sequence of rose poems, addressed to Rosa Baring, as 'inert',[11] and declares, with truth, that they lack the depth of feeling of those written on the death of Arthur Hallam. Martin does not include *Maud*, which he believes to have been only partially inspired by the friendship. The sequence of rose poems begins with a conventional address on Rosa's birthday, 23 September 1834:

> Thy rosy lips are soft and sweet,
> Thy fairy form is so complete,
> Thy motions are so airy free,
> Love lays his arrows at thy feet
> And yields his bow to thee;
> Take any dart from out his quiver
> And pierce what heart thou wilt for ever.

('Thy Rosy Lips are Soft and Sweet', Ricks, II, 60)

Here the reference to the rose is perfunctory, a mere sign of the recipient's identity. In other poems, Tennyson begins to revel in the word for its own sake:

> Rose of roses, bliss of blisses,
> Rosebud-lips for honey-kisses;
>   East and West and North and South
> Bear not such a rose as this is.

('Early Verses of Compliment to Miss Rosa Baring', Ricks, II, 60)

Tennyson loved flowers and knew them well from childhood studies. Flower imagery proliferates in his work, reaching an apotheosis in *Maud*. He was far from unique in this respect. An increasing number of publications identified the significance of particular flowers, and, through the middle years of the century, portrait painters exploited an implicit parallel between the beauty of young girls and that of the flowers which they carried or wore.

In Christian signification, the rose stands for the Virgin Mary or for martyrdom. Tennyson gives it its older, pagan, meaning as the emblem of Venus, goddess of love. In 'The Rosebud', which Cecil Lang and Edgar Shannon describe as 'perhaps the most erotic verses surviving by Tennyson' (Letters, I, xxi), the rose stands for the girl and for the promise of love. Here, at least, Martin's criticism of inertness is inappropriate.[12]

> As in the flowers by night I kneeled,
> The night with sudden odour reeled,

The southern stars a music pealed,
Warm beams across the meadow stole;
For Love flew over grove and field,
Said, 'Open, Rosebud, open, yield
Thy fragrant soul'.

(Ricks, II, 61)

A more extended use of the rose as an emblem of love comes in the central section of 'The Gardener's Daughter'. Here, the painter's lover, Rose, moves, like Maud twenty years later, through a garden of roses. Elizabeth Barrett Browning was unimpressed by this clichéd association of women with flowers, seeing in it a denigration of true womanhood: 'his women are too voluptuous, . . . however of the most refined voluptuousness – His gardener's daughter, for instance, is just a rose; and "a Rose" one might beg all poets to observe, is as precisely *sensual* as fricasseed chicken, or even boiled beef & carrots.'[13]

The 'rose' poems seem to relate to a love affair which flourishes for a time, and then ends in the poet's disillusionment with the girl's worldliness:

The form, the form alone is eloquent!
A nobler yearning never broke her rest
Than but to dance and sing, be gaily drest,
And win all eyes with all accomplishment.

('Three Sonnets to a Coquette', Ricks, II, 78)

The story of love thwarted by the opposition of a rich girl's family is one which Tennyson told in a number of his narrative poems, among them 'Locksley Hall', 'Edwin Morris', 'Maud', 'Pelleas and Etarre' and 'Aylmer's Field'. The theme was a popular one in nineteenth-century literature, but the persistence with which Tennyson returned to it suggests that this relationship and its bitter ending left a deep mark.

The division of opinion about the nature and intensity of Tennyson's relationship to Rosa Baring reflects a broader uncertainty about the young poet's emotional life. Among recent writers, Robert Martin concludes that Tennyson was without a strong sexual drive. Alan Sinfield wonders whether the relationship to Arthur Hallam, although 'not directly sexual' was perhaps 'just momentarily so (at Cauteretz?)'.[14] Before the 'discovery' of Rosa, the biographical material provided few indications that Tennyson was sexually attracted towards women. That he had some kind of empathy with them is beyond doubt. The female voice of his finest early poems may be a surrogate for his own, but few readers have detected masculinity in the lady of Shalott or Mariana. Poems like 'Eleonore' or 'Madeline' may be dismissed as mere exercises in a conventional mode, but they are also a useful reminder that Tennyson's social experience brought him into contact with many young girls. The Cambridge environment was largely masculine, but among the houses of his friends it was decidedly not. Most had sisters, and Tennyson had four of his own. Among the girlfriends whom they brought home were Rosa Baring and Emily Sellwood.

Many Victorians lived a double life, often concealing the dark side of it so thoroughly that only the persistence of modern biographers has brought it back to light. It was taken for granted that men sowed wild oats when young, but that this took place out of the public eye, and often with girls of a lower social class. Some remarks of Arthur Hallam in a letter to Robert Monteith are often quoted: 'I drop you a line', Hallam wrote, 'to say that Alfred went this morning to Richmond, intending to write an Innkeeper's Daughter at the Star & Garter'. Hallam tells Monteith that, if he wants to see Tennyson, 'you had best not delay too long as by the time the Innkeeper's Daughter is written the poet may be off to some other *star*, & be occupied on some remoter *garter* than that which encircles the fair leg of the Richmond barmaid who doubtless will serve as the prototype of his ideal creations'.[15]

Hallam's jocular tone allows for the usual reading of the sentence, that Tennyson had gone to Richmond to gather material for one of his 'Daughter' poems, but it *is* possible that he went to look at a barmaid who pleased him. That he would have entered into any serious involvement with her is unlikely. When Tennyson later confessed that his wife was the only woman he had ever truly kissed, he seems to have been telling the truth.

During the 1830s, Tennyson began to develop a vein of rural and domestic subject-matter in a group of pastoral narratives. Love and marriage are central issues in these poems, which 'treat in various ways the frustrations, sorrows, and joys of sexual and/or romantic or erotic love'.[16] The reputation of such poems as 'The May Queen', or 'The Talking Oak', plummeted in the early twentieth-century, when they were regarded as sentimental in the worst sense. More recently, William Fredeman has argued that there is a need to re-assess the group which Tennyson called 'English Idyls': 'the domes-tic element in Tennyson's poetry goes well beyond matters relating to the hearth, the heart, and the home: it is the stabilizing force in individual life, the protection afforded by a civilised order in society, and the assurance of a purposeful meaning in the universe.'[17]

A version of one of the earliest pastoral poems, 'The Miller's Daughter', was included in the 1832 volume, but it was extensively revised before republication in 1842. 'The Gardener's Daughter', begun at Cambridge, was written and rewritten over a long period. In its final form it is associated with Rosa Baring, but she was not in Tennyson's mind when he began it. Among the others in the group, 'The Lord of Burleigh' was begun in 1833, 'Dora' in 1835.

Tennyson was an admirer of George Crabbe's narratives of sea-coast life in East Anglia, though his work has little in common with that of the older poet. Tennyson's rural vein is softer, without the streak of violence which is characteristic of Crabbe. Tennyson was drawing less upon local stories than existing literary texts: Mary Russell Mitford's *Our Village* for 'The Miller's Daughter' and 'Dora', and a story told by Susan Ferrier and Thomas Moore, reprinted by Hazlitt in *The Picture Galleries of England*, for 'The Lord of Burleigh'.

Of the four, 'The Miller's Daughter' is the most untroubled. The speaker, a country squire, tells how, in youth, he saw the miller's daughter, Alice, tending her window-box of flowers. The image of the woman looking out of a window, and so inside a double frame, is a traditional motif in Dutch paintings like the famous Rembrandt *Girl leaning on a stone pedestal* at Dulwich, where beauty and dignity are found within the context of ordinary domestic life. Typically, Tennyson frames Alice with flowers:

> For you remember, you had set,
>   That morning, on the casement-edge
> A long green box of mignonette,
>   And you were leaning from the ledge.

(81–4)

Like 'The Miller's Daughter', 'The Gardener's Daughter' is a poem of love in an idyllic world. The influence of Theocritus and the Greek pastoral poets is felt, not just in individual lines, but in the relationship of the natural scene, and of the activities of the countryside, to the undramatic but striking events of the love story in the foreground.

The suitors of 'The Miller's Daughter' and 'The Gardener's Daughter' both marry for love, choosing their brides from a class below their own. The titles indicate the trades, and so the social position, of the girls' fathers. Mobility between classes was a standard subject for the romantic novels of the 1830s, and 'The Lord of Burleigh' and 'Dora' take up the same pattern, but here the misalliance is attended with sadness and irreparable division and loss. The death of Arthur Hallam may mark the division between the poems of love fulfilled, and of love disappointed. In 'The Lord of Burleigh', the village girl wedded by an aristocrat (who pretends to be a humble landscape painter), is unable to cope with the demands of her new life. The romantic story of Burchell and Sophia in Goldsmith's *Vicar of Wakefield*, is retold with a more sombre outcome.

'Dora' reverses the pattern of 'The Miller's Daughter', where the squire's mother greets her new daughter-in-law with a gesture of reconciliation:

> [she] rose, and, with a silent grace
> Approaching, press'd you heart to heart.

> (159–60)

In 'Dora', the estranged son, William, 'half in love, half spite . . . woo'd and wed/A labourer's daughter'. (37–8) This is no romantic love story and, when reconciliation comes at the end of the poem, William is dead, and the old man's rapprochement with his grandchild is shot through with remorse.

'Dora' is often regarded as Tennyson's most Wordsworthian poem, and has been compared to the older poet's 'Michael'. The story was told that Wordsworth wished that he had written it. In actual fact, the Poet Laureate was far from enthusiastic when Spedding tried to interest him in Tennyson's work. Aubrey de Vere, who was more persistent, got him to agree that two of the political poems were 'very solid and noble in thought', but this was scarcely true warmth (*Memoir*, I, 209). Matthew Arnold thought 'Dora' far inferior to comparable works by Wordsworth, and faulted it for having *'simplesse'* (false simplicity) but not true *'simplicité'*.[18] In Arnold's terms, 'Dora' was a trivial modern work, without the classic nobility which he found in 'Michael', and which, in his 1853 'Preface', Arnold declared to be an essential element in true poetry.

These poems of everyday life, like his scientific references, were part of Tennyson's response to the problem of writing in the nineteenth-century. In narratives revolving around the traditional patterns of parenthood and marriage, he sought to touch his readers' hearts with moving accounts of human relationships. For all his difference from Dickens, they have this in common. 'Dora', the most disturbing of the group, reminds us how much Tennyson's own experience of family conflict (like Dickens's) had conditioned his outlook and feelings. The old man's remorse over his dead son, and his new affection for his grandson, these may have figured in the poet's fantasies, but any such wish for the future went unfulfilled.

Soon after his son's death, Henry Hallam expressed a 'fear' that the 'solitary life' of the country was 'sadly unpropitious' for Alfred and Emily Tennyson (*Memoir*, I, 106). Alfred broke up the long periods of work and study at home with solitary journeys or visits to friends. In July 1834 he was with John Heath at Kitlands, near Leith Hill, in Surrey. A letter to Tennyson recalls an expedition they made to Worthing: 'The sea was much more boisterous and yellow than it was with you on that beautiful calm night three weeks ago. There were no boys bathing in no glowing sunset, but all things were enveloped in a thick drizzling mist' (Letters, I, 114).

In the autumn, Tennyson was at Tintern Abbey, where he wrote *In Memoriam* XIX, and one of his most poignant lyrics, 'Tears, Idle Tears': 'This song came to me on the yellowing autumn-tide at Tintern Abbey, full for me of its bygone memories. It is the sense of the abiding in the transient'. Tintern is rich in association, though Tennyson had mixed feelings about Wordsworth's famous poem. More telling was the relative proximity of Clevedon, and the grave of Arthur Hallam, recalled in the ruined tombs of the long gone monastic community:

> 'O let the simple slab remain,
> The MERCY JESU in the rain!
> The MISERERE in the moss!'
>
> (Ricks, III, 597)

In April 1835, Tennyson was the guest of James Spedding in the Lake District. The Spedding family had risen from agents to country gentlemen. Captain John Spedding farmed a large estate, and his home, Mirehouse, still stands on the shore of Lake Bassenthwaite, overlooked by Skiddaw. Tennyson's holiday was marred by constant rain. In the drawings Spedding produced at the time, he appears hunched in his huge cloak, sheltering in a shed, or seated by the fireside with a book. He worked on several poems, including 'Morte d'Arthur', drawing on his experience of the Lakes for landscape passages. He read aloud, either his own compositions or poems by Milton, Keats and Wordsworth. One of his fellow guests was Edward Fitzgerald, who had seen but never spoken to Tennyson. When the three men moved to Windermere for a week's further holiday, Spedding was soon called home, while the remaining two struck up a warm friendship.

That Tennyson was short of cash was obvious to all. He had paid for his long-promised visit to the Lakes by selling the gold Chancellor's medal for £15. Spedding collected up a pile of holed socks, which he laid out on Tennyson's bed sixteen years later 'in order to emphasise his friend's change in fortunes'.[19] After their return, Fitzgerald generously wrote offering to help him out financially. What transformed Tennyson's position was the death of old George Tennyson in July 1835, when Tennyson inherited an estate worth approximately £500 a year to add to an allowance of £100 a year from his aunt, Elizabeth Russell.

Tennyson travelled to London intermittently, establishing a familiar round of existence which was to continue until his marriage. He stayed with friends or in lodgings, dining at 'Dick's', 'The Rainbow', 'The Bell and Crown' in Holborn, or Bertolini's in Leicester Square. At the Cock Tavern in Fleet Street (to whose head waiter he devoted a poem), Tennyson was once reported to have ordered two chops, one pickle and two cheeses, a pint of stout, a pot of port and three cigars. Later, he would sometimes walk in the streets: 'When all the scum of night & hell boils from the cellar & the sewer'.[20]

The theatre continued to draw him. In 1837, he was at the Olympic in the Strand to see John Oxenford's version of Pope's *Rape of the Lock*: 'lumpish sylphs hanging plumb-heavy over the toilette, sesquipedalian gnomes, the clumsy conduct of unclouded Caves, and Pope every way travestied' (Letters, I, 150). W. F. Pollock remembered sitting on the 'narrow and uncomfortable benches of the pit at the Olympic to see [William] Farren and [John] Liston and [Lucia Elizabeth] Vestris and many another good performer in the charming light pieces which used to be played there before the days of legs, breakdown dances, and coarse burlesques'.[21]

Most of Tennyson's friends commented on his habit of heavy pipe-smoking to late hours, and some found it exhausting. Fitzgerald's comments in 1838 are echoed by several others: 'We have had Alfred Tennyson here; very droll, and very wayward: and much sitting up of nights till two or three in the morning with pipes in our mouths: at which good hour we would get Alfred to give us some of his magic music, which he does between growling and smoking; and so to bed. All this has not cured my Influenza as you may imagine: but these hours shall be remembered long after the Influenza is forgotten'.[22]

On 24 May 1836, Charles Tennyson, who had taken the name of Turner on inheriting his uncle's estate, married Louisa Sellwood, daughter of Henry Sellwood, a Horncastle solicitor. Her mother had been a sister of Sir John Franklin, the explorer. Louisa, Anne and Emily Sellwood were friends of the Tennyson girls, and Alfred Tennyson first saw Emily when she visited Somersby. Their meeting in a wood is described by Hallam Tennyson: 'At a turn of the path they came upon my father, who, at sight of the slender, beautiful girl of seventeen in her simple gray dress, moving "like a light across those woodland ways," suddenly said to her: "Are you a Dryad or an Oread wandering here?"' (*Memoir*, I, 148).

After his brother's wedding, Tennyson, as best man, wrote a sonnet addressed to the bridesmaid, Emily. The sestet is a declaration of love, a 'pleasant' love stimulated by the woman's emotion, not by a spontaneous surge of feeling:

> And all at once a pleasant truth I learn'd,
> For while the tender service made thee weep,
> I loved thee for the tear thou couldst not hide,
> And prest thy hand, and knew the press return'd,
> And thought, 'My life is sick of single sleep:
> O happy bridesmaid, make a happy bride!'
>
> (9–14)

The returned press of the hand told Tennyson that Emily was prepared to care for him, that here, at least, there was no risk of rejection. 'There is the glory of being loved, for so we have "laid great bases for Eternity"', he told her in a letter of the late 1830s (*Memoir*, I, 172). Only short passages from these early letters to Emily survive, but, even as fragments, they are demonstrably the work of the poet, not of the man who resented and disliked letter writing:

> Dim mystic sympathies with tree and hill reaching far back into childhood. A known landskip is to me an old friend, that continually talks to me of my own youth and half-forgotten things, and indeed does more for me than many an old friend that I know. An old park is my delight and I could tumble about it for ever. (*Memoir*, I, 172)

The departure of the Tennyson family from Somersby, long threatened, finally took place in late May or June 1837, when the new rector married and took over the house. In *In Memoriam* CII the contending memories associated with the place, those of childhood and of Arthur Hallam, finally blend into one:

> These two have striven half the day,
>   And each prefers his separate claim,
>   Poor rivals in a losing game,
> That will not yield each other way.
>
> I turn to go: my feet are set
>   To leave the pleasant fields and farms;
>   They mix in one another's arms
> To one pure image of regret.

(17–24)

Alfred, continuing to take responsibility for the family, rented them a new house at High Beech in Epping Forest. It had the advantage of being near London, but Tennyson found the forest disappointing and monotonously flat. The prospect from his study was over a 'muddy pond' with 'two little sharp-barking dogs' . . . 'no sounds of Nature and no society; equally a want of birds and men' (*Memoir*, I, 168 and footnote 23). Social relations were: 'artificial, frozen, cold and lifeless . . . Large set dinners with store of venison and champagne are good things of their kind, but one wants something more' (Letters, I, 158). Later, lodgings were taken in Mornington Crescent, near Camden Town, and used at various times by members of the family. On one journey home to High Beech, Tennyson, looking back at the city, conceived a line he used in 'Locksley Hall', combining it there with a recollection of his first visit to London in 1827:

Eager-hearted as a boy when first he leaves his father's field,

And at night along the dusky highway near and nearer drawn,
Sees in heaven the light of London flaring like a dreary dawn.

(112–4)

Moving to Europe, where living was cheaper, appealed to impecunious English authors. The idea attracted Tennyson and the suggestion, probably from Spedding, that he should go down to the Mediterranean, prompted a poem:

You ask me, why, tho' ill at ease,
Within this region I subsist,
Whose spirits falter in the mist,
And languish for the purple seas.

('You ask me, why', 1–4)

His answer is the stability of British democracy. Only if the growth of socialism threatens and 'banded unions' stifle freedom of speech, will he consider exile:

When single thought is civil crime,
And individual freedom mute.

(19–20)

A fear of violent revolution continues to emerge sporadically in Tennyson's poetry of the 1830s, but radicalism was not the only threat. An expansion of commerce, 'filling' and 'choking' the state's harbours with the 'golden sand' of money, would also send him in search of 'a warmer sky', to

see before I die
The palms and temples of the South.

(27–8)

In a recent study, Alan Sinfield has related Tennyson's periodic dreams of exile to his awareness of the alienation suffered by writers moving on the margins of society.[24] Tennyson's poems do indeed imply that political disturbance at home might drive him away, rather than encouraging him to play an active part himself. In *In Memoriam*, he speculates on Arthur Hallam's bright prospects as a public figure, but it was not something that he wished for himself. Yet indications that this was a turbulent period in British political history are common in Tennyson's work of the 1830s and 1840s.

Queen Victoria came to the throne in 1837. Her name is now associated with an era of unprecedented national prosperity and imperial expansion. For the early years of her reign, however, British social and political life was dominated by insecurity, poverty, and threats of insurrection. 'The hungry forties' was a period of economic depression, with the Irish potato famine of 1845 and 1846 driving more immigrants into the already overcrowded industrial towns on the mainland. There were reforming factory acts in 1833, 1844 and 1847, but the novels of Elizabeth Gaskell and *The Condition of the Working Class in England* by Friedrich Engels both describe the horrifyingly insanitary conditions in which large numbers of people were living.

Like many of his contemporaries, Tennyson was exhilarated by the idea of technological change. In 'Godiva', the seemingly casual opening lines allude to the poet's wait at a railway station. His response to the power of industry is more apparent in the final lines of 'The Golden Year', written soon afterwards, where discussion about a possible golden age ends resoundingly as the blast of

The steep slate-quarry, and the great echo flap
And buffet round the hills, from bluff to bluff.

(75–6)

The social discussion of 'The Golden Year' reaches no conclusions, but the poem retains an air of balanced and civilised disagreement.

By contrast, 'Locksley Hall', written in 1837–8, expresses a disjointed social philosophy through the persona of a disappointed and bitter man. Towards the end of the poem, the speaker has a vision of a future of expansive commercial enterprise, and of violent conflict:

For I dipt into the future, far as human eye could see,
Saw the Vision of the world, and all the wonder that would be;

Saw the heavens fill with commerce, argosies of magic sails,
Pilots of the purple twilight, dropping down with costly bales;

Heard the heavens fill with shouting, and there rained a ghastly dew
From the nations' airy navies grappling in the central blue.

(119–24)

Like Thomas Carlyle, the speaker of 'Locksley Hall' proclaims his belief in the power of productive work to engender a better future:

Men, my brothers, men the workers, ever reaping something new:
That which they have done but earnest of the things that they
    shall do.

(177–19)

Yet Tennyson himself was far from convinced by this. He had already attacked rampant commerce in 'You ask me why', and his own experience had left him with a hatred of the 'gold that gilds the straiten'd forehead of the fool! . . . Every door is barr'd with gold, and opens but to golden keys'. (62; 100) In theory Tennyson believed in the benefits accruing from industrial and commercial expansion; in practice he knew that it meant unacceptable privileges for the rich, and abundant opportunities for dishonest speculators.

In Parliament, friction between industrial and agricultural interests focused on moves to repeal the corn laws, originally introduced to protect the interests of British farmers. Since 1815, legislation had kept bread prices high, and had restricted overseas trade by provoking retaliatory tariffs. In Tennyson's 'Audley Court', written in 1838, one speaker supports a change in the law but his friend Francis Hall, a farmer's son, disagrees. When, after years of wrangling, the Tory prime minister, Sir Robert Peel, finally repealed the corn laws in 1846 (in the wake of the Irish famine), Tennyson supported him. His liberalism placed him with the industrialists, and the poor, rather than with the landed and agricultural interests so strongly represented in his native county.

The Chartist movement, founded in 1838, demanded electoral reform, with universal male suffrage, the ballot, annual parliaments, and payment of Members of Parliament. Chartism expressed the anger of the working classes, demanding parliamentary representation and a larger share of the nation's growing wealth. When Parliament rejected a Chartist petition in 1839, riots followed. Another petition was presented in 1842, and a third in 1848, the 'Year of Revolutions' in Europe, and of the publication of Karl Marx's *Communist Manifesto*. In London, the army was called in to suppress threatened demonstrations.

In Tennyson's 'Walking to the Mail', Sir Edward Head has gone abroad for 'fear of change at home' (l. 60). Such anxieties cannot have been uncommon at the time, and the vigour of Tennyson's language captures the disquiet and insecurity stimulated by apprehensions of a new French Revolution:

> I once was near him, when his bailiff brought
> A Chartist pike. You should have seen him wince
> As from a venomous thing: he thought himself
> A mark for all, and shudder'd, lest a cry
> Should break his sleep at night, and his nice eyes
> Should see the raw mechanic's bloody thumbs
> Sweat on his blazon'd chairs; but sir, you know
> That these two parties still divide the world –
> Of those that want, and those that have.

> (62–70)

In the 1840s, political parties were not rigidly aligned as they are today, and it is by no means easy to define Tennyson's political position. He came from a liberal family, and would have rejected the labels of Tory or Radical. Describing him as a radical Tory, or a conservative Liberal may seem a tautology, but it is probably not far from the truth. He believed that change was both necessary and inevitable, but that it must be carried through slowly and carefully, not abruptly by violent means.

Hallam Tennyson, writing many years later, summarised his father's memories of the unrest of the 1840s in his *Memoir*:

> My father thought they should be met not by universal imprison-
> ment and repression, but by a widespread National education, by
> more of a patriotic and less of a party spirit in the Press, by partial
> adoption of Free Trade principles, and by an increased energy and
> sympathy among those who belonged to the different forms of
> Christianity.
>
> (*Memoir*, I, 185)

Tennyson's friendship with Thomas Carlyle, whom he met in the late 1830s, undoubtedly influenced his social thinking, encouraging him to attack abuses (as he did in *Maud*) and to demand more vigorously that the moneyed classes should demonstrate responsible leadership. Carlyle came from outside the charmed circle of Tennyson's early friendships. By the 1830s and 1840s, Tennyson's Cambridge contemporaries were aspiring lawyers, politicians, churchmen or scholars. But, by heredity as well as upbringing, Tennyson had not that earnest sense of endeavour, of steady achievement, which marks the lives of so many educated men of the Victorian age. Carlyle was energetic and earnest enough, but he was also a writer and a prophet, a contentious polemicist and idealist. Both Carlyle and Tennyson had been struggling for years to gain public recognition, which Carlyle, fourteen years the elder, had recently achieved with *The French Revolution*.

There was an instant sense of affinity on both sides. Carlyle was attracted to Tennyson by his openness and simplicity. As Tennyson modestly expressed it: 'He seemed to take a fancy to me'.[25] Carlyle left some of the best pen-portraits ever written of Tennyson: 'One of the finest-looking men in the world. A great shock of rough dusty-dark hair; bright-laughing hazel eyes; massive acquiline face, most massive yet most delicate; of sallow-brown complection, almost Indian-looking; clothes cynically loose, free-and-easy; smokes infinite tobacco'.[26]

Personally, they seemed to have little in common, save a taste for tobacco. Tennyson's 'indolence' was unlikely to appeal to an apostle of the puritan virtues of industry and enterprise, and Carlyle had no liking for lyric poetry. His description of Tennyson's use of classical subjects as sitting 'on a dung-heap, among innumerable dead dogs' (*Memoir*, I, 340), seems to have amused the poet, but it was hardly ingratiating. Carlyle was surprised by his own enthusiasm for Tennyson's 1842 volume, where he particularly admired the poems which posed moral questions; 'Ulysses', 'Dora' and 'The Vision of Sin'.

As an outspoken opponent of ideas of immortality, Carlyle was a disturbing companion for Tennyson, struggling with doubt in the *In Memoriam* poems. Carlyle told him to get 'Old Jewish rags' out of his mind: 'Why should we expect a hereafter? Your traveller comes to an inn and he takes his bed. It's only for one night, and another takes it after him'. Tennyson was proud of his reply: 'Your traveller comes to his inn and lies down in his bed almost with the certainty that he will go on his journey rejoicing next morning'.[27] The friendship flourished for a time and then gradually lapsed. In 1845 Tennyson told Elizabeth Rundle: 'You would like him for one day . . . but then get tired of him: so vehement and destructive' (*Memoir*, I, 279). There was no permanent break, however. Tennyson was still visiting Carlyle and talking with him until near Carlyle's death in 1881.

Tennyson never became a disciple of Carlyle. He was no polemicist, although poems like 'Walking to the Mail' or 'Locksley Hall' raise topical issues. 'Walking to the Mail' is one of a group of poems with an air of masculine conviviality characteristic of Tennyson's work in the later 1830s. The others were 'Audley Court', 'The Golden Year', 'Edwin Morris', and 'The Epic' all written in the late 1830s, but published in the 40s and 50s. Drawing upon the model of Theocritus's *Idylls*, he developed a new kind of conversation poem, a form sufficiently flexible to incorporate references to public and private preoccupations. Formally, the poems are quite unlike the highly wrought lyrics for which reviewers had been criticising him, seeming, by contrast, to have no structure at all. Groups of educated young men (standing for the shepherds or cow-herds of the Greek originals) picnic, walk in the mountains or sit up together on Christmas Eve. Their talk turns over their own affairs, those of friends and neighbours, glancing, as such conversations often do, at matters of wider moment like the role of women, the advance of science, or the decline of Christian faith. The issues are raised with seeming artlessness, too lightly, perhaps, for the twentieth-century reader to grasp their importance.

When he wrote these poems, Tennyson was in his late twenties. Those *In Memoriam* elegies on which he was working at the same time use a tighter verse form, but some of the ideas are similar. What would Arthur Hallam have contributed to public life? Was there a threat of revolution? What were the implications of modern science? Was faith in decline? Tennyson's problem was to find a way of introducing these things, while still writing poetry. It was a problem which was to dominate his work during the 1840s.

5

The Poet of the Age

The early 1840s was a period of depression and creative inactivity for Tennyson. His work remained largely unacknowledged, and inspiration seemed to be failing him. Apart from revisions of earlier work, few new poems can be dated to the period between 1840 and 1845. Tennyson's unsettled personal life, a loss of direction and sense of failure contributed to his writer's block. As early as 1837, he had replied sarcastically to the 'prosperous and talented' Richard Monckton Milnes, who had annoyed him by demanding a poem for a journal: 'Had I been writing to a nervous, morbidly-irritable man, down in the world, stark-spoiled with the staggers of a mismanaged imagination and equally opprest by Fortune and by the Reviews, it is possible that I might have halted to find expressions more suitable to his case' (Letters, I, 148).

By 1840, Tennyson's engagement to Emily Sellwood had come to an end. It was later said that the poet could not afford to keep a wife, but this cannot have been the only reason. Elizabeth Tennyson was so happy with the idea of Emily as a daughter-in-law that she even offered to give up some of her own income to help them. The embarrassment of Charles Tennyson Turner's recurring opium addiction was probably a more serious obstacle. His wife, Louisa, broke down under the strain of his addiction, and the couple remained separated until 1849. Henry Sellwood might well feel that one Tennyson son-in-law was more than enough.

There remain other possibilities. Did Tennyson himself begin to fear the tie of marriage and slowly disentangle himself from Emily, possibly pleading poverty as a reason? Or was he, with his self-destructive instincts, deliberately inflicting pain upon himself? How serious were the Sellwoods' doubts about his religious faith? Tennyson's poem 'Love and Duty' struggles to express the auguish of a parting which the speaker believes to have been forced upon him:

> For Love himself took part against himself
> To warn us off, and Duty loved of Love –

O this world's curse, – beloved but hated – came
Like Death betwixt thy dear embrace and mine,
And crying, 'Who is this? behold thy bride,'
She pushed me from thee.

(45–50)

Whatever the actual chain of circumstances, the lovers parted, and
Emily remained at home with her father. Tennyson continued to
wander restlessly, searching for somewhere to write and settle. In
August 1840, Spedding reported, with dry wit, that Tennyson was
going 'to Florence, or to Killarney, or to Madeira, or to some place
where some ship is going – he does not know where'.[1] Days later,
Tennyson passed through Southampton, where he saw his old friend,
William Brookfield, and announced that he was going to Le Havre.
Some change of plan must have come about, however, for the journey was abandoned.

A year later, Tennyson returned to two cities associated with
Arthur Hallam, Paris and Rotterdam. In the Louvre, he was capti-
vated by Poussin's painting *Echo and Narcissus*, a work known to
have been influenced by Titian. He was responding to rich colour
and sensuous feeling. Narcissus, either dead or dying, lies beside
water, while, behind him, the pining Echo fades away. Tennyson
particularly delighted in the third figure, Cupid, the 'ferocious little
Love' (*Memoir*, I, 277): 'Standing over the dead body he looks like a
little god of the world'. In 1868, and again in 1869, Tennyson took
Frederick Locker to see the Poussin, but the latter was disappointed:
'[Tennyson] gazed at this picture with delight, but I confess I saw
little to admire' (*Memoir*, II, 67).

Tennyson's letters in these years were directed from a variety of
locations, Mablethorpe in 1841 and 1843, Yorkshire in 1841, Eastbourne in 1842 and 1845, Killarney in 1842, St Leonard's in 1843,
Barmouth in 1844. He meant to travel to Ireland with the poet,
Aubrey de Vere, in 1842, but missed him in London and so went on
by himself. The Ballybunion caves, on the coast of Kerry, inspired
lines which later became a simile for Merlin's prevision of Vivien's
treachery:

So dark a forethought roll'd about his brain,
As on a dull day in an Ocean cave

The blind wave feeling round his long sea-hall
In silence.

(*Merlin and Vivien*, 228–31)

In 1840, on medical advice, the Tennysons left High Beech for 5
Grove Hill, Tunbridge Wells, a town which Tennyson particularly
disliked, and avoided as much as possible. Far from benefiting from
the change, they found themselves 'half killed by the tenuity of the
atmosphere and the presence of steel more or less in earth, air and
water' (Letters, I, 178).

The family was contracting. Frederick settled in Italy, where he
married in 1839. Charles, still separated from his wife, was at Grasby,
and Horatio tried his hand, unsuccessfully, at farming in Tasmania.
In 1841, Emily Tennyson announced her engagement to a naval
lieutenant, Richard Jesse. Jesse's garrulity irritated Tennyson, but
there is no evidence that he opposed the marriage. If he had any
thoughts about Emily's 'disloyalty', he kept them to himself. Both
Emily and her youngest sister, Cecilia, were married in 1842, and, in
the following year, Arthur and Septimus joined Frederick in Italy.
Septimus returned home after a few years, but Arthur, an alcoholic,
stayed abroad until the later 1850s.

The marriages of his brothers and sisters, and those of his friends,
highlighted Tennyson's single state. Among his friends to marry
were Jack Kemble, Francis Garden, Robert Tennant and William
Brookfield. Those who stayed as bachelors, like Spedding and
Fitzgerald, were in more affluent circumstances than Tennyson,
and able to maintain independent households. The breaking of
Tennyson's engagement cut him off from hopes of domestic felicity.
In theory he still had a home with his mother, but her frequent
changes of house gave an increasingly nomadic flavour to his life.

By the time of his sisters' marriages, Tennyson's mental health
had been further undermined by acute financial anxiety. During the
High Beech period, the family had formed an unwise friendship
with a neighbour, Dr Matthew Allen, the director of a progressively
run lunatic asylum. Allen, in his early fifties, had an unsavoury past
which he carefully concealed. His medical qualifications were purely
nominal, and he had been imprisoned for debt.

Allen established himself in High Beech in 1825, and proceeded to
put into practice ideas which he had learnt as apothecary to the York

Lunatic Asylum. He dispelled the usual prison atmosphere by encouraging his patients to walk in the fresh air and to take frequent baths. By 1837, his asylum was widely admired for its progressive forms of treatment, though, in reality, it was poorly run.

Septimus Tennyson was an occasional patient of Allen's, and Alfred stayed with him intermittently during the early 1840s. Tennyson's friends joked about the possibility that he was a patient. Fitzgerald told William Hepworth Thompson in September 1840: 'old Alfred living for a fortnight at a madhouse. We did not want that to finish his education'.[2] Tennyson later drew upon his memories of the asylum when describing the speaker's insanity in *Maud*.

In August 1840, Spedding saw Tennyson in London, 'greatly taken' with Allen.[3] On the same visit Allen and Tennyson went together to visit the Thomas Carlyles, whom Allen already knew. Around this time, the 'speculative' and 'hopeful' Allen conceived a plan to make a fortune out of mechanised wood-carving (*Memoir*, I, 187). He persuaded Tennyson to invest in what seemed a golden opportunity, and £3000 was eventually handed over, together with about £5000 from other members of the Tennyson family. The only security was an insurance policy on Allen's life. Allen himself initially paid the premium, but in 1843 Edmund Lushington took over the payments, and continued them until Allen died in 1845.

By the middle of 1842, Tennyson had serious doubts about the scheme. Caught between desperate hopes and encroaching despair, he wrote to Mrs Allen, begging her to prevent her husband from borrowing £1000 from Septimus Tennyson and describing himself as 'a penniless beggar and deeply in debt besides' (Letters, I, 213). By March 1843, the crash was inevitable. Frederick came back from Italy and tried unsuccessfully to rescue the family's money from Allen's clutches. In December, Fitzgerald found Tennyson looking very ill: 'I have never seen him so hopeless: and I am really anxious to know how he is. But he would scarcely see any of us, and went away suddenly'.[4]

The supportive friendship of Edward Fitzgerald helped to raise Tennyson's spirits during these unhappy years. Often low-spirited himself, Fitzgerald had particular sympathy with depression. He formed strong attachments to younger men, but found them unable or unwilling to return his emotion. Tennyson's role in his life was very different, but the outcome was much the same. The wayward poet had neither the resources of affection, nor the unselfishness, which Fitzgerald craved, and it was the latter who did most of the giving.

One bond between them was a common love of paintings and they made at least two expeditions to the Dulwich Art Gallery. Like the National Gallery, the collection was strong in work by Canaletto, Claude, Poussin, Rembrandt, Van Dyck, Murillo and the English eighteenth-century masters, Reynolds and Gainsborough. One of the pictures which caught Tennyson's attention was Murillo's *Madonna del Rosario*, 'her eyes fixed on you . . . "Yes",' said Tennyson, '"but they seem to look at something beyond – beyond the Actual into Abstraction. I have seen that in a human face."'[5] In the decade since he had first seen the Louvre, something in Tennyson's nature had changed. He now found pleasure in a sublime religious work, as a medium for the exploration of the spiritual and unearthly.

In June 1840, the two friends met by chance in Warwick, where they spent the evening together:

> I went thro' Warwick Castle. It is certainly a noble specimen of old feudalism, and the views from the windows would be of unrivalled loveliness if the river were only clearer. I and Fitzgerald also [climbed] up Guy's tower, and had 'large prospect' of the surrounding country: but nothing pleased me better on the whole than two paintings I saw in the castle: one, an Admiral van Tromp by Rembrandt, the other Macchiavelli by Titian, both wonderful pictures, but the last grand beyond all words. (*Memoir*, I, 175–6)

The attributions, whether made by Fitzgerald or given out at the castle, were quite inaccurate. The so-called Macchiavelli was by the Dutch painter, Adrian Hanneman, and Rembrandt never painted Tromp, nor is any portrait of the Dutch seaman known to have been at Warwick.

After Warwick, they went on to view the ruins of Kenilworth Castle. Tennyson, whose expectations had been aroused, probably by Walter Scott's novel, was disappointed. In Stratford-upon-Avon, he wrote his name up in Shakespeare's birthplace. 'I was seized with a sort of enthusiasm, and wrote mine, tho' I was little ashamed of it afterwards: yet the feeling was genuine at the time, and I did homage with the rest' (*Memoir*, I, 176).

Tennyson's uneasy relations with Fitzgerald were not repeated in another close friendship of this time, with Edmund and Henry Lushington, sons of a prosperous lawyer. Edmund was a brilliant classicist, while Henry, who succeeded Arthur Hallam as Tennyson's most valued critic, followed his father into the law. Tennyson visited the Lushingtons' Kentish home for the first time around 1840. He became a regular guest, both there and at the chambers in the Temple which Henry Lushington shared with George Venables, a Cambridge friend and fellow lawyer. 'When light was to be seen in their windows it was always a tempting invitation to go up and enjoy a Cambridge evening'.[6] Venables was closely attached to Henry Lushington, and his diary suggests that Tennyson's company could be wearisome to him: 'A. Tennyson came and sat all day'; 'Again idled all morning talking with him'; 'interrupted by Tennyson who staid all morning'.[7]

In 1841, the Tennysons moved to Boxley, near Maidstone, which brought them close to the Lushingtons at Park House. A guest remembered Alfred sitting 'on a garden seat on the grass, in a brown suit, looking somewhat grave and silent' (*Memoir*, I, 205). He sternly rebuked those who spoke lightly of industrial distress. Within months, Edmund Lushington, now squire of Park House and Professor of Greek at Glasgow University, had fallen in love with Cecilia Tennyson. In the closing section of *In Memoriam* Tennyson transforms their wedding, which took place on 14 October 1842, into a visionary apotheosis of the future, an event which in some way compensates for the frustrated marriage of Hallam and Emily. Edmund, a man of 'graceful, though shy, charm',[8] devoted to his livelier wife, was probably the subject of the lines about friendship in *In Memoriam* LVIII. Unfortunately, Cecilia, a hypochondriac in the Tennyson mould, found that spending half of every year in the smoke of Glasgow did not agree with her. She took to living in Edinburgh, or passing the winter in the south. Of their four children, only one daughter survived into adulthood, rendering sadly ironic the joyous concluding lines of *In Memoriam* about the birth of their son.

It was once common to describe the period between the publication of the two sets of *Poems*, in 1832 and 1842, as Tennyson's 'ten year silence'. The death of Hallam and the onslaughts of the reviewers were believed to have cast a blight over the poet's inspiration and creativity. In fact, the first years after Hallam's death were those in which Tennyson wrote some of his greatest poetry, as well as making significant revisions to earlier work. It was a time of varied experiment in form and subject, as he responded, not only to personal circumstances, but to the demands of public and critics. Perhaps stung by attacks on his complicated rhyme schemes, perhaps simply reflecting a change in himself, Tennyson moved away from intricate verse patterns in his new poems, revised others, and eventually omitted several works of this kind from the two volume edition of 1842.

Tennyson's friends had been trying for years to encourage him to publish his work once more. He resisted, apparently fearing a critical onslaught. In 1839, Fitzgerald complained: 'I want A. T. to publish another volume: as all his friends do: especially Moxon, who has been calling on him for the last two years for a new edition of his old volume: but he is too lazy and wayward to put his hand to the business. He has got fine things in a large Butcher's Account book that now lies in my room.'[9] This was one of the account books in which Tennyson wrote his poems, often using the edges of the sheets as pipe cleaners.

In 1838 C. C. Little of Boston proposed an American edition of the earlier volumes. Tennyson managed to stave off the scheme until Charles Stearns Wheeler wrote early in 1841, offering to see an American volume through the press. The poet's reply represented a change of heart:

> I am conscious of many things so exceedingly crude in those two volumes that it would certainly be productive of no slight annoyance to me, to see them republisht as they stand at present, either here or in America. . . . I have corrected copies of most that was worth correction in those two volumes and I will in the course of a few months republish these in England with several new poems and transmit copies to Little and Brown.
>
> (Letters, I, 187)

This plan was carried out, with Ticknor's, not Little and Brown, as the American publishers.

The claim that it was the Americans who had pushed him into publication was one which Tennyson continued to make, as though unwilling to take responsibility himself. It had some validity. In the absence of a new publication, there was a real danger of a pirated American edition of the earlier poems. Charles Dickens reported in 1842 that Tennyson's work was 'wholly unknown' in America: 'except by a few of his pretty poetical conceits'.[10] Given his financial position, he could not risk the initiative passing into other hands.

This was not the sole impetus, however. Other poets were appearing on the scene. Robert Browning, though with little critical success, had been publishing regularly since 1833. When Elizabeth Barrett brought out *The Seraphim* in 1838, one critic accused her of having 'modelled herself upon the very worst portions of Keats and Tennyson, in labouring for outlandish compound words, picking up obscure phrases, and accenting every unnecessary syllable'.[11] Comparisons with Tennyson apart, the reviews of her work were enthusiastic. Tennyson would have noticed that Bulwer Lytton, who had scourged his own work, called *The Seraphim* 'a poem of high excellence, but still higher promise'.[12] Having published only two poems since 1832, Tennyson was in danger of being forgotten. George Venables told him: 'If you do not ever publish, do not you think you will have even that which you have published taken out of its napkin and given to him who has published ten volumes?'[13]

Tennyson worked on the new volumes throughout 1841, as revision took the place of composition. On 2 March 1842, Fitzgerald led him 'with violence' to Moxon, and by 17 March the proofs had arrived: 'Poor Tennyson has got home some of his proof sheets: and now that his verses are in hard print, thinks them detestable'.[14] Although Fitzgerald had taken over Hallam's role as negotiator, he had not Hallam's enthusiasm for Tennyson's poetry. If he decided that the volume would be a great one, Fitzgerald regretted the inclusion of some of the early poems: 'the Merman, the Mermaid, and those everlasting Eleanores, Isabels, – which always were, and are, and must be, a nuisance'.[15]

Moxon printed 800 copies of the two-volume edition, of which 500 were sold within four months. There were further printings in 1843, 1845 and 1846. The figures testify to Tennyson's growing popularity, and Edgar Shannon argues that the largely favourable reviews helped to stimulate public support. The critics were broadly in agreement that the volumes represented an advance on the earlier work, and the revisions were seen as improvements: 'There are some additions of verses and stanzas here and there, many minute changes, and also beneficial shortenings and condensations'.[16] Most reviewers had doubts about particular poems, 'Audley Court', the 'Epic' (the modern frame to 'Morte d'Arthur') and 'Walking to the Mail' were described as 'slight'. Almost everybody objected to the two short comic poems, 'The Skipping Rope' and 'The Goose', as too trivial for inclusion in a serious volume.

Four major reviews were written by fellow Apostles; Francis Garden in the *Christian Remembrancer*, John Sterling in the *Quarterly*, Richard Monckton Milnes in the *Westminster*, and James Spedding in the *Edinburgh Review*. In different ways all four put forward the same ideal for poetry, that, in Spedding's words, 'All that is of true and lasting worth in poetry, must have its root in a sound view of human life and the condition of man in the world; a just feeling with regard to the things in which we are all concerned'.[17]

Comparisons with Wordsworth persisted. Leigh Hunt described Tennyson as a poet able to mix 'thought and feeling, more abundant in the former respect than Keats, and more pleasurable and luxuriant in the latter than Wordsworth'.[18] John Sterling found the 'Ode to Memory' inferior to the 'Immortality' ode, the 'English Idyls' accessible, but less 'profoundly reflective' than Wordsworth's 'Michael, The Brothers, the story of Margaret in the beginning of The Excursion, Ruth'.[19]

Sterling, writing in the same Tory magazine which had printed Croker's scathing attack in 1833, was instructed not to praise any poem which Croker had criticised. The restriction created difficulties for him, but Sterling's review was seen by many, including the angry Croker, as a recantation on the part of the Quarterly. The message was clear. Tennyson, no longer regarded as a dangerous radical, was now widely accepted as a major poet.

Tennyson's fellow authors were generally enthusiastic about the volumes. Elizabeth Barrett was 'rapt . . . in Elysium'[20] and Dickens was bowled over. He told John Forster from Broadstairs that he had been 'reading Tennyson all this morning on the seashore'.[21] On the other side of the Atlantic, Ralph Waldo Emerson, impressed by 'Godiva' and 'Oenone', declared that '"Ulysses" belongs to a high class of poetry, destined to be the highest, and to be more cultivated in the next generation' (Memoir, I, 182). As a whole, American readers 'enjoyed the poems for what they were – lyrics, idyls, and short narratives of extraordinary beauty. The British were disappointed; they wanted something grander – an epic, a great moral or philosophical work'.[22] Sales in America nearly equalled those in Britain.

Not everybody liked the revisions. Browning thought them 'insane. WhatEVER is touched is spoiled. There is some woeful mental infirmity in the man – he was months buried in correcting the press of the last volume and in that time began spoiling the new poems (in proof) as hard as he could'.[23] Tennyson himself was equally discontented. Faced with his proofs, he sided with Fitzgerald in finding them 'too full and complicated'. Once again he wished that 'he had never been persuaded to print'.[24]

For all Tennyson's doubts, the publication of the 1842 volume was a milestone in the establishment of his reputation. When Bulwer Lytton published an anonymous attack in 'The New Timon', he was seen to be out of step with public opinion, and heavily criticised for it. Overwhelmed by the Matthew Allen débâcle, Tennyson was too low-spirited to recognise the slow up-turn in his fortunes. Writing to Fitzgerald in February 1844, he was usually direct about himself: 'The perpetual panic and horror of the last two years had steeped my nerves in poison . . . my nerves were so bad six weeks ago that I could not have written this and to have to write a letter on that accursed business threw me into a kind of convulsion. I went through Hell' (Letters, I, 222–3).

In the interests of economy, the Tennysons moved from Boxley to Cheltenham in 1843. Shortly afterwards, Alfred left them to begin a 'water-cure' at nearby Prestbury. Quantities of cold water were applied to the body by showering, immersion or wrapping in blankets. The aim was to stimulate the circulation, and so purify the system. It is possible that other aspects of the cure, the ban on coffee, tobacco and alcohol, and the emphasis on walking and exercise, did more to improve Tennyson's health than the water. The cure was temporary, Tennyson was soon smoking and drinking as hard as ever.

Tennyson left, intending to return, but never did. Three years later, in the spring of 1847, he tried again at another establishment, Umberslade Hall, near Birmingham. At the end of the year he moved to Malvern, where he was treated by one of the best-known practitioners of the day, Dr James Gully. Robert Martin argues that Tennyson took the water cure because he feared that he had inherited epilepsy, possibly misreading the symptoms of gout. The treatment does not seem to have benefited his spirits and it cut him off from the company of his friends.

There were some encouraging gleams amid the poet's gloom. For one thing his financial situation was gradually improving. From the second, third and fourth editions of *Poems* he received £746.8s.1d., two-thirds of the profits. In 1845, the year of the third printing, Matthew Allen died, and Tennyson was able to collect £2000 from the insurance policy. Something of his reaction is described in the poem, 'Sea Dreams'. Then, in October, the Prime Minister, Sir Robert Peel, finally granted him the pension of £200 a year for which his admirers had been pressing.

Sounder finances allowed Tennyson to consider Europe once more. In August 1846, he travelled with the publisher Edward Moxon through Belgium, Germany and Switzerland. The unfailingly cheerful Moxon had a difficult job in keeping up the spirits of his companion. Tennyson's brief journal is dotted with irascible comments. In

Bruges, the dinner was 'not very good', and the night was 'hot' and 'nervous . . . man hemm'd overhead enough to shake the walls of Jericho'. The tea in Ghent was unsatisfactory, and in Louvain he passed another 'nervous night, bath doesn't answer' (Letters, I, 258–9).

Germany was better, with 'nice rooms' in Cologne, but there were 'three Hyde Park drawling snobs stinking of perfumed soap' on the hot Rhine boat. Fortunately, these undesirables disembarked at Mainz. Tennyson was returning to the Rhine for the first time since his journey there with Arthur Hallam, fourteen years before. In Cologne, he found the cathedral completed: 'splendid but to my mind too narrow for its breadth' [*sic*]. Nonnenworth and the Drachenfels brought back 'sad recollections', and Koblentz, where they had a 'horrid row' at one hotel, was as hateful as ever. From Mannheim, Moxon and Tennyson went on by rail to Kehl, Basle and Lucerne where they spent three days (Letters, I, 259). Lucerne is one of Europe's loveliest towns. Two enclosed wooden bridges, decorated with paintings, cross wide rivers as they flow into the lake. Tennyson made the usual excursions to the Rütli, where Swiss independence was first declared, and to William Tell's Kapel, another national shrine.

Two large mountain massifs overlook Lake Lucerne, the Pilatus and the Rigi. Viewing the sunrise from the summit of the Rigi was *de rigeur* for the Victorian tourist. Moxon and Tennyson hired horses for the ascent at Weggis. At the Kaltbad Hotel on the way up, Tennyson complained of the 'infernal chatter of innumerable apes'. The view down over the lake was 'very fine', 'little coves and wooded shores and villages under vast red ribs of rock', but the sunset was 'feeble', and the room 'fleabitten'. Dawn, for once, lived up to expectations: 'sunrise, strange look of clouds packed on the lake of Egeri, far off Jungfrau looking as if delicately pencilled . . . began to descend at nine – strange aspect of hill, cloud and snow as if the mountains were on fire . . . We watch the clouds opening and shutting as we go down and making framed pictures of the lake etc.'. Even now, Tennyson's pleasure was marred by an 'infamous Swiss boy' the nature of whose sins is not disclosed. Back in Weggis, they were offered a choice of live fish, but Tennyson was too tender-hearted to order their destruction (Letters, I, 260).

Following a well-trodden path, Moxon and Tennyson made their way into the Bernese Oberland. This was a great age of British Alpinism, when numerous peaks were scaled for the first time. It was also the age of Thomas Cook, who helped to make Switzerland one of Europe's leading tourist attractions. From Interlaken they made two expeditions into the mountains, one to Grindelwald and its glaciers, the other through Lauterbrunnen to the Wengern Alp and the Eiger Glacier. The region is famous for the spectacular prospect of three distinctive peaks, the Eiger, Mönch and Jungfrau, but Tennyson also noted the 'beautifully shaped snow peak' of their lesser neighbour, the Silberhorn, still unclimbed in 1846 (Letters, II, 49).

Thirty years before, Byron had come the same way, finding in the Oberland 'a range of scenes beyond all description or previous conception'.[25] Tennyson's reaction was very different. 'Mountains, great mountains, disappointed me', he told Edward Fitzgerald, before going on to praise the Valley of Lauterbrunnen. Mont Blanc (which he saw later) was 'very sulky – kept his nightcap on – doff'd it one morning when I was knocked up out of bed to look at him at 4 o'clock. The glance I gave did not by any means repay me for the toil of travelling to see him' (Letters, I, 264).

One result of Tennyson's visit to Switzerland was the song 'Come Down, O Maid' from *The Princess*, which he said was written in Grindelwald and Lauterbrunnen, 'descriptive of the waste Alpine heights and gorges and of the sweet rich valleys below'. (VII) The song gives new force to Tennyson's preference for valley over high mountain as the shepherd tells the maid (the Jungfrau) to leave the 'height and cold' of the mountain top for the rich 'Plenty' of love and family life in the valley below.

> And come, for Love is of the valley, come,
> For Love is of the valley, come thou down
> And find him.

> (VII, 183–5)

On their road to Geneva, Tennyson and Moxon crossed the Gemmi Pass into the Valais. Tennyson was impressed by what he saw, with the Oberland behind and, ahead, the great peaks of the Valais Alps, Monte Rosa, the Weisshorn and the Matterhorn. From Geneva, they took a day trip to Lausanne, to visit Charles Dickens. Tennyson and Moxon (whom Dickens thought an 'odd companion for a man of genius') did not arrive until evening, when they were entertained with Liebfraumilch, biscuits and 'cigars innumerable'.[26]

Tennyson evidently liked Dickens as a man, if not as a writer. In September 1845, he travelled up from Cheltenham to see a private production of Ben Jonson's *Every Man in his Humour*, put on by Dickens and John Forster at Miss Kelly's theatre. Another member of the audience, Jane Carlyle, described how Tennyson leant against a wall in the interval: 'with his head touching the ceiling like a caryatid, to all appearance asleep, or resolutely trying it under most unfavourable circumstances'.[27]

Tennyson and Moxon returned home after a holiday of two weeks. For Tennyson other travels followed, often undertaken alone. In the early summer of 1848 he was in Cornwall, thinking 'of again taking up the subject of Arthur'. Arriving in Bude, Tennyson 'askt girl way to sea, she opens the back door . . . I go out and in a moment go sheer down, upward of six feet, over wall on fanged cobbles. Up again and walked to sea over dark hill' (*Memoir*, I, 274). His leg troubled him for some time afterwards.

Tennyson recorded precise observations of the Cornish scene in his journal, with a few additional comments on the local people and their occupations. 'Rainy and bad, went and sat in Tintagel ruins, cliff black and red and yellow, weird looking thing'. 'Large crimson clover; sea purple and green like a peacock's neck'. 'Tamarisk hedge in flower. Round Pentreath beach, large crane's bill near Kynance, down to cove. Glorious grass-green monsters of waves. Into the caves of Asparagus Island. Sat watching wave-rainbows'. According to Caroline Fox, Tennyson stayed 'with little grocers and shopkeepers along his line of travel'. He passed from one to another through a chain of introductions begun by the surgeon who had treated his leg: 'They all knew about Tennyson, and had read his poems, and one miner hid behind a wall that he might see him' (*Memoir*, I, 274–5).

Later in the same summer, Aubrey de Vere persuaded Tennyson to return to Ireland, travelling initially to the de Veres' family home at Curragh Chase, near the Shannon estuary. On a stormy evening, Tennyson and de Vere climbed the Holy Mountain, Croagh Patrick, and looked down over Clew Bay: 'The sunset was one of extraordinary but minatory beauty', wrote de Vere, 'It gave, I remember, a darksome glory to the vast and desolate expanse with all its creeks and inlets from the Shannon, lighted the green islands in the mouth of the Fergus, fired the ruined Castle of Shanid . . . The western clouds hung low, a mass of crimson and gold' (*Memoir*, I, 291).

Still in search of dramatic seascapes, Tennyson went south to

Valencia Island, where the cliffs rise as high as 800 feet. 'At Valencia the sea was grand, without any wind blowing and seemingly without a wave: but with the momentum of the Atlantic behind, it dashes up into foam, blue diamonds it looks like, all along the rocks, like ghosts playing at hide and seek' (*Memoir*, I, 196–7). In Killarney a bugle call 'beneath the "Eagle's Nest",' gave 'eight distinct echoes' (*Princess*, IV), transformed into one of Tennyson's best-known lyrics, 'The splendour falls on castle walls'.

Tennyson ranked the sea at Valencia with those of Mablethorpe and West Cornwall. In comparison, the English Channel struck him as 'not a grand sea', 'only an angry curt sea' (*Memoir*, I, 196). He was often on the south coast in the 1840s, sometimes staying with the Lushingtons at St Leonards or Eastbourne, or, in 1845, living in one of a row of cottages there. Edmund Lushington still remembered it clearly in the 1890s. 'A little garden lay in front of the cottages, beyond that a cornfield extended some way till it was stopt by a path on the edge of the cliff, which overlooked the sea, and continued its course on to Holywell . . . He had then completed many of the cantos of "In Memoriam" and was engaged on "The Princess" of which I had heard nothing before' (*Memoir*, I, 203).

After visiting Robert Monteith at Carstairs in the summer of 1849, Tennyson spent a few days on the Clyde. On the outbreak of a cholera epidemic, he fled north to the cathedral town of Dunkeld and from there made a coach expedition to the Pass of Killiecrankie. Another traveller, W. W. Mitchell, noticing Tennyson's books and his 'studious and intellectual look', 'judged him to be a learned college pundit who was travelling in the highlands to refresh his jaded mind' (Letters, I, 300). When he discovered his companion's identity, Mitchell cried out in amazement, and felt 'heartily ashamed of the liberty' he had 'used' on an enjoyable and friendly day. 'Nothing wrong', was Tennyson's reply (Letters, I, 303).

From Oban, Tennyson sailed to Skye, passing through the Inner Hebrides. 'I think I saw more outlines of hills than ever I saw in my life – and exquisitely shaped are those Skye mountains' (Letters, I, 305). In retrospect, his favourite memory of his Scottish journey was of Alloway, 'by the monument of poor Burns and the orchards, banks and braes of bonny Doon. I made a pilgrimage thither out of love for the great peasant – they were gathering in the wheat and the spirit of the man mingled or seemed to mingle with all I saw. I know you do not much care for him but I do and hold that there never was immortal poet if he be not one' (Letters, I, 305–6).

As the decade went on, Tennyson began to be lionised on his visits to London. In 1847, Carlyle complained that he was 'dining daily till he is near dead',[28] and journal entries for May 1848 confirm that Tennyson was out almost every night. In the company of friends and writers, Tennyson remained easy and relaxed, but, in the wider world, he became a figure of mystery, never an easy guest. His attitude to celebrity was equivocal. He continued to accept invitations, but complained about the company he was keeping. '[Tennyson] said that he could not stand the chattering and conceit of clever men, or the worry of society, or the meanness of tuft-hunters, or the trouble of poverty, or the labour of a place, or the preying of the heart upon itself'.[29]

Tennyson was also widening his acquaintance in the literary world. As a guest at a Hampstead dinner of the Society of Authors, he was received with tumultuous enthusiasm. Among his contemporaries, he warmed to Robert Browning, although privately confessing that he found the poetry difficult to understand. To another rival, Henry Taylor, Tennyson took an instant dislike, later modified. Coventry Patmore, fourteen years his junior, became a devoted disciple and friend until they fell out in the 1860s. Patmore later described their frequently silent relationship to Edmund Gosse:

> Tennyson often sank into a sort of gloomy reverie, which would fall upon him, in Keats' phrase – 'Sudden from heaven, like a weeping cloud', and put a stop to all conversation. While they walked the streets at night in endless perambulation, or while they sat together over a simple meal in a suburban tavern, Tennyson's dark eyes would suddenly be set as those of a man who sees a vision, and no further sound would pass his lips, perhaps for an hour.[30]

Among the older authors, Tennyson was a frequent guest of Samuel Rogers. The friendship lasted until Rogers's death in 1855, despite periods of estrangement. According to Tennyson, Rogers 'was a kindly old man, excepting when he was bilious' (*Memoir*, II, 72). Through Rogers, Tennyson met Thomas Moore, author of the famous *Irish Melodies*. 'Rogers is not as good as Moore,' he said, after both men were dead. 'Moore had a wilder fancy, but still hardly anything that Moore wrote is altogether what it should be' (*Memoir*, II, 71). Other figures of the older generation with whom Tennyson became acquainted were Walter Savage Landor and Thomas

Campbell. In the summer of 1843, Moxon, Campbell and Tennyson made an expedition to Birdlip Hill, near Cheltenham. Campbell was seeking to restore his health, but died in the following year.

The most significant literary encounter was that with William Wordsworth. Tennyson's name appears in the visitors' book at Rydal Mount for 1835, but it is generally assumed that the two poets met for the first time at Samuel Hoare's house in Hampstead in May 1845. Tennyson was disappointed in the lake poet, though he told de Vere that 'Mr W. improved upon him'. Two days later, both poets were guests at a dinner given by Moxon. This time Wordsworth seemed to warm towards the younger man, calling him 'brother bard'. The diffident Tennyson, 'ashamed of paying Mr Wordsworth compliments', finally found himself able to express 'the pleasure he had had from Mr Wordsworth's writings'. Wordsworth took his hand, and 'replied with some expressions equally kind and complimentary. Tennyson was evidently much pleased with the old man, and glad of having learned to know him'.[31] 'I shall never forget my deep emotion the first time I had speech with him', Tennyson later told Frederick Locker (*Memoir*, II, 70).

This is the best of Tennyson. The worst emerges in an account of another dinner-party, given by Samuel Rogers for eight authors on 26 January 1845. Seven men had assembled and gone into dinner when the eighth guest, Caroline Norton, arrived. Famous as a poet, and as a campaigner for women's rights, she had been accused by her husband, in a bitterly contested legal case, of committing adultery with Lord Melbourne. Tennyson, appalled at being introduced to a 'scarlet woman', turned his back on her. Such behaviour is all the more unexpected since the poem on which he was working at this time, *The Princess*, has been associated with Caroline Norton.

Tennyson had been planning to write a poem about women's education since 1839. The first party of *The Princess* was completed by the summer of 1845, the second by the following January. The whole poem was in proof by May 1847, when Tennyson was seized with his usual hesitations, and set about making substantial revisions. As a result, Moxon only brought the volume out on 25 December, and missed the Christmas gift market.

The Princess represented a considerable departure in the poet's style. A few years before, Tennyson had felt that: 'if I meant to make my mark at all, it must be by shortness, for the men before me had been so diffuse, and most of the big things except "King Arthur" had been done'. (*Memoir*, I, 166). Yet *The Princess* was by far Tennyson's longest poem to date, comparable only with two unfinished works: 'The Devil and the Lady' and 'The Lover's Tale'. More surprising still, the poem is an attempt to dramatise a contentious problem, the relationship between the sexes and the place of women in the modern world. Tennyson may have been taking up the challenge made to him by many friends and critics, to find 'objects of high imagination and intense popular feeling for his art to work upon. If . . . an artist could only now find out where these objects are, he would be *the* artist of modern times'. Tennyson, George Venables was arguing here, had the intellectual and moral power to weld together 'convergent tendencies of many opinions' into great poetry (*Memoir*, I, 123).

The issue chosen for *The Princess* was topical. Since the publication of Mary Wollstonecraft's *Vindication of the Rights of Women* in 1792, there had been an increasing demand for reform in the relations between the sexes. In France, some advanced socialist thinkers wanted complete social equality between men and women, and writers of the period often compared women, with their restricted educational and vocational opportunities, to the working classes. 'Knowledge is now no more a fountain seal'd', declares Tennyson's Ida, and she is in the vanguard of change (II, 76). Queen's College, Harley Street, was founded by F. D. Maurice in the year after the poem's publication, 1848; Girton College more than 20 years later, in 1869.

Ida, the heroine of Tennyson's poem, has set up a women's university, and has decreed that men enter only on pain of death. The Prince, betrothed to Ida since childhood, braves the statute and enters the university with two friends, all disguised as women. The war which breaks out when they are discovered is won by the Princess's army. However, after nursing the wounded Prince, she falls in love with him, abandons her university and chooses marriage after all.

Tennyson's problems in constructing his narrative were considerable and he never succeeded in resolving them. As his storyteller recognises, he was trying too hard to please everybody: 'What style could suit?' (l. 9), the speaker asks, men would think a 'mock heroic' mode appropriate (l. 11), and women (seeing the subject differently) would demand seriousness.

> I moved as in a strange diagonal,
> And maybe neither pleased myself nor them.

> ('Conclusion', 27–8)

Tennyson evades some of his difficulties by the use of a framing device set up in a 'Prologue'. Seven separate narratives, each devised by an undergraduate, make up a serial story, told to a group of women, guests and family, at Vivian Place. The subtitle, 'A Medley', implies that this multiple narrative is a mere literary miscellany, and that the absence of coherence is deliberate. By this means, the mingling of medieval and modern, burlesque comedy and social commentary, is excused and accounted for. To late twentieth-century readers, these things are far less unfamiliar and disturbing than they were for the Victorians, but difficulties remain even today.

In his own notes to *The Princess*, Tennyson explained the importance of the idea of the child to his argument: 'The child is the link thro' the parts, as shown in the Songs . . . which are the best interpreters of the poem' ('Introductory Notes'). The frequent references to childhood and motherhood are an indication that he sees this bond as central to the true meaning of womanhood. The story of Ida's friend, Psyche, dramatises the contention. The abduction of her child, Aglaia, turns this competent woman, well-versed in recent scientific research, into an abject figure of terror and despair. But the idea of the child can have more than one interpretation. In Ida's terms, as in Ibsen's *Doll's House*, first performed thirty years later, the state of woman is analogous to the childish:

> they had but been, she thought,
> As children; they must lose the child, assume
> The Woman.

> (I, 135–7)

The songs were inserted into *The Princess* in 1850. Still unsatisfied, Tennyson then made an addition of more doubtful value, the Prince's 'weird seizures'. These cataleptic attacks, when the victim is unable to tell shadow from substance, underline the vulnerable nature of the hero at moments of crisis, and, by blurring the issue at these points, give the poet a further opportunity for evasion.

In political terms, Ida has created a world where she can rule without interference, reproducing in miniature the hierarchy of her father's kingdom. Tennyson's use of 'mock heroic' discourages the reader from taking the heroine's psychology seriously, but the background pattern is clear. A strong-minded girl reacts against her dynastic role. She is to be a pawn in a marriage game, while her brother, physically strong but without intelligence, will succeed their ineffectual father. Ida herself recognises that she 'sought far less for truth than power/In knowledge' (VII, 221–2). The historical prototype for the strong-minded woman ruler was Elizabeth I. Like many of his contemporaries, Tennyson was inclined to see her as a surrogate man, a 'man-minded offset' (l. 51) of Henry VIII, as he describes her in 'The Talking Oak'.

The Princess, if not a feminist work, is not a celebration of masculinity. Ida and Lady Blanche are not the only characters criticised for being 'man-minded'. The Prince's father, who states the most extreme case for not taking women seriously, is condemned for it. This is not, as some writers have suggested, a comic passage:

> Man is the hunter; woman is his game:
> The sleek and shining creatures of the chase,
> We hunt them for the beauty of their skins;
> They love us for it, and we ride them down.

> (V, 147–50)

Lines from the 1832 version of 'A Dream of Fair Women', suggest that there was indeed a parallel in Tennyson's mind between male chauvinism and materialism. 'I think women much better (morally) than men' was Tennyson's later statement on the subject, and from the start he believed that female gentleness must moderate the greed and irresponsibility of the commercial ethic.[32]

> In every land I thought that, more or less,
>   The stronger sterner nature overbore
> The softer, uncontrolled by gentleness
>   And selfish evermore.

> (Ricks, I, 481)

Tennyson was well aware that a true poet must possess feminine as well as masculine characteristics. When hostile critics apportioned his lyrical gifts to his female aspect and called him 'Miss Alfred Tennyson', they must have provoked the poet's anger against their own masculine aggression.

Sexual reversal is abundant in *The Princess*. Walter Vivian, in the framing 'Prologue', talks of an ancestress who fought off an army and an unwanted marriage. Lilia, his sister, says that such women are not uncommon, but have been beaten down by 'convention':

> It is but bringing up; no more than that:
> You men have done it: how I hate you all!

('Prologue', 129–30)

The Prince, with his lengths of 'yellow ringlet, like a girl' (I, 3), plays the woman's part to woo Ida, inverting the devices of *As You Like It* and *Twelfth Night*. Only when he is wounded and vanquished does Ida, like Charlotte Brontë's Jane Eyre, declare her love for a dependent suitor.

In mock heroic style, the poem insists that separating women from men is a hopeless enterprise, and that those who attempt it are misguided. In ending *The Princess* with a marriage, Tennyson sets his programme of change within the stable limits of home and family. Later in the century, similar arguments were being used to make a case against women's suffrage. George Eliot, among others, believed that woman is different from man, and that her power to bring about good in the world would be impaired if she entered the masculine arena. By the 1870s, when he supported the enfranchisement of single women and told his son that the higher education of women was one of the 'great social questions "impending in England"'.[33] Tennyson's approach was decidedly more progressive than George Eliot's.

Even for 1847, the message of *The Princess* is a liberal one. The poem does not advocate that women should give up plans for education and self-fulfilment, but that they should bring these qualities into married life. In the closing stages, the Prince sets out a new future, in which the sexes will take an equal part:

> Henceforth thou hast a helper, me, that know
> The woman's cause is man's: they rise or sink
> Together, dwarf'd or godlike, bond or free.

(VII, 242–5)

On the other side, women readers were not slow to see that the poem proposed no more than an amended version of the status quo. Elizabeth Barrett Browning, 'a good deal disappointed', thought that

Tennyson had merely reproduced a masculine university 'which is a worn-out plaything in the hands of one sex already, & need not be *transferred* in order to be proved ridiculous?'[34] Her own narrative poem, *Aurora Leigh*, setting out the struggles of a female poet in her attempt to find independence and recognition, was in some ways a riposte to Tennyson.

That *The Princess* was not regarded as subversive is clear from the reviews. Most critics responded warmly to the richness of the poem's imagery and language: 'there is in this production a wealth and pictorial beauty and a delicate apprehension of motive and feeling to which our current poetry can furnish few parallels'.[35] The same writer, John Westland Marston in the *Athenaeum*, goes on, however, to complain of the 'incoherency' of the design;[35] 'consciousness of an eccentric plan can scarcely excuse it'.[36] There was a general feeling that Tennyson had not fulfilled his promise as the great poet of the age, and that *The Princess* did not mark a significant advance upon his 1842 volume. Marston's complaint that it was incoherent was echoed by many others.

Among those who did accept the poem as 'an essentially modern one', was Charles Kingsley. Writing after the emendations of 1850, he came close to seeing the poem as Tennyson might have wished. 'Tennyson shows himself more than ever the poet of the day. In it more than ever the old is interpenetrated with the new – the domestic and scientific with the ideal and sentimental. He dares, in every page, to make use of modern words and notions, from which the mingled clumsiness and archaism of his compeers shrinks, as unpoetical.'[37]

There is evidence that, by now, Tennyson's popularity had diverged from his reputation in the periodicals and newspapers. Although more reviews of *The Princess* were favourable than otherwise, the work could hardly be accounted a critical success. The public, on the other hand, had no doubts. By 1853, the book had gone into five editions (all of 1500 or 2000). By 1854, his usual two-thirds share of the profits had brought in over £600 for Tennyson.

Tennyson had been writing his 'elegy' poems for Arthur Hallam since 1833, circulating them or reading them aloud among their mutual friends. By 1845, he had completed many sections of the work which became *In Memoriam*. The history of the elegy as a poetic form goes back to the Greeks, and Tennyson was conversant with numerous examples: Milton's 'Lycidas', Moschus's 'Lament for Bion' (to which he had introduced Hallam), 'Adonais', (which Hallam had helped to publish), are all obliquely mentioned in *In Memoriam*. A host of other texts are also echoed, including the Bible, the Apocrypha, Hallam's beloved Dante, Shakespeare's sonnets and the works of Goethe.

Unlike Milton or Shelley, Tennyson makes little reference to the traditional symbolism of elegy, scarcely bowing to the convention that poet and friend appear as musical shepherds, piping and singing in Arcady. Where the subject had been a close friend, these devices were inappropriate. The heart of the poem, for all its wide range of reference, lies in grief at a human loss. Coleridge's definition of elegy as 'the form of poetry natural to the reflective mind',[38] conveys the broader effects of *In Memoriam*, but Tennyson had no need to drum up feelings for the purposes of reflection or composition. His niece recalled that: 'In after years he would frequently talk to me about the friends of his youth, especially Arthur Hallam, of whom he spoke as of one who had died but yesterday'.[39]

Technically, *In Memoriam* is not one poem but 133, including a 'Prologue' and an 'Epilogue'. Written on different occasions and in differing moods, there is no obvious sequence, and Tennyson himself is known to have arranged the separate poems in more than one order. A few were added after publication to make the overall meaning clearer. According to the poet, he did not initially envisage the creation of a larger work, although the choice of a common stanza form, abba, implies that the parts were consciously related to each other from the beginning.

In its finished form, there is a broad shape to *In Memoriam* which moves from shattering, chilling, grief to the affirmation of a continuing evolution towards human perfection. Certain poems provide signposts to this progression, those associated with Christmases over a period of years, or the two contrasting pairs which describe Wimpole Street in a rainy dawn and on a fresh spring morning, or a yew tree in winter and spring.

In Memoriam XLVIII explicitly considers the question of form. For a work, 'of Sorrow born', the poet has rejected the grand manner in favour of a series of brief lyrics. Comparisons between Shakespeare's sonnets and *In Memoriam* have often been made, and the 'generic structured collection',[40] particularly the sonnet sequence, was a popular genre with several poets including Elizabeth Barrett Browning, Dante Gabriel Rossetti and George Meredith, all of whom used it for extended analyses of human relationships. Tennyson discusses his reasons for preferring the lightness and openness of lyric to the weightier lines of blank verse or the hexameter. Even the sonnet would have seemed to him too formally concentrated:

> Nor dare she trust a larger lay,
>   But rather loosens from the lip
>   Short swallow-flights of song, that dip
> Their wings in tears, and skim away.

(XLVIII, 13–16)

The same poem, XLVIII, begins with a declaration that if these 'brief lays', proposed 'Grave doubts and answers' to the problems raised, then they would be 'such as men might scorn' (1–4). The poet does not state a philosophy in *In Memoriam*; his frequent use of intransitive verbs, or of the subjunctive with 'if' and 'whether', frustrates the reader who reaches out for certainties.

In the tenth poem, Tennyson writes of the power of traditional religious patterns, as he contemplates his anxiety that Hallam should be buried in English earth. Yet, *In Memoriam*, as T. S. Eliot famously said, is also a poem of 'doubt'.[41] It is reasonable to associate some of the poem's attitudes with the central contention of the German idealist philosophers that truth cannot be apprehended by rational means but must be perceived through the inner reason. It is to such intuitive truth that Tennyson often turns. His knowledge of German philosophy had been revived in the 1840s through friendship with George Venables and the Lushingtons. Venables' translation of the work of the Christian idealist, Johann Gottlieb Fichte, was in process at the very time when Tennyson, who saw Venables frequently, was writing the later parts of *In Memoriam*.

The ideas of Arthur Hallam himself provided another source of inspiration. Hallam's essay, 'Theodicaea Novissima', was published in the first edition of his *Remains* only at Tennyson's insistence, and it is by no means surprising that it has its effect on the elegy. In the essay, Hallam argues that reason alone cannot establish the existence of God. Trying to explain the presence of evil in the world, he decides that Christ could only equal God by fighting evil, and that man was created, not for his own sake, but to fulfil the perfection of Christ. Man can approach God only through his capacity to love, the quality epitomised by the divine.

It is part of the progression of *In Memoriam* that the poet first denies and then upholds Hallam's position. Man, who trusted that

'God was love indeed', finds much in the universe to undermine that belief (LVI, 13). Instances of sudden death are described to parallel the shocking waste of Hallam. Scientific discovery, and the laws of nature, open up the prospect of an uncaring, arbitrary world. Tennyson never did manage to convince himself that evil was necessary to create good. But he had always before him the memory of Hallam fighting off the assaults of doubt with his eyes wide open:

> He fought his doubts and gather'd strength,
> He would not make his judgment blind,
> He faced the spectres of the mind
> And laid them: thus he came at length
>
> To find a stronger faith his own.
>
> (XCVI, 13–17)

The 'elegies' had been combined into a fair copy by February 1849 when Tennyson sent Coventry Patmore to search for a 'butcher's account book' in his former lodgings. Having forced his way past the landlady, Patmore found the book in a drawer: 'if I had been a little later it would probably have been sold to a butter-shop'.[42] Emily Patmore copied the poems out for Moxon, who gave Tennyson a £300 advance. By the winter, Tennyson was considering publishing a very limited edition of the elegies for his friends. Six copies were apparently printed and distributed under very strict instructions. Tennyson told Aubrey de Vere: 'I believe I am going to print them and then I needn't tell you that you will be perfectly welcome to a copy – on the condition that when the book is published, this vaunt courier of it shall be either sent back to me, or die the death by fire in Curra[g]h Chase' (Letters, I, 321).

Encouraged by his friends' reactions and by the approval of Emily Sellwood, Tennyson agreed to the publication of 1500 copies. By Christmas, 8000 had been printed. The title *In Memoriam* is said to have been chosen by Emily for what was initially an anonymous poem. Hallam's identity, however, was clearly stated, so that Tennyson's authorship was scarcely a secret. Several of the first reviewers openly referred to him. Not everyone knew the truth, however. The critic of the *Literary Gazette* assumed that the author was a woman, and another that 'these touching lines come from the full heart of the widow of a military man'.[43] Until recently, these mistakes have provoked only merriment, but, in a changing climate of opinion, it is possible to approach them more sensitively, as a response to Tennyson's openness of feeling and emotion.

The warmth of the reviews marked the decisive turn in Tennyson's critical reputation. Most responded to the quality of the poetry, praising the choice of stanza. There was a general sense that Tennyson had at last proved himself by writing a poem for the public as a whole. If the critic of the *English Review* believed that 'Mr Tennyson will always be a *class poet*; he will never be *very generally popular*',[44] he was quite wrong. George Henry Lewes was nearer the truth in *The Leader*: 'We shall be surprised if it does not become the solace and delight of every home where poetry is loved. A true and hopeful spirit breathes from its pages . . . All who have sorrowed will listen with delight to the chastened strains here poured forth *In Memoriam*'.[45] A few critics, including the reviewer in *The Times*, felt that the grief was exaggerated and excessively drawn out, or wondered whether the poem worked as a whole. Considering the religious controversies of the age, surprisingly few took up the question of 'doubt'.

In the five years from 1850–54, the poem brought Tennyson £1176, in addition to the £300 advance. This was comparable to the sums earned by writers of fiction. The poet's wider frame of reference, literary, philosophical, and scientific, cannot have been accessible to all, but his broad meaning was readily comprehensible. The domestic vignettes, drawing parallels with the love of parents and children or husband and wife, pointed towards archetypal patterns of human emotion. Today, *In Memoriam* is subjected to scholarly and critical scrutiny, as alternative readings and levels of meaning are proposed, but ordinary readers still feel able to approach it as a statement of human grief. This quality did much to create its early success with the Victorian public, more prepared than twentieth-century readers to contemplate the religious and personal implications of death and loss.

6

Marriage and Farringford

Tennyson's growing prosperity revived his thoughts of marriage. He put the case dramatically to Lady Harriet Baring in 1845, saying that he 'must have a woman to live beside; *would prefer a lady*, but cannot afford one; and so must marry a maidservant'.[1] In the same year, Aubrey de Vere found him, 'much out of spirits, and said that he could no longer bear to be knocked about the world, and that he must marry and find love and peace or die'.[2]

Tennyson did not conform to the conventional image of a paterfamilias. He smoked heavily, was undomesticated and far from presentable. Colonel Weston Cracroft, who met him in Lincolnshire in 1849, found him 'dirty looking'. 'On the whole his features coarse, and complexion dirty and sallow – he wears spectacles – conversation agreeable. I was amused when the Poet put his feet up on the sofa and Mrs Rawnsley, careful soul, whom I had observed to grow fidgetty, all of a sudden quietly warned him off'.[3]

Tennyson saw Emily Sellwood in September 1847 when both were guests of the Lushingtons at Park House. It was an uneasy meeting. Emily had come to believe that 'they two moved in worlds of religious thought so different that the two would not "make one music" as they moved'.[4] There is some evidence that Tennyson proposed again and was refused. In 1849 he sent her the versions of his poem, 'Sweet and Low', asking her to select one for publication in *The Princess*. In the following spring she read a draft of 'Elegies'. In sending it back, she told the poet: 'I am the happier for having seen these poems and . . . I hope I shall be the better too'.[5] It is often said that the 'Elegies' calmed Emily's religious doubts about her suitor, but it is hard to believe that the revelation of his capacity for tenderness and love was not equally persuasive.

Tennyson was now forty, Emily thirty-six, and, after the disappointments of the preceding decade, their hesitations were natural. The first move came from Tennyson, strongly supported by the Rawnsleys and by their friend, Charles Kingsley, a vigorous advocate for the married state. There was another meeting at Park House, when financial difficulties were again aired. The decision to marry was finally taken in the Rawnsleys' parsonage at Shiplake.

Once it became clear that Emily would accept him, her suitor, predictably, began to waver. Having obtained a licence, he delayed fixing the date. Charles Tennyson Turner (now reunited with Louisa) found his position as Emily's brother-in-law awkward: 'after what happened before, we kept a strict eye upon him, in case he should take it into his head to bolt!!!'[6] Other members of the Tennyson family were kept in the dark about the arrangements. Those in Cheltenham knew that he meant to marry, but had no idea when the ceremony would take place. Mary Tennyson, who disliked Emily, believed that her brother's secrecy was a reflection of his doubts: 'Poor thing, I daresay he is miserable enough at times, thinking of what he is about to do' (Letters, I, 325).

Afraid that the press would report the marriage, Tennyson did not inform friends or relatives until after the event. Many of them had never heard of Emily and were greatly surprised by the news. Some, including John Forster, were angry. The wedding, on 13 June 1850, was without conventional trappings: 'neither the cake nor the dresses arrived in time, and the white gloves were lost' (Letters, I, 327). The party was small: Emily's father, her brother-in-law, Charles Weld, Edmund and Cecilia Lushington, the Rawnsley family, whose daughters and niece were bridesmaids, and their curate, Greville Phillimore. *In Memoriam* extolls the importance of the marriage bond and the marriage ceremony, but the hasty, secretive way in which the wedding was arranged suggests deep insecurities on Tennyson's part.

Letters written by both bride and groom on the day after the wedding express a sense of relief. Emily told Catherine Rawnsley that she was 'as happy and comfortable as even you could wish me', and Alfred sent a joking one line letter to Sophy Elmhirst (the former Sophy Rawnsley): 'We seem to get on very well together. I have not beaten her yet' (Letters, I, 327–8). A letter to Drummond Rawnsley was accompanied by one of Tennyson's most affectionate pieces of occasional verse, 'To the Vicar of Shiplake'.

Like other Victorians of their class, the Tennysons took a long honeymoon. From the home of the Eltons at Clevedon Court on the Bristol Channel, they made a pilgrimage together to the grave of Arthur Hallam. They were delayed at Weston-super-Mare 'because we both needed rest not because it is beautiful'.[7] They explored the village of Lynton on the North Devon coast, and then Glastonbury, traditionally associated with both King Alfred and King Arthur. A visit to Elizabeth Tennyson in Cheltenham followed, and from there they moved to the Lake District. Finding them in a hotel, James Spedding took them off to Mirehouse for a stay of several days. There were 'excursions on lake and mountain' and a 'family circle which could not fail to be interesting' (*ET, Journal*, p. 18).

From Mirehouse they travelled to Tent Lodge on Lake Coniston, one of the estate houses belonging to James and Mary Marshall, sister and brother-in-law of Tennyson's Cambridge friend, Stephen Spring-Rice. Today Tent Lodge seems a sizeable residence, but Thomas Carlyle wrote to his wife: 'I should judge it much more charming for the Marshalls than for him [Tennyson]: "Sir, we keeps a Poet!" Softest of soft sowder [flattery] *plus* a vacant Cottage and to dinner as often as you like.'[8] Tennyson told his aunt, Elizabeth Russell, who had paid for the journey: 'We found the seat of a Marshall on almost every lake we came to, for it seems there are several brothers who have all either bought or been left estates in this country; and they are all, report says, as wealthy as Croesus'. He was entranced by the views over 'crag, mountain, woods and lake, which look especially fine as the sun is dropping behind the hills' (*Memoir*, I, 333).

When she married, Emily Tennyson intended to 'soon take a home and probably near town'.[9] But that was not Tennyson's way. Six months after the wedding the couple were still living as the guests of others. Tent Lodge had been offered as a permanent home, but rejected on account of the damp. When they finally left Coniston in October on their way to Cheltenham and Park House, Emily was pregnant and Tennyson's letters were full of inquiries about houses in the south of England. In January 1851, they moved into The Hill at Warninglid near Horsham in Sussex, only to leave again two weeks later, driven out by the leaking roof, smoky chimney and howling wind. They were anxiously trying to dispose of the remainder of the lease for months afterwards. The Rawnsleys, followed by the Lushingtons, took them in once more.

While the Tennysons were at Park House, Alfred took another major step towards social recognition: he accepted nomination as Poet Laureate. William Wordsworth had died on 23 April 1850, and in May the post was offered to Samuel Rogers, who declined on grounds of age. A number of alternatives were floated, among them Leigh Hunt, Martin Tupper, Henry Taylor and Elizabeth Barrett Browning. It was the publication of *In Memoriam*, and Prince Albert's enthusiasm for the book, which swung the balance in Tennyson's favour. He liked to imply that the appointment had taken him by surprise, but, on the night of 8 November, just before the offer was made, he dreamt that Queen Victoria and Prince Albert called upon him, and that Albert kissed him.

Two replies were written, 'one accepting and one declining'. Tennyson 'threw them on the table, and settled to decide which I would send after my dinner and bottle of port'.[10] The choice, he informed James Knowles, was made because George Venables 'told me, that, if I became Poet Laureate, I should always when I dined out be offered the liver-wing of a fowl' (*Memoir*, I, 336). A different explanation went to Sophy Elmhirst: 'I would rather not have been made Laureate if I could have helped it: but I was told by those who know these matters that being already in receipt of a pension I could not *gracefully* decline the Queen's offer. As for writing court odes except upon express command from Headquarters, that I shall not do. Pretty things they are likely to be.' (Letters, I, 343)

Tennyson's decision cannot have resulted either from flippancy or expediency. He was profoundly aware of the traditions of English poetry, and conscious of what it meant to succeed a man of Wordsworth's stature. He more than lived up to expectation. For over forty years Tennyson placed the laureateship at the centre of national life, establishing himself as the greatest of all laureates, the man with whom the title itself will always be most closely associated. The opportunity to write about contemporary events accorded with his own growing predilection. Such poems as the 'Ode on the Death of the Duke of Wellington' and 'The Charge of the Light Brigade' were not written from a sense of duty (like some of the Royal Family poems) but from genuine creative excitement.

One of the drawbacks of the job was the upsurge of unsolicited mail: 'My complaint against the time and my office of Poet Laureate is not so much that I am deluged with verse as that no man ever thinks of sending me a book of prose – hardly ever. I am like a man receiving perpetual parcels of currants and raisins and barley sugar and never a piece of bread' (Letters, II, 196).

At the time of his appointment, Tennyson took a lease on Chapel House in Montpelier Row, Twickenham. Built in 1720, as part of a magnificent terrace, Chapel House had many advantages. Only 300 yards from the river, a mile from Richmond Park, it was easily accessible to London by rail. Convenient as it was, it never gained the Tennysons' affection. Six weeks after they moved in, on Easter Sunday, their first child, a boy, was born dead. For the rest of his life, Tennyson recalled the lost son with poignancy: 'he looked (if it be not absurd to call a newborn babe so) even majestic in his mysterious silence after all the turmoil of the night before' (Letters, II, 15). Emily never saw her child, but Alfred thought the boy like himself in power and spirit, a true heir of the Tennysons.

After this tragedy, and in a particularly cold and wet English summer, Tennyson decided that the moment had come to make his long postponed journey to the south. After Paris, with further visits to the Louvre and a meeting with Robert and Elizabeth Browning, the Tennysons travelled down to the South of France, and from there to Genoa. It was their first visit to Italy:

> What slender campanili grew
> By bays, the peacock's neck in hue;
> Where, here and there, on sandy beaches
> A milky-bell'd amaryllis blew.

> ('The Daisy', 13–16)

Having lived so long with Italy in his imagination, Tennyson found the reality disconcerting: '"Flies, fleas, filth, flame" and "fraud"' were words frequently on his lips. Browning had recommended Bagni di Lucca, a summer resort popular with expatriates, and the Tennysons moved there with a small party of relatives and friends. At first Emily found the deep valley claustrophobic with 'nothing but very steep wooded heights and a few houses', but, once settled, they enjoyed walking in the surrounding hills.[11]

From Bagni, the couple made their way to Florence, about which Arthur Hallam had enthused twenty years earlier. For once, they were not disappointed:

> At Florence too what golden hours,
> In those long galleries, were ours;
> What drives about the fresh Cascinè,
> Or walks in Boboli's ducal bowers.

> In bright vignettes, and each complete,
> Of tower or duomo, sunny-sweet,
> Or palace, how the city glitter'd,
> Thro' cypress avenues, at our feet.

> ('The Daisy', 41–8)

They stayed with Frederick Tennyson and his Italian wife at the Villa Torregiani, just outside the city. While there, Tennyson had two remarkable dreams involving his brother Septimus. In one, the dying Septimus (he lived until 1866) was bidding Alfred farewell, and in the other Septimus, having been seriously ill, recovered. In twice dreaming of Septimus as near death, while in the house of his irascible eldest brother, Tennyson was perhaps associating his sweet-tempered and unstable younger brother with his own lost son. If, as some believe, the dreamer is transformed into the personalities of the dream, then Tennyson was preoccupied with his own death. Some confirmation for this comes in 'The Brook', written a few years later, where a poet lies:

> Not by the well-known stream and rustic spire,
> But unfamiliar Arno, and the dome
> Of Brunelleschi.

> (188–90)

Instead of going on to Rome and Venice, as planned, the Tennysons, mistakenly believing that Emily was pregnant again, and fearing Italian uprisings, returned to the north. Franklin Lushington suggested that the about turn reflected Tennyson's craving for English tobacco. Reggio, Parma, Lodi, Piacenza and the Lombardy plain they saw in 'a plague of rain' (l. 50). At Milan the sun shone at last, and Tennyson delighted in the Cathedral with its 'mount of marble, a hundred spires!' (l. 60) As always, he noticed the stained glass, 'the giant windows' blazon'd fires' (l. 58):

> I climb'd the roofs at break of day;
> Sun-smitten Alps before me lay.
> I stood among the silent statues,
> And statued pinnacles, mute as they.

> ('The Daisy', 61–4)

The Tennysons returned home to a peripatetic existence. They disliked Chapel House, but were unable to settle on an alternative. Spring 1852 found them in Malvern, and in the autumn they rented Seaford House on the Sussex Coast. Tennyson made two trips north in the summers of 1852 and 1853, to Yorkshire and Scotland. He was incurably restless.

A second son was born to the couple soon after Tennyson's return from Yorkshire, on 11 August 1852. The father's letters reveal a touching and tender pleasure: 'I have seen beautiful things in my life, but I never saw anything more beautiful than the mother's face as she lay by the young child an hour or two after, or heard anything sweeter than the little lamblike bleat of the young one' (*Memoir*, II, 356).

Emily, in poor health for weeks after the birth, was sufficiently recovered to give a baptism party on 5 October. There was talk of calling the child Alfred, but when the clergyman asked for the name, 'A. [Alfred] with a loud voice said "Hallam"' (*ET, Journal*, p. 28). Among the guests were Jane Carlyle, a fund of 'brilliant anecdotes' and Robert Browning, who insisted upon bouncing the baby up and down (*Memoir*, II, 488).

Hallam Tennyson's godparents were Henry Hallam, James Marshall and Frederick Denison Maurice, Maurice being Emily's particular choice. The choice was a significant one, for Maurice, a former Cambridge Apostle, was associated with the Broad Church movement, and that was where the Tennysons' sympathies lay. Emily was a deeply religious woman, always hoping to bring her husband more firmly into the Anglican fold. Maurice believed that Christianity must be intellectually honest, exploring rather than ignorantly rejecting the findings of science and the works of the German 'higher critics' (who looked upon the Bible as a historical rather than a supernatural work). Such theories, often associated with the avant-garde Sterling Club, brought down the wrath of both tractarians and evangelicals upon him.

What finally undermined Maurice's position at the conservative King's College, London, was the publication of his *Theological Essays* in June 1853. Both friends and enemies were baffled by his prose, but the Council of King's eventually concluded that in the essay on 'Eternal Life' Maurice cast doubts upon the doctrine of eternal damnation. Later in the year, he was dismissed from his professorship. The offending book was dedicated to 'Alfred Tennyson, Poet Laureate', and made special mention of the author's relationship to Tennyson's son. The tribute to Tennyson's 'writings', which 'have taught me to enter into many of those thoughts and feelings', placed Tennyson himself squarely in Maurice's camp. 'Will you forgive me', Maurice goes on, 'the presumption of offering you a book which at least acknowledges them [Tennyson's writings] and does them homage?'[12] Referring to unwelcome controversies, which he hoped would be a thing of the past when Hallam grew up, Maurice closed with a quotation from *In Memoriam*:

> Ring out the darkness of the land
> Ring in the Christ that is to be.

> (CVI, 31–2)

This was not the first attempt to appropriate *In Memoriam* as a broad church poem. Charles Kingsley, reviewing it for *Fraser's* in 1850, spoke of the blessing of finding 'the most cunning poet of our day able to combine the complicated rhythm and melody of modern times with the old truths which gave heart to martyrs at the stake, to see in the science and the history of the nineteenth-century new and living fulfilments of the words which we learnt at our mothers' knee!'[13] Another member of the broad church group was Frederick William Robertson, whom Tennyson had known in Cheltenham. In 1852 Robertson lectured on *In Memoriam* to an audience of working men in Brighton, telling them that the poem fell 'back upon the grand, primary truths of our humanity; those first principles which underlie all creeds, which belong to our earliest childhood, and on which the wisest and best have rested through all ages: that all is right: that darkness shall be clear: that God and Time are the only interpreters: that Love is King: that the Immortal is in us'.[14]

Tennyson's own attitude to the Church had been essentially liberal since his boyhood. In the 1830s he had supported the moves to abolish subscription to the 39 Articles for Oxford and Cambridge undergraduates, and he entirely concurred with Maurice's views on eternal punishment:

> With loathsome, loveless prate of Hell
> Each bigot makes his infidel,
>   Claps Calvin in God's chair and bids us
> Honour the Devil and all is well.

> (Ricks, II, 497–8)

Even so, Tennyson was cautious about signing a petition in support of Maurice's reinstatement (although he eventually did so): 'I will only add that the veneration for Maurice which induced me to pass by all my family claims and select him as Godfather to my child remain unabated – I may say increased' (*Letters*, II, 76).

It might have been expected that marriage and a child would mellow Tennyson. On the contrary, the political and social events of this time excited and enraged him. The crisis which led to his first outpourings was the 1848 revolution in France which resulted in the fall of Louis Philippe. Tennyson, initially uninterested in European revolutions, turned down a suggestion that he travel to Paris with Ralph Waldo Emerson in that year, telling the American writer that they would never come back alive. When Tennyson did reach Paris for a few days in November 1848, he spent his time in the Louvre, looking at Poussin's *Death of Narcissus* and at the *Venus de Milo*, and apparently taking little interest in the political situation.

In December 1848, a plebiscite was held to elect a President of France. The man elected was Louis Napoleon, son of the former King of Holland, and nephew of Napoleon I. The new president found his position frustratingly nominal, and, three years later, in December 1851, he seized absolute power in a *coup d'état*, holding a referendum which allowed him to re-draw the constitution. In 1852, he proclaimed himself Emperor of the French as Napoleon III. Although there were some liberal social reforms, his enemies across the Channel were horrified by the new emperor's despotic acts: the ban on political meetings, imprisonment of opponents, censorship of the press and institution of a secret police. Coming after Russian repression in Poland, and Austrian attacks on Italy and Hungary, it seemed to Tennyson that Europe needed to be defended against such tyranny.

Tennyson's distaste for Napoleon III was shared by many Englishmen. Well known in London from his years in exile, he was widely regarded as a corrupt adventurer, a verdict which subsequent events did little to change. Tennyson abused him to John Forster as 'that French Dutch pseudo-Corsican-bastard-blackleg kite-eaglet' (*Letters*, II, 47), and, in his poem 'Britons, Guard your own', accused him of manifold dishonesty:

> We hate not France, but France has lost her voice,
> This man is France, the man they call her choice.
>   By tricks and spying
>   And craft and lying,
> And murder, was her freedom overthrown.
>   Britons guard your own.

(Ricks, II, 471)

As Poet Laureate, Tennyson felt himself unable to enter into the political arena. The force of his feeling, however, was not to be denied. Using the pseudonyms, 'Merlin' and 'Taliessin' (both ancient bards), he wrote a series of poems for the press, appealing to the Liberal government under Lord John Russell to recognise the danger. Few would have detected the author of *In Memoriam* in these strident verses, which even recommended military intervention. Tennyson played a game with his readers when he accompanied 'Suggested by Reading an Article in a Newspaper' with this letter: 'Sir, – I have read with much interest the poems by *Merlin*. The enclosed is longer than either of those, and certainly not so good; yet as I flatter myself that it has a smack of Merlin's style in it, and as I feel that it expresses forcibly enough some of the feelings of our time, perhaps you may be induced to admit it. Taliessin.' (*Letters*, II, 26)

Fears of a French invasion were rife, as Napoleon III revived ideas of empire. Fitzgerald, visiting Seaford in December 1852, found Tennyson: 'full of *Invasion*; and I believe truly is more wise and grave about it than any of our Ministers'. Nobody, Tennyson told him, 'listens or cares'.[15] In fact, Tennyson was far from alone. Several paintings exhibited at the Royal Academy during this period conveyed the same warning. Among them were Sir Edwin Landseer's *Time of Peace* and *Time of War* (1846, formerly in the Tate Gallery, since destroyed) and *Our English Coasts* (1852, Tate Gallery) by the Pre-Raphaelite painter, William Holman Hunt. Hunt, like Tennyson, was alarmed by Napoleon III's close relation with the Roman Catholic Church, which had recently established an English hierarchy.

> The Jesuit laughs, and reckoning on his chance
>   Would unrelenting
>   Kill all dissenting,
>
> ('Britons, Guard Your Own', Ricks, II, 471)

was Tennyson's version of this threat.

Southern England was indeed exposed to attack. Most of the regular army was stationed either in the colonies or in Ireland, and few reserves were kept at home. The Militia Bill, which proposed voluntary enlistment, was initially thrown out by the Commons after extensive debate, and then accepted in late May 1852. Army men felt that this 'Home Guard' would not provide adequate defence, while free-thinkers, like John Bright and Richard Cobden, resisted the idea of war for fear of damaging trade. Tennyson called these groups 'babbling Peace Societies,/Where many a dreamer trifles!' ('The Penny-Wise', Ricks, II, 468). When Coventry Patmore set up a volunteer rifle group, the Tennysons subscribed £5, and Tennyson wrote an inflammatory poem on the sins of the French.

The 'invasion' poems were anonymous, but Tennyson was tempted to vent his feelings about Napoleon III in a public work, his 'Ode on the Death of the Duke of Wellington'. In a first draft, he warned the British to beware of the 'silent man beyond the strait', with 'all the powers of the state' and 'all the passions of the rabble'. (Ricks, II, 488) Tennyson wisely omitted this passage before the poem was published. More general admonitions against complacency in a national crisis remained. The British, the poem declares, are a people of 'sober freedom', but others 'their nobler dreams forget,/Confused by brainless mobs and lawless Powers' (164; 153–4).

According to Francis Palgrave, the 'Wellington Ode' was the one poem which caused Tennyson 'a certain anxiety' (*Memoir*, II, 488). Palgrave is not always very perceptive, but Edgar Shannon agrees with him: 'Two years of domesticity, with its concomitant house-hunting, travel, child-birth, and visitors, had not been conducive to poetry . . . For the first time in his literary life Tennyson was truly under pressure'.[16]

In conception, the 'Ode' follows in the tradition of Pindar and of Horace, celebrating the life and greatness of a hero through the rhetoric of praise and through recollections of his achievements. Tennyson had known Horace's *Odes* since his boyhood, when he had translated them for his father. He takes as his model here, not the largely private early *Odes* (echoed in 'The Daisy' and 'To the Rev. F. D. Maurice'), but the more formal and political Roman *Odes*. By adapting the Horatian mode to celebrate the virtues of a victorious British commander, Tennyson was following in the footsteps of Andrew Marvell, whose 'Horatian Ode upon Cromwell's Return from Ireland' is perhaps the greatest example of its kind in the language.

Tennyson's 'Ode' is more rhetorical than Marvell's. The sound of the dead march is heard throughout, no mean technical achievement, yet the controlled measure is one of power rather than mere convention. Not surprisingly, it was among those poems which Tennyson regularly chose to read aloud.

Wellington died on 14 September 1852, and was buried in St Paul's Cathedral two months later, on 18 November 1852. Tennyson saw the procession pass Somerset House in the Strand, but was not present at the interment. His poem had, in any case, been published two days before, at one shilling a copy, Moxon having paid him £200 for an edition of 10 000. Two months is a very short gestation for a major poem, and Tennyson made numerous emendations prior to publication and in subsequent editions. Some of the later additions reflect his experience of the actual procession, others sound a more confidently Christian note, perhaps in response to criticisms in the press.

For all its rhetorical solemnity, the poem is not without a personal note. 'Streaming London's central roar' reflects Tennyson's own lifelong response to the capital. (l. 9) As a boy his imagination had been fired by St Paul's and by the tomb of Nelson. In the 'Ode', the admiral's spirit greets Wellington's cortège. 'The doings of Wellington and Bonaparte' had been the subjects of 'story and verse' at Somersby (*Memoir*, I, 5), and early poems like 'The Invasion of Russia by Napoleon Buonaparte' and 'Buonaparte' reveal the force of the young Tennyson's patriotism. His reference to the 'Pyrenean pines,/Follow'd up in valley and glen', (113–14) associates the scene of some of Wellington's triumphs with Tennyson's own cherished memories. Cecil Lang has pointed out the importance of Wellington's Christian name, Arthur, in connecting the 'Ode' with *In Memoriam* and with the *Idylls*, although the name itself is not used in the poem.[17]

Critical reaction to the 'Ode' was divided, which the sensitive Tennyson construed as hostility. His detractors felt that his work was written in defiance of his lyrical gifts, and that such nobility of subject was beyond his reach. Several twentieth-century commentators have come to the same conclusion, if by a different route, deciding that the poem was part of an 'establishment' straitjacket which Tennyson made for himself.

Tennyson's was not the only poetic tribute to the Iron Duke. Throughout his time as laureate, he was shadowed by an unofficial 'double', Martin Farquar Tupper. A year younger than Tennyson, Tupper had been publishing prolifically from an early age. His best-known work, *Proverbial Philosophy: A book of Thoughts and Arguments*, became an immense popular success. Tupper's career as a chronicler of national events opened with Queen Victoria's coronation of 1838, and his success in the years when Tennyson was in the critical wilderness gives an indication of popular taste. Four thousand copies of Tupper's 'Dirge for Wellington' were sold soon after the Duke's death, and, while acknowledging the superior quality of Tennyson's version, Tupper remarked that the Laureate had given himself far more time to complete it.

In October 1853, Tennyson returned to the Isle of Wight, which he had first visited in 1849, with ideas of settling there. He based himself with friends at Bonchurch, on the south-east coast. Hearing of a house to let at Farringford Hill, near Freshwater, 'He went, and found it looking rather wretched with wet leaves trampled into the [lawns]' (ET, *Journal*, pp. 30–2). A regency building with gothic windows and castellation, Farringford may have distantly reminded him of Somersby. Emily was summoned to inspect the property, and, having seen the view over Freshwater Bay to Afton Down, she decided in favour.

The Tennysons rented the house for three years at £2 a week, with an option to purchase. Elizabeth Tennyson took over the remaining lease of Chapel House, but talked of moving to Farringford herself. Emily was left, during one of her husband's absences, with the embarrassment of fending her off. Fortunately, Tennyson approved: 'You have done quite right I think in respect to Mother . . . I was afraid if she came to live with us the rest would flock there' (Letters, II, 72).

The rent for Farringford was roughly twice that of Chapel House. As usual, Tennyson was a prey to financial anxieties: 'We are going to buy this house and little estate here, only I rather shake under the fear of being ruined' (Letters, II, 75). Farringford was indeed an 'estate', with a home farm, cottages and a thatched farmhouse, leased out to a Mr Merwood. 'We love our picturesque fields,' wrote Emily, 'each would have had its own little romance had we been born among them' (ET, *Journal*, p. 238).

In the 1850s, Farringford was so remote that the domestic staff, used to the proximity of London, were reduced to tears at the sight of the place. Tennyson had his own strategy for overcoming the problem. When boredom set in, he would leave Yarmouth pier for a spell in London, seeing his friends, having his teeth attended to, buying new books, and organising the publication of his poetry. Emily hated his absences, but she knew that she must endure them.

Farringford was an ideal place for a compulsive walker. Behind the house, above a patch of tangled woodland known as the 'wilderness', is the high down which today bears Tennyson's name. At the summit stood an old beacon, popularly associated with the Spanish Armada, and now displaced by Tennyson's memorial. From there the land falls slowly to the series of stacks known as the Needles, the westermost point of the island. All along the south coast, easily reached on foot from Farringford, are magnificent chalk cliffs, dangerously friable for those who venture too close to the edge. He went further afield as well, to Newport, ten miles away, or to Bonchurch.

The countryside offered a wealth of natural phenomena to stimulate Tennyson's imagination. With his wonted precision, he noted birds, animals, butterflies and wild flowers. From the start he enjoyed studying fossils with the scientific writer, Dr Robert James Mann, and later he befriended the rector of Brighstone, Mr Fox, who collected fossil dinosaurs. Clear skies also encouraged him to return to astronomy, and in 1859 a platform was built at the top of the house so that he could watch the stars. Emily's journal records several evenings when they studied cosmic events, the most dramatic being the passing of the great comet in 1858.

Over the years, the Tennysons entertained numerous friends at Farringford, some staying in the house, and others calling in on visits to the island. Plumbley's Hotel in Freshwater became a regular haunt for their guests. Seven months after the move to the Isle of Wight, Sir John Simeon, the squire of Swainston Manor, called to greet the newcomers. Swainston is on the road to Newport, further inland than Farringford, but with a distant view over the Solent. Tennyson would sometimes walk there, and friendly relations were established between the two households. Simeon was a Roman Catholic, but Tennyson overcame his religious prejudices, and became attached to 'the Prince of courtesy', as he later dubbed his friend ('In the Garden at Swainston', 10).

Five months after their arrival at Farringford, the Tennyson's youngest child was born, on 16 March 1854. The boy was christened Lionel because of Tennyson's observation of Mars in the constellation of the Lion on the night of his birth. Lionel was never to be as dearly loved as Hallam. To his father, he did not stand comparison with the dead first-born: 'If my latest born were to die to-night, I do not think that I should suffer so much as I did, looking on that noble fellow who had never seen the light' (*Memoir*, I, 375).

At Farringford, Tennyson discovered a new outlet for his creativity, gardening. When he did not walk in the afternoon, he would dig, hoe, organise the compost pit and set out new beds. In summer he rolled the lawns, and cut the grass with a scythe, 'carefully removing every dandelion' (*Letters*, II, 258). Both Tennysons spread the ground with ashes and lime, and watered their flowers. The poet would buy shrubs and trees; oleanders, rhododendrons, laurels, barberry (berberis), lilacs, and mezereon are among those which he is known to have planted at Farringford. By 1856, there was a stove in the greenhouse, from which plants were put out in the spring.

The grounds were planned as a small landscape garden, dotted with favourite perennials like Russian violets, primroses, cowslips, narcissus, hyacinths, irises and lilies of the valley. Tennyson found these either on his own land or in the surrounding country. 'I hope no one will pluck my wild Irises which I planted,' he wrote in 1863, 'if they want flowers there is the kitchen-garden – nor break my new laurels etc. whose growth I have watched . . . I don't quite like children croquetting on that lawn. I have a personal interest in every leaf about it' (*Letters*, II, 337–8). Magnolias and roses grew in front of the house, and gates, walks and seats were carefully placed for the best views.

Tennyson's 'careless-order'd garden' was an old fashioned one ('To the Rev. F. D. Maurice', 15). By the 1850s, the concept of formal flower-gardens was gaining ground everywhere, while the Farringford scheme, with its 'natural' shrubs and lawns, and its trees planted to conceal surrounding buildings, was laid out in the manner of the 1820s and 1830s. In his poem, 'Amphion', probably written in the late 1830s, Tennyson had satirised the growing prevalence of exotic plants in English gardens, mocking the idea of gardening by 'Botanic Treatises' (l. 77). On his own estate he attempted to exclude the artificial.

Tennyson's deep love and knowledge of flowers is evident from his poems. In later life, he disapproved of picking wild flowers, but, in these years, he often brought a handful indoors for Emily's pleasure and delight. At Farringford, flowers were planted in the walled garden where an arbour was later built. The kitchen garden was a common feature of country house gardens, but Tennyson's relegation of both colourful flowers and human activity there, out of sight of the house windows, was again old-fashioned. Victorian gardeners were bringing them into view, as Tennyson himself would do at Aldworth. In his kitchen garden, vegetables and fruit trees grew behind the herbaceous borders, and Tennyson himself planted potatoes there in 1855. Helen Allingham's painting (from a much later date) shows a riot of brilliant flowers, with aubretia, irises, geraniums, tulips, wallflowers and pansies among them.

Help with the garden was greatly appreciated, and guests and tutors found themselves roped in as free labour. In 1854, the young painter, John Everett Millais, joined Tennyson in sweeping up and burning leaves. A year later he began one of his most famous paintings, *Autumn Leaves* (Manchester City Art Gallery), where a group of four girls stand by a heaped bonfire.

On his travels Tennyson made a point of looking at gardens. He wrote to Emily from Lisbon in 1859 of the Botanic Gardens with their palms, prickly pears and cactuses: 'and enormous oleanders covered all over with the richest red blossom and I thought of our poor one at Farringford that won't blossom' (*Memoir*, I, 140). Palgrave remembered him in Paxton's greenhouse at Chatsworth in 1862: 'The great conservatory, – Archetype, as is well known, of the Exhibition Building of 1851 . . . I think was Tennyson's greatest enjoyment . . . this acre of the Tropics enshrined under glass was planted so closely with palm and fern, that Tennyson found in it some faint but attractive image of those gorgeous southern forests which he drew with masterly hand in "Enoch Arden"'.[18] The formal gardens at Chatsworth he found less pleasing: 'were I the Duke . . . I would make my first expenditure on undoing it,' he told his companion.[19]

From 1861 to 1869, the Tennysons took over management of their farm, but this they relinquished in 1869 to their former gardener, Charles Heard. Emily's words on the subject reveal how much she had relied upon the garden to keep her husband in good humour: 'The Farm is not the source of out of doors interest to A. which I had hoped it might have been when we had no longer that of making new lawns & glades & otherwise altering the grounds at Farringford'. (ET, *Journal*, pp. 298–9)

The Tennysons' early years in remote and peaceful Farringford were punctuated by news of war. In October 1853, just before their arrival, Turkey had opened hostilities against Russia, protesting at the Russians' occupation of Moldavia and Wallachia (now Romania). By late February, a booming of cannon from across the Solent could be heard at Farringford, and, a few weeks later, Britain and France entered the contest on Turkey's side, the ancient enemies drawn together by a common alarm at the prospect of Russian expansion. Intending to halt the Russian advance, they found that their enemy had withdrawn into the Black Sea province of the Crimea, where the ensuing war took place.

Tennyson's dislike of Russia has been ably charted by Patrick Waddington.[20] The poet's first reactions to the Russian war were, however, less patriotic than personal. Writing to his aunt he expressed a fear that it might 'go far to knock my profits on the head' (*Letters*, II, 83), and, as late as 23 October, two days before the charge of the Light Brigade at Balaclava, Tennyson was still writing to Moxon in the same terms: 'I should like to know how my books are going on or off rather, and whether the Russian war has interfered with their sale' (*Letters*, II, 98).

At the time, Tennyson was at work on a new poem, which became his favourite, *Maud*. In the final section he captures the warmongering mood of the time, as the unnamed speaker of the poem decides to enlist. His tone is matched by newspaper reports of the scenes in the centre of London in February 1854, which the Scots, Grenadier and Coldstream Guards paraded to Buckingham Palace, before sailing from Southampton.

There is some confusion about the inception of *Maud*, but it is accepted that the germ of the poem lay in the lyric of lost love, 'O that 'twere possible', unwillingly surrendered to Lord Northampton in 1837 for publication in *The Tribute*. Late in 1853, Emily Tennyson's father made a copy of 'O that 'twere possible', in response to a request from Farringford. Sections of *Maud* were written early in 1854, but the work was then laid aside. It was apparently at this time that friends persuaded Tennyson to complete it, each believing that he or she was the instigator of the poem.

The prevailing mood of *Maud* is in a markedly different vein from that of the haunting early lyric. The political poetry of the early years of the decade reflects Tennyson's uncharacteristic ferocity. The internal storm culminated in the writing of this most experimental and challenging of all his great poems. The fuel for *Maud* seems to have come from the private frustrations of the 1830s and 1840s, but the public events and the evils of urban society in the 1850s supplied the tinder.

Maud is an extended monologue which painfully explores the mind of a deeply disturbed man, and, at the same time, opens up an explosion of anger against the mammonism of the age. According to one source, *In Memoriam*, a poem of grief, now seemed to Tennyson 'too hopeful . . . more than I am myself'.[21] *Maud* is a poem with little, if any, sense of consolation. It opens with an account of the suicide of the speaker's father after a financial disaster. Such collapses were common enough at the time, and Tennyson himself had suffered one when Matthew Allen's business failed. In this case, a partner seems to have profited from the father's fall:

But that old man, now lord of the broad estate and the Hall,
Dropt off gorged from a scheme that had left us flaccid
   and drain'd.

(Part I, I, 19–20)

For the speaker's denunciation of ostentatious wealth and 'gewgaw' castles, Tennyson drew upon recollections of his father's disinheritance, of Bayons Manor, and of his aunt's mine-owner husband (Part I, X, 347). Memories of Rosa Baring apparently lie behind the story of the poor suitor for a rich girl, although romantic novels of Tennyson's youth, like Sir Walter Scott's *Bride of Lammermoor* or Bulwer Lytton's *Falkland*, probably had a part to play in the creation of the plot.

   In terms which sometimes echo Carlyle, the speaker denounces commercial greed and its terrible side effects, poverty and crime:

And the vitriol madness flushes up in the ruffian's head,
Till the filthy by-lane rings to the yell of the trampled wife,
And chalk and alum and plaster are sold to the poor for bread,
And the spirit of murder works in the very means of life,
. . .
When a Mammonite mother kills her babe for a burial fee,
And Timour-Mammon grins on a pile of children's bones,
Is it peace or war? better, war! loud war by land by sea,
War with a thousand battles, and shaking a hundred thrones.

(Part I, I, 37–40; 45–8)

The adulteration of food was a topical issue. A parliamentary committee was debating the subject, and the use of sulphate of lime to whiten bread was under investigation. Infanticide was also common, and 'Mammonite mothers' who killed their children 'for a burial fee' were another subject for public outcry. Carlyle cites one such case in *Past and Present*.

   The complexity of *Maud* makes it impossible for the reader to settle down to reading the poem in a particular way. It is written in a variety of verse forms and styles encompassing denunciatory verses, the lyricism of a love poem like 'Come into the Garden, Maud', and searing accounts of madness:

And the hoofs of the horses beat, beat,
The hoofs of the horses beat,
Beat into my scalp and my brain.

(Part II, V, 246–8)

Here, Tennyson was drawing on his recollections of instability within his own family and among the patients at Matthew Allen's asylum. Throughout the nineteenth-century, doctors analysed madness, attempting to categorise its varieties, and to establish its causes and possible remedies. Public interest was maintained through articles on the subject, new asylums were set up and old ones were reformed. Charlotte Brontë's Bertha Rochester, Mary Braddon's Lucy Audley, Browning's speaker in 'Porphyria's Lover', are all literary creations reflecting the public fascination with the insane.

As the writing of *Maud* continued, Tennyson, like the rest of the nation, was dependent upon the press for news of the war. Brief despatches, often inaccurate, reached Whitehall from sources in Eastern Europe, but full accounts of actions took two or three weeks to appear. At first, these confirmed the public mood of optimism. A victory at the River Alma had opened the way to the Russian stronghold of Sebastapol. There were persistent rumours that the city had fallen. Emily Tennyson wrote in her journal of 'great disappointment' darkening 'England on learning that the news that Sebastapol had fallen was false' (ET, *Journal*, p. 39).

A note of caution had already been sounded by the *Times* correspondent, William Howard Russell. On arrival at Gallipoli in April, Russell told his readers of 'the privation to which our men were at first exposed' . . . 'the inefficiency of our arrangements' and the sharp contrast with the 'excellence of the French commissariat administration'.[22] The strictures are characteristic of Russell's reports throughout the war. British troops were scandalously ill-equipped, and attempts to improve the position were bedevilled by periodic bad luck with the weather, which disrupted supply vessels, and, far more seriously, by bureaucratic incompetence. Russell reported that the commander-in-chief, Lord Raglan, spent most of his time at his desk, valiantly trying to tackle a mountain of paper.

In the winter of 1854–5, Russell wrote of a 'system of "requisitions", "orders", and "memos", which was enough to depress an army of scriveners'. As a result the troops were cold, wet, and without adequate food or medical support. 'I had an opportunity of seeing several lighters full of warm great coats, etc., for the men, lying a whole day in the harbour of Balaklava beneath a determined fall of rain and snow . . . no one would receive them without orders'.[23] From the start of the campaign, cholera, exacerbated by poor sanitary conditions, had killed as many men as the war. The Tennysons read Russell's despatches with horror: 'my heart almost bursts with indignation at the accursed mismanagement of our noble little army, that flower of men', was the poet's response (*Letters*, II, 104). Like many others, he rapidly turned from patriotic enthusiasm to a mood of frustration and despair.

In November 1854, Tennyson wrote a short poem, on which, as he said, he did not 'pique' himself (*Letters*, II, 114). As it turned out, this was to be his greatest popular success, 'The Charge of the Light Brigade'. On 25 October 1854, the Russians had attempted to reduce the pressure on Sebastapol by attacking the British forces outside Balaclava. They were driven off by the Heavy Cavalry Brigade, and Lord Raglan then gave an order for the Light Brigade, under Lord Cardigan, to prevent the Russians from removing certain British guns. The order was misunderstood to mean that the Light Brigade was to attack the main Russian gun emplacement. Of the 670 soldiers who charged, 552 survived, but the initial *Times* report gave 607 as the number of soldiers involved, and 198 for those who returned. These figures were later modified, but Tennyson's poem was written with the original, more shocking, casualty figures in mind.

News of the 'charge' took some time to arrive in Britain. On 3 November, *The Times* briefly announced the total defeat of the light cavalry on 25 October. Short notices were published over the next few days, but Russell's full account did not appear until 13 November, nearly three weeks after the event. His style sets the scene for Tennyson's poem: 'Two great armies, composed of four nations, saw from the slopes of a vast ampitheatre seven hundred British cavalry proceed at a rapid pace, and in perfect order, to certain destruction . . . Causeless and fruitless, it stands by itself, as a grand heroic deed . . . The British soldier will do his duty, even to certain death, and is not paralyzed by feeling that he is the victim of some hideous blunder'.[24] Russell's was not the only eye-witness account to be published. Two days later an officer's letter appeared, telling readers: 'We all knew that the thing was desperate even before we started; and it was even worse than we thought . . . I do not think that one man flinched in the whole brigade, though every one allows that so hot a fire was hardly ever seen. We went right on, cut down the gunners at their guns (the Russians worked the guns till we were within ten yards of them)'.[25]

Tennyson later said that he wrote his poem 'in a few minutes, after reading the description in the *Times* in which occurred the phrase "some one had blundered", and this was the origin of the metre of his poem'. (*Memoir*, I, 381) In fact, although Russell employs the word 'blunder' in the passage quoted above, together with 'error', 'fatal movement' and 'misconception', the actual phrase used in Tennyson's poem does not appear. The poem was written on 5 December, altered, then re-altered over the next two days, and published in John Forster's magazine, *The Examiner*, on the ninth. Tennyson signed it with his initials, relegating it to somewhere between his anonymous newspaper poems and his 'serious' works.

The poem attracted little notice to begin with. The poet was persuaded to remove the line 'someone had blundered' for the first book publication of 1855, because it did not rhyme with 'hundred'. As a Lincolnshire man, Tennyson would have said 'hunderd', and it has been suggested that he was embarrassed by this exposure of his regional accent. Fortunately, he changed his mind again when the Society for the Propagation of the Gospel asked to distribute sheet copies to the troops in the Crimea. 'I declare I believe it is the best of the two and that the criticism of two or three London friends . . . induced me to spoil it'. (*Letters*, II, 117) John Ruskin agreed with him: 'It was precisely the most tragical line in the poem. It is as true to its history as essential to its tragedy.' (*Memoir*, I, 411)

It was Tennyson who made this comparatively minor incident into one of those momentous British defeats claimed as a moral victory. More than twenty years later, he wrote a poem about another, the sinking of the *Revenge* during the Spanish wars of the sixteenth-century. Paradoxically, 'The Charge of the Light Brigade' also established the action's subsequent history as a military disaster, a judgement which more recent historical accounts have queried, suggesting that the 'charge' was even a partial success, a blow to the confidence of the Russian cavalry.

Tennyson had a large part to play in building up the titanic nature of this engagement, which is far better known today than any of the Crimean victories. Paintings like Elizabeth Butler's popular *Roll Call* (*Calling the Roll after an Engagement, Crimea*, 1874 Royal Collection) and Richard Caton Woodville's *Charge of the Light Brigade* (1897,

National Army Museum) had their basis in the popularity of his poem, and in the passionate curiosity it aroused in the public.

After writing 'The Charge of the Light Brigade', Tennyson turned back to *Maud*, and worked on it throughout the winter of 1854 to 1855. He continued to make minor changes right down to proof stage, but the volume, *Maud, and other Poems*, finally appeared on 28 July 1855. To Tennyson's surprise, several critics were hostile to his poem. When Tennyson wrote of the speaker's decision to put madness and despair behind him, and to enlist for the Crimea, he captured the national mood at the outbreak of war:

> For the peace, that I deem'd no peace, is over and done,
> And now by the side of the Black and the Baltic deep,
> And deathful-grinning mouths of the fortress, flames
> The blood-red blossom of war with a heart of fire.

> (Part III, VI, 50–3)

By 1855, such passages made Tennyson sound like a warmonger, and his poem struck a note of distasteful chauvinism.

Voicing a common reaction, George Eliot prefaced her commentary with praise of the 'true' Tennyson, with 'his wonderful concentration of thought into luminous speech, the exquisite pictures in which he has blended all the hues of reflection, feeling and fancy'.[26] In contrast, she found *Maud* 'harsh' and 'rugged', it set her teeth on edge, and roused her disgust: 'it remains true, that the ground-notes of the poem are nothing more than hatred of peace and the Peace Society, hatred of commerce and coal-mines, hatred of young gentlemen with flourishing whiskers and padded coats, adoration of a clear-cut face, and faith in War as the unique social regenerator'.[27]

George Eliot's response was echoed throughout the press. Charles Kingsley was typical in praising the lyrics and disliking the rest. 'Incomplete and unsatisfying . . . not to be accepted as an equivalent for that great master-work . . . which the world expects from him', was the *Quarterly's* verdict.[28] William Gladstone, who wrote anonymously in 1859 that *Maud* was the 'least popular, and probably the least worthy of popularity' among Tennyson's 'more considerably works',[29] later explained that he had been 'disabled' and 'dislocated' by 'a feeling, which had reference to the growth of the war-spirit in the outer world' (*Memoir*, I, 398–9). Some critics associated the poem with the Spasmodic group of poets, now largely forgotten, but well regarded in the 1840s. The Spasmodics also addressed the great issues of the day, writing in an intense post romantic style. Such excess was already under attack in 1855, and those who found *Maud* problematic or disappointing used the supposed association with the Spasmodics (for which there was some justification) as a way of belittling Tennyson.

The effect of the critical onslaught on the sensitive Tennyson is incalculable. 'There has been from many quarters a torrent of abuse against it; and I have even had insulting anonymous letters: indeed I am quite at a loss to account for the bitterness of feeling which this poor little work of mine has excited', he wrote in August (*Letters*, II, 124). News of the death of Henry Lushington in Paris, on his way home from Malta, came just as Tennyson was struggling to regain his equilibrium in the face of these attacks.

Those who knew Tennyson well were deeply concerned. Benjamin Jowett wrote to praise *Maud* warmly, telling Tennyson that 'No poem since Shakespeare seems to show equal power of the same kind, or equal knowledge of human nature' (*Memoir*, I, 396). He accounted for the problems of *Maud*'s reception with admirable lucidity: 'The vulgar don't see this psychological truth & they have not imagination enough to fill up the interstices of the tale. They are incapable of feeling the continuous effect of the whole. Also they confuse the hero with the poet & get so disappointed that they cannot absolutely identify them.'[30] Jowett's only regret was that the violence of the poem did not have the beauty found in *Macbeth*.

Jowett's references to Shakespeare go to the heart of the matter. *Maud* is essentially a dramatic work, the projection of a personality into a role. *Romeo and Juliet* may have been one source for the lovers from warring families, and Tennyson himself called his poem 'a little *Hamlet*' (*Memoir*, I, 396); '*Hamlet* (if it came out now) would be treated in just the same way, so that one ought not to care for their cackling, not that I am comparing poor little "Maud" to the Prince' (*Memoir*, I, 406).

The 1850s saw a number of significant experiments with narrative voice, both in poetry and in fiction. Charlotte Brontë's first-person masterpiece, *Villette*, was published in 1853. Dickens's *David Copperfield* (with its single narrator), and his *Bleak House* (with its inventive double narration) came out in 1850 and 1853 respectively. Most relevant of all is the comparison with Robert Browning, whose volume of dramatic monologues, *Men and Women*, also published in 1855, ran into a comparable critical storm. Browning projects the personalities of a range of speakers, of whom some, like the speaker in *Maud*, are apparently subject to mental disorder. Tennyson himself had written dramatic monologues, among them the diatribe of the self-deluded 'St Simeon Stylites', a piece of contorted self-analysis which prefigures the intensity of *Maud*. Significantly, the Brownings were among the few people who genuinely liked *Maud*.

Tennyson himself consented to a comparison between *Maud* and another relevant genre, the monodrama. This type of entertainment became popular in England in the late eighteenth-century. In monodrama, a single performer displays a wide variety of moods through a single discourse. Figures from classical legend, Pygmalion, Ariadne, Proserpine, were often invoked. Some monodramas were performed in London where the speaker was either displaying symptoms of madness or surrounded by lunatics. Earlier works of Tennyson, particularly 'Oenone', combine the qualities of monodrama with those of the dramatic monologue.[31]

The term 'mono-drama' was first used of *Maud* by Dr Robert James Mann, a Ventnor scientist, whose *Tennyson's "Maud" Vindicated*, published in 1856, apparently quotes Tennyson himself. Mann counters the charges that Tennyson had attacked the Quakers, and had glorified war, as well as explaining the poem's meaning. For the 1856 edition, Tennyson made a number of changes in the text, some in response to hostile criticism. At a later stage, he divided the poem into two sections (later three) in order to clarify the progression.

Maud is unique in Tennyson's oeuvre. Did it represent a new path from which the poet was deflected by the outcry? The answer will never be known, but Tennyson's attachment to it is well documented. He told Marian Bradley to 'always stand up for "Maud" when you hear my pet bantling abused. Perhaps that is why I am sensitive about her. You know mothers always make the most of a child that is abused'. (*Memoir*, I, 468) *Maud* was his favourite child, as *David Copperfield* was Dickens's, and, until the end of his life, Tennyson delighted in reading it aloud. It has been suggested that this passion was a way of forcing his audiences to accept the poem. Tennyson would often interpolate his readings with comments, explaining the poem or praising his own skill. Gladstone, present on one such occasion, said that he only understood and appreciated *Maud* after hearing it in this way. Even George Eliot, whose review, like Gladstone's, had been anonymous, found herself sitting through it. Not everyone was as polite. Carlyle, for one, made for the door when a reading was announced.

One of the most remarkable of the readings was one of the first, held in the Brownings' lodgings at 13 Dorset Street on 27 September 1855. Dante Gabriel Rossetti, another guest, told William Allingham: 'I never was more amused in my life than by Tennyson's groanings and horrors over the reviews of *Maud*, which poem he read through to us, spouting also several sections to be introduced in a new edition . . . His conversation was really one perpetual groan . . . he repeated the same stories about anonymous letters he gets, etc. – at the very least six or eight times in my hearing.'[32] These letters were presumably those which Tennyson continued to quote for many years. One of the most offensive read: 'Sir, once I worshipped you – now I loathe you! So you've taken to imitating Longfellow, you BEAST!'[33]

The first edition of *Maud and other poems* numbered 10 000 copies (more than six times the first edition of *In Memoriam*), selling at five shillings each. Eight thousand copies were sold in just under three months. A considerably revised second edition appeared in 1856, and there were reissues every year until 1862. If the critical reception distressed Tennyson, it had little effect upon the sales or the profits.

Tennyson always told his friends that *Maud* paid for Farringford. This was partially true. The figure of over £2000 which he received from Moxon in 1856 went towards the purchase price. Not all the money came from *Maud*, however. In 1854, Tennyson bought £1700 worth of East Lincolnshire Railway shares, presumably with money from the sales of *In Memoriam*. He made the purchase after considerable hesitation, since he feared that the coming war would depress their value, and even wondered whether the broker would abscond with his money. The latter proved honest, but the war did indeed lower the value of the shares. After the sale, Tennyson told the broker: 'I have no doubt that you have managed for me as well as possible under the circumstances. It is of course rather annoying to lose so much, but I had made up my mind to lose – it could not be helped.' (Letters, II, 165–6)

Earlier in 1856, just before the publication of *Maud*, Tennyson had faced the prospect of a far worse loss, when it seemed that his bank might collapse, taking his savings with it. Bank collapses were a regular feature of nineteenth-century life, and Tennyson's anxieties were not exaggerated. In the end, the loss was limited to £200, and, with the help of the money from his shares and from *Maud*, Tennyson eventually put up the asking price for Farringford, which had now risen to over £6000.

7

Tennyson and the Arts

The years after 1857 were some of the happiest in Tennyson's life. The traumas of the Crimean War and of *Maud* were behind him. He could enjoy the comforts of Farringford, under the protection of Emily, who took charge of everything, acting as secretary as well as housekeeper. Aubrey de Vere thought the poet 'very greatly blessed in his marriage . . . He is much happier and proportionately less morbid than he used to be; and in all respects improved'.[1] Tennyson was never really at peace for long, however, and Emily had to struggle to maintain a balance between boredom and restlessness. Tennyson established the practice of working in the morning and evening, and walking or talking with friends in the middle of the day.

These were also years when, probably under Emily's influence, Tennyson was drawn into closer contact with artists and connoisseurs of art, whether as the subject of portraits, a visitor to exhibitions, or simply as a friend of young painters and sculptors. For book illustration, which represents the closest relationship between literature and the visual arts, Tennyson had little enthusiasm. He expressed an admiration for Turner's landscape engravings to Samuel Rogers's *Poems*, but this was exceptional. Rogers, he believed, had had particular advantages: 'On the whole I am against illustrators, except one could do with them as old Mr Rogers did, have them to breakfast twice a week and explain your views to them over and over again' (*Memoir*, II, 43). Tennyson's dislike of illustrations to his poems became proverbial. His illustrators did not (and could not) match up to his own imaginative vision.

Edward Moxon had a hard battle to win Tennyson's agreement to an illustrated edition of the 1842 *Poems*. What finally pushed the unwilling poet into the project was the promise of £2000 at a time when he was worrying about the purchase of Farringford. Moxon's bravado in offering such a large sum probably doomed the project as a financial venture from the start.

With Tennyson's help, Moxon contacted a number of illustrators. One group, Clarkson Stanfield, Thomas Creswick, William Mulready, and J. C. Horsley, were all well established. Tennyson thought Creswick 'a capital broad genial fellow', Mulready 'an old man . . . full of vivacity', and was delighted when the 'amiable' Horsley told him that he was 'the painter's poet' (*Memoir*, I, 375–6). Had this group illustrated the whole volume, it would have been a more consistent, if less remarkable, work. What makes it interesting is that Moxon also employed three young Pre-Raphaelite artists, D. G. Rossetti, John Millais and William Holman Hunt, probably on Tennyson's recommendation. Emily wanted Elizabeth Siddal, later Rossetti's wife, to be approached, but to this Moxon would not agree, even when Emily offered to pay for the drawings herself. The Pre-Raphaelite Brotherhood, founded in 1848, was a radical group of young artists, reacting against conventional academic values. They were committed to ideas of 'truth to nature', and to establishing closer links between literature and the fine arts.

It is customary to describe the old stagers as uneasy bedfellows to the younger men, a view with which Hunt, writing many years later, concurred. Hunt believed that the book's financial failure resulted from the division of styles, that those who wanted traditional illustrations were upset by the Pre-Raphaelite work, and vice versa. The illustrations themselves, however, are far more varied in technique than this simple explanation would suggest. Creswick, and, to some extent, Horsley and Stanfield, did indeed contribute drawings in the conventional picturesque style of the day, but Mulready and Daniel Maclise are less easily categorised. Maclise's fine illustrations to 'Morte d'Arthur' are similar in style to Hunt's blocks for 'Oriana'.

Moxon allowed the artists to chose their own subjects, which most of them agreed to do promptly enough. John Millais, then 26, and a great admirer of Tennyson's poetry, was particularly enthusiastic. The respect was mutual. Hearing that the artist was painting a subject from Coventry Patmore's *The Woodman's Daughter* (1851, Guildhall Art Gallery), Tennyson expressed a hope that Millais might 'do something from me'.[2] Millais' *Mariana* (private collection), exhibited at the Royal Academy in 1851, *should* have appealed to Tennyson as a faithful rendering of his poem.

Tennyson singled out two paintings by Millais at the Royal Academy exhibition of 1852. One was *Ophelia* (Tate Gallery), and the other *A Huguenot, on St Bartholemew's Day, refusing to shield himself from danger by wearing the Roman Catholic badge* (private collection). *The Huguenot* had begun life as an illustration to a line from Tennyson's 'Circumstance', 'Two lovers whispering by an orchard wall', but had then developed into a history piece. Tennyson argued with Millais about the 'limits of realism in painting', telling him that 'if you have human beings before a wall, the wall ought to be picturesquely painted, and in harmony with the idea pervading the picture, but must not be made too obtrusive by the bricks being *too* minutely drawn, since it is the human beings that ought to have the real interest for us in a dramatic subject picture' (*Memoir*, I, 300–1).

Millais' eighteen illustrations to the Moxon edition are among the finest examples of Victorian draughtsmanship. Friends commented on his persistence as he drew directly onto the tiny wood-blocks, three or four inches square. The concentration and emotional intensity of the best of them, those to 'Locksley Hall', 'The Death of the Old Year', 'Dora', 'The Miller's Daughter' and 'The Lord of Burleigh', rise to match Tennyson's own quality, making this the most successful pairing of poet and artist in the Victorian period. For 'Locksley Hall' Millais shows the speaker and his cousin Amy together on the seashore, before their love is blighted by the girl's parents. The faces of the lovers are concealed, and the dominant feature of the drawing is the enclosing and protective gesture of the young man's arms. The wide sky and the open sea behind prefigure the melancholy outcome of the story. Emily and Hallam Tennyson posed for 'Dora', where Millais expresses the theme of restored family unity through four figures clasped together in a tight oval.

Tennyson asked Millais to persuade Hunt to contribute illustrations, and Millais invited Rossetti to join them: 'Tennyson seems enclined [*sic*] to give the greater part to us, and would I think be thankful for my suggesting another person.'[3] The illustrators were paid £25 for each drawing (apart from Rossetti who negotiated £30). Hunt and Rossetti made fewer drawings than Millais, Hunt seven and Rossetti five, but they have achieved far greater celebrity. Hunt's Lady of Shalott, with her hair flying out around her, appalled Tennyson who asked the artist why he had made 'her hair wildly tossed about as if by a tornado? . . . I didn't say that her hair was blown about like that . . . Why did you make the web wind round and round her like the threads of a cocoon?' Hunt defended himself by quoting the line, 'Out flew the web and floated wide', only to hear the response, 'but I did not say it floated round and round her'. Tennyson laid it down that 'an illustrator ought never to add anything to what he finds in the text.'[4] For all the difficulties over 'The Lady of Shalott', Hunt, like Millais, became a family friend, and Tennyson remained, with some reservations, an admirer of his paintings.

When Rossetti came to choose his subjects, he discovered that the best had been reserved by other artists. In consequence he decided that he would have to 'allegorize' on his 'own hook'.[5] His 'Palace of Art' drawings are not illustrations to the poem but to the imaginary pictures which Tennyson describes within the palace. One shows St Cecilia high on a castle wall over a river, with a brooding angel on the point of kissing her. Tennyson liked Rossetti's other 'Palace of Art' block, where the weeping queens gather round the body of King Arthur, but his high church Sir Galahad, crossing himself with holy water in a tractarian chapel, is not in the spirit of Tennyson's muscular knight, whose 'strength is as the strength of ten' (l. 3).

The Tennysons' evident distaste for the illustrated edition was widely discussed in the Pre-Raphaelite circle. Emily told Thomas Woolner (a close friend of Millais and Hunt) that the book would probably be a failure: 'even in those things that are fine in themselves there is for the most part some departure from the story'.[6] Mulready's block for 'Sea Fairies' and Hunt's for 'Mariana' appealed to her, but she objected to 'The Lord of Burleigh', asking why 'she is in a cottage surrounded by peasants instead of Burleigh with her own weeping Lord by her side'.[6] Millais, anxious to protect Tennyson's feelings, offered to alter his block for 'The Miller's Daughter', and to include 'a view of the mill', but it was by then too late for the change to be made.[7]

Publication was delayed as Moxon tried to extract the woodblocks. Disgusted with the work of the engravers, the Dalziel brothers, whom he accused of wrecking his designs, Rossetti was slow to submit his drawings, and never fulfilled his undertaking. Christmas 1856 was missed, and the book came out in May 1857, priced at 31s. 6d. By July only 1300 copies out of 10 000 had gone, and, a week later, Tennyson accepted an offer of the £2000 originally promised him. At a later date, Routledge, who specialised in relatively cheap gift books, bought up 5000 of Moxon's remaining stock and sold them for a guinea each. They printed a further 5000 in both 1865 and 1869, so that, for Tennyson at least, the edition finally returned a reasonable profit.

Moxon determinedly pursued the idea of illustrated editions. His project for *The Princess*, with 26 drawings by Daniel Maclise, was still in hand at the time of his death in 1858. Emily later told John Forster that Tennyson had never given permission for the volume: 'On the contrary we were utterly astonished when we heard that Maclise was in Italy or had been there drawing for it.' (Letters, II, 211) Maclise's visit to Italy took place in 1855, which may date the beginning of the project. Moxon, the Tennysons later discovered, had intended the volume as a surprise.

The majority of Maclise's woodcuts are medieval in inspiration. In 1847 he had made the drawings for *Leonora*, a gothic poem by the German writer, Gottfried Bürger, in a translation by Julia Margaret Cameron. For that work, the pages were set up in a style typical of German illustration, with integrated text, border and drawing. If Maclise's later work for *The Princess* is less overtly German in manner than that in the Bürger edition, the drawings are still markedly historicist in character. The scenes in the university are set against romanesque arches, and the style of the women's costumes is a cross between medieval and Tudor, topped by mid-Victorian hair-styles. Armour was a popular accessory for painters in the later 1850s, and Maclise exploits its decorative effects, as he had done in his 'Morte d'Arthur' drawing. The tournament scene is a complex pattern of men and horses writhing on the ground, the swirling design reminiscent of his fantastic title page to Dickens's *The Chimes*. In a quite different vein are the vignettes for the songs, pleasing evocations of loving relationships. Tennyson's attitude to the volume, however, was predictably hostile: 'too wide of the text' was his verdict (Letters, II, 211). He complained that the couple in the drawing for 'As through the land at eve we went' were too young, and felt considerable irritation that Maclise, although staying nearby at Ventnor, had never consulted him.

After a long illness, Edward Moxon died in 1858. In the months which followed, Moxon's heirs and the Tennysons all took up entrenched positions. Failing health had loosened Moxon's hold upon the publishing business, and his affairs were in disorder. Bradbury and Evans, the managers of *Punch*, took over the firm in the name of Moxon's son, and Moxon's brother, William, attempted to sort out the tangled finances. William Moxon's first move was to demand £8886. 8s. 4d from Tennyson for the illustrated edition, which he insisted the poet had set in train. Through John Forster, and their brother-in-law, Charles Weld, Tennyson and Emily managed to set the record right with Bradbury and Evans. The available evidence was not, however, watertight, being reports of undocumented conversations, and intermittent statements of account. The Moxons would have been foolish to alienate their leading author, and Tennyson, understandably, threatened to withdraw. In the end, the Moxons remained his publishers until 1868, partly because he disliked change, and partly because of his concern for Emma Moxon, to whom he continued to send an allowance for many years.

Tennyson's uneasy relationship with his Pre-Raphaelite illustrators was motivated by a number of aesthetic and financial anxieties. That his objection to illustrations was by no means total, even in the 1850s, is clear from his dealings with Eleanor Vere Boyle (EVB), an amateur artist married to a son of the 8th Earl of Cork and Orrery, Revd Richard Boyle. When she asked permission to illustrate 'The May Queen', Tennyson told her 'I would rather you than any one else should do it.'[8] Sending her designs to him, Eleanor Boyle was humble about her abilities, telling him that she felt 'only too well, *how unworthy* my illustrations are, and I must trust to your goodness, to forgive me, for having ventured to place them with your Poem'.[9] Eleanor Boyle's work is charming, her numerous angels are in the 'fairy' style, while other cuts are more naturalistic, presenting 'The May Queen' in the manner of a rural idyll. It is possible that Tennyson really did find a reflection of his own image of 'The May Queen', but it seems more probable that he liked the artist personally, and was prepared to apply less critical standards to the daughter-in-law of a peer.

The frontispiece to the Moxon illustrated *Poems* was not a woodcut, but an engraving of a medallion by Thomas Woolner. Dissatisfied with the scale of a medallion modelled in the Lake District in 1851, Woolner, on returning from a fruitless journey to the Australian goldfields, asked permission to work on a new version. 'Very beautiful very fine & shiny, the best likeness that has been made', was Emily Tennyson's verdict. (ET, *Journal*, p. 43). The 1856 medallion and the bust which Woolner modelled a year later are the most powerful records of Tennyson's middle age, sculpted when he was still clean-shaven. It is one of the paradoxes of Tennyson's career that, with the exception of the Samuel Laurence oil portrait of around 1840 (National Portrait Gallery), the most familiar images of him are those of the ageing laureate, not of the lyric poet. From the mid-1850s, portraits of him proliferate, but by then he had grown a straggly beard. Those who met him in later life were often amazed at his unkempt and untidy appearance. Woolner's images, by contrast, are stern and heroic. Tennyson's hair, so unruly in the photographs of the period, is aesthetically ordered, and even his disarranged shirt collar is incorporated into the design of the bust. The original 1857 bust was bought, after considerable hesitation, by Trinity College, Cambridge. A few other versions exist, and there were to be numerous casts of the medallion, in both bronze and plaster.[10] Even so, the currency of such works was obviously limited, and most people came to be familiar with Tennyson's features from the portraits made in the latter half of his life, when photography and new engraving processes made mass circulation possible.

Since the advent of photography in the early 1840s, professional photographic studios had mushroomed, and Tennyson attended a number of these. He was at Mayall's in Regent Street in 1855, and at Cundall and Howlett's in New Bond Street in 1857. In the 1860s and 70s, both men photographed him again, and the whole Tennyson family were at Jeffrey's in Great Russell Street in 1862. These studio portraits, with their air of formality and constraint, were widely reproduced and disseminated. Far more revealing are the handful of portrait photographs by 'art' photographers. The Tennysons were 'taken' by three of the greatest, Charles Dodgson (Lewis Carroll), and Oscar Rejlander in the 1850s, and by Julia Margaret Cameron in the 1860s.

Dodgson's first photographs of the Tennysons were taken in September 1857, when they were again guests of the Marshalls in the Lake District. Dodgson had made portraits of Agnes Weld, Emily Tennyson's niece, the year before, and it was on the strength of Tennyson's known admiration for these that Dodgson introduced himself to the family. He was granted permission to photograph Hallam and Lionel, 'the most beautiful boys of their age I ever saw'.[11] To his delight, Tennyson also agreed to pose, seated, and wearing his black hat.

The difference between Dodgson's photographs of the Tennysons and those by Oscar Reijlander is instructive. Swedish by birth, Reijlander had settled in England after training as a painter in Rome. He was well known for his photographic genre scenes, with models posed naturally as they went about their everyday business. Reijlander's first photographic portrait of Tennyson is dated 1859, and he made further studies of him in the 1860s and 1870s. Reijlander was at Farringford in May 1863, on his way to the Royal Family at Osborne. It was then that he made his romantic portraits of Hallam and Lionel, with their long jackets, lace collars, knickerbockers and flowing hair. The images delighted Emily Tennyson, who had chosen to dress her sons in these unmasculine costumes, very much in the style of the aesthetic movement. Reijlander's study of the family, taken in the garden, is a remarkable document. With Emily admiring her husband, Hallam looking at this parents, and Lionel and his father gazing straight out at the photographer, it precisely charts the relationships within the group.

Reijlander was a pioneer of art photography. Among his successors and friends was Julia Margaret Cameron. The Tennysons had met the Camerons long before Julia Margaret was given a camera, apparently introduced by the poet Henry Taylor in 1850. In the later 1850s the Tennysons and Camerons were both intermittent tenants of Lord and Lady Ashburton at Ashburton Cottage, Putney Heath, and in 1857 the Cameron family rented lodgings in Freshwater with the intention of being near Farringford. In 1860, they bought two houses of their own there, knocking them together to form 'Dimbola', and, for more than a decade, Emily Tennyson's journal is full of accounts of visits from the Camerons and their children.

It was at 'Dimbola' that Julia Margaret Cameron became a photographer, ruthlessly seizing upon interesting faces for her work. Most famous as a portraitist, she also created photo-montages, sometimes posing her models in scenes from Tennyson's poems. Like the painter, George Frederic Watts, whom she knew well, she was a chronicler of the great men and women of the Victorian era, and an apostle of 'high art'. In contrast to the other great woman photographer of the age, Clementina, Lady Hawarden, Julia Margaret Cameron had no desire to restrict herself to the family circle, and she was fearless in stalking the famous. Surprisingly, Tennyson consented to be photographed on numerous occasions. In a series of portraits of the 1860s, Mrs Cameron pictured him in vaguely artistic dress, with a black beret, or a pleated collar. Her best-known image of Tennyson, the so-called 'dirty monk' print, shows him grasping a book, his face wrapt in intense concentration.

Julia Margaret Cameron was one of the seven lively and intelligent daughters of James Pattle, an Indian Civil Servant. She was the wife of Charles Hay Cameron, a jurist and later a member of the Supreme Council of India, twenty years older than herself. Her sister Sara was married to another Indian administrator, Thoby Prinsep, and, on their return to England, the Prinseps made their home at Little Holland House on the edge of the Holland estate in Kensington. The other Pattle sisters were often to be found there and they were recorded for posterity by Watts, Sara's painter-in-residence. He had come, it was said, with a little exaggeration, for three days and had stayed for 30 years.

Sara Prinsep was known as a 'lion hunter', one who sought out distinguished men and women to give lustre to her own salon. Tennyson, an obvious 'lion' and a source of inspiration to the artists of the Pattle circle, soon became one of the household's chief attractions. The young artist, George Du Maurier, told his mother that it was 'a nest of proeraphaelites [*sic*], where Hunt, Millais, Rossetti, Watts, Leighton etc., Tennyson, the Brownings and Thackeray etc. and tutti quanti receive dinners and incense, and cups of tea handed to them by these women almost kneeling'.[12]

Tennyson received practical help from Sara Prinsep. In 1857, she took him to Little Holland House, suffering from an ingrowing toe-nail and probably from gout as well. A year later, in July 1858, she had to rescue her poet again. This time she took the whole family from damp lodgings in Hampstead, where they were staying near Elizabeth and Matilda Tennyson. While Hallam and Lionel played in her large garden, their father kept Mrs Prinsep happy by sitting to Watts, the apostle of high art. Like the Venetian painters whom he admired, Watts posed his sitter against a rich magenta curtain, throwing the poet's dark jacket and hair into relief, and creating a sensitive study in the style of Van Dyck.

This was perhaps Watts's most successful oil portrait of Tennyson, but the sitter and his wife did not like it. Julia Margaret Cameron took up the cudgels on the artist's behalf, protesting against a refusal to sanction an engraving, but the mild Watts disassociated himself from his champion: 'I quite agree with you that a very much better head might be painted of Mr Tennyson, & I hope he will give me an opportunity of trying to improve upon the present one, meantime I hope neither of you have been seriously vexed by your joust with Mrs Cameron, you know how she delights in a passage of arms!'[13]

It was while this portrait was in progress that Tennyson apparently composed a passage that portraiture for *Lancelot and Elaine*, lines which insist that an artist should paint the soul as well as the face of his subject:

> As when a painter, poring on a face,
> Divinely through all hindrance finds the man
> Behind it, and so paints him that his face,
> The shape and colour of a mind and life,
> Lives for his children, ever at its best
> And fullest.

(330–5)

Watts *did* try again in March 1859, when Tennyson extended his stay in London to allow for the completion of a second work, the so-called 'moonlight' portrait. This much-reproduced image of the poet is softer and closer to the iconography of Christ. The *Art Journal* rightly commented that: 'it scarcely conveys to our mind a satisfactory expression of his intellectual qualities: the eyes are comparatively lustreless, while the general character of the features is indicative of austerity'.[14] Predictably, Emily Tennyson admired this 'beautiful and touching' work, which cannot possibly have represented the poet as he was in life.[14] Watts expressed pleasure that her 'poetic imagination' had completed his inadequate suggestion.[15] This was indeed Tennyson as the Little Holland House group would have wished to find him.

The kindness of the Pattles and their friends went a long way towards transforming Farringford into a palace of 'high art'. It was the Prinseps who organised the mounting of Tennyson's bust of Dante, and Julia Margaret Cameron provided a vivid blue wallpaper, with a border based on the Elgin Marbles. Another Cameron gift was a photograph of her own version of the Raphael *Sistine Madonna* in a frame decorated with stars. The Tennyson home slowly filled with icons of aesthetic taste. Francis Palgrave and Arthur Butler both sent reproductions of the Sistine Chapel frescoes, and from another friend, Charles Wynne, the MP for Caernarvon, came an engraving of a work then almost as famous as the *Sistine Madonna*, the so-called *Beatrice Cenci* by Guido Reni (now thought to be neither by Guido nor of Beatrice Cenci on her way to execution). Woolner sent photographs of Michaelangelo's Medici tomb and of the *Victory* of Phidias, and it was probably he who dispatched a cast of the *Venus de Milo*.

Records of these years are scattered with references to museums and exhibitions. In July 1857, Tennyson went several times to the Art Treasures exhibition in Manchester, where he particularly admired a sketch then thought to be by Michelangelo, but since reattributed. Paintings by William Mulready and Holman Hunt, sketches by Turner, and two famous Gainsboroughs, *The Blue Boy* and *Mrs Graham*, were among his favourites. The following year saw the arrival at Farringford of Dr Tennyson's picture collection. Then, in June, Tennyson spent a whole day in the new South Kensington Museum, and enjoyed 'fine pictures' at the British Institution (Letters, II, 202). In August, the family went with Woolner to the Crystal Palace, where the sculptor made them look carefully at a cast of Verrocchio's famous statue of Bartolomeo Colleoni. In October, Alfred read Giorgio Vasari's account of the life of Raphael to Emily, along with a sonnet by Michelangelo. Three years before, when Tennyson received an honorary degree, they had studied the Raphael drawings together in the Ashmolean Museum in Oxford. The language of 'high art' began to influence their conversation. While Alfred described the moon rising over the down as 'like Michael Angelo's sunrise in the Medici Chapel at Florence. The head over the giant shoulder' (ET, *Journal*, p. 50), Emily reported that Annie Fields, the wife of Tennyson's American publisher, had 'a face like the old Italian Masters' faces' (ET, *Journal*, p. 138).

Many of Tennyson's fellow guests at Little Holland House were already known to him, but in these relaxed surroundings he was to establish friendships with a number of artists and critics, including John Ruskin. By the time that Tennyson met the Pre-Raphaelites, the first thrust of the movement was over, and the members were pursuing their own careers. Nevertheless, this was a period when the younger painters who frequented Little Holland House were briefly united against the Royal Academy. They exhibited together at the Hogarth Club from the late 1850s, and many were separately or jointly involved in schemes for book illustration.

At home in the Isle of Wight, Tennyson put into practice a Pre-Raphaelite dictum, expressed by Rossetti in the Preface to the Pre-Raphaelite magazine, *The Germ*: 'to obtain the thoughts of Artists upon Nature as evolved in Art, in another language, besides their *own proper* one'.[16] Tennyson, who presumably knew nothing of the short-lived *Germ*, began in January 1856 to carve 'some ivy leaves from nature in Apple-tree wood. In spite of its hardness they are very well carved' (ET, *Journal*, p. 59). Terracotta casts from these patterns of intertwined leaves were placed round the doors of farm cottages on the Farringford estate near the end of Tennyson's life, and can still be seen there.

Holman Hunt, visiting Farringford in 1858, found that Tennyson had been painting 'writhing monsters of different sizes and shapes, swirling about as in the deep', onto panes of glass 'which would have had no outlook but on bare brick'.[17] Hunt was impressed by Tennyson's 'taste and judgement', and noticed the success with which the poet had combined colours to 'make mysterious tints', without destroying the 'decorative quality . . . by over-elaboration'. 'The definition of forms had been judiciously relinquished when only a general suggestion had been achieved'.[17] Tennyson's paintings for his summer-house, which no longer survive, may have been to the same designs, with dragons, sea-serpents and kingfishers, appropriate subject matter for a period when Tennyson was taken up with his Arthurian project.

During February and March 1856, Tennyson completed a new

poem which was to become *Merlin and Vivien*, the sixth book of the *Idylls of the King*. From as far back as the 1830s, he had conceived the idea of an Arthurian cycle of poems, originally envisaged as an allegory, with Arthur as religious faith, Merlin as science, and Mordred representing sceptical understanding. Tennyson wrote a number of early poems with Arthurian subjects, but always claimed that he gave up the plan for a longer work because of hostile reviews of 'Morte d'Arthur'.

In the 1850s, Tennyson's plans for a 'serial poem' were uncertain, but he already had a cycle of some sort in mind. As well as reading extensively in Arthurian material, he was at Glastonbury again in August 1854, and in Wales for two months in 1856, visiting places associated with Arthur and his knights. *Enid* was written between April and August 1856, *Guinevere* followed in July 1857, and then came *Elaine*, begun at Little Holland House in July 1858, and completed by February 1859. These four books were published together in 1859, as *Idylls of the King*.

Tennyson's chosen subjects for his first books are taken from a variety of sources. *Enid* came from the Welsh poem, the *Mabinogion*, in the recent translation by Lady Charlotte Guest. The story of Lancelot and Elaine was based upon a passage in Malory, while *Vivien* and *Guinevere* are almost entirely Tennyson's invention, drawing upon brief references in *Morte Darthur*. All four books have as title a woman's name. Enid and Elaine, the ideals of womanhood, are balanced by two destructive and unchaste women, Vivien and Guinevere. Tennyson's development of the idea of the seductress in *Vivien* is in many ways a new departure, seen by some writers as an indication of his growing anxiety about sexual morality. Ironically, there were those who felt that a poem on this subject was not fit for family reading. *Vivien* sets the stage for Tennyson's treatment of the kingdom of Arthur, an ideal commonwealth destroyed by disloyalty within. Like the serpent in *Paradise Lost*, a poem to which the themes and structure of the *Idylls* can be related, Vivien makes her way into Camelot, and conquers by means of her tongue and her beauty.

By contrast with Vivien's wiles, Elaine 'the lily maid of Astolat' (*Lancelot and Elaine*, 2) is powerless. Her love cannot turn the tide and break the hold of Lancelot's love for Guinevere. The poem is related to 'The Lady of Shalott', but, where the earlier poem is written in a tight stanza, and is limited in scope, *Elaine* is a long blank-verse poem of hopelessness and passivity, opening with a chilling description of the wasteland landscape where Arthur finds an ominous treasure, a dead king's crown.

Enid and *Guinevere* repeat the pattern of opposites. Enid is the perfect type of female obedience, whether living in poverty with her father or as the wife of a demanding and jealous husband. Like the later *Gareth and Lynette* this is the story of a knightly quest, where Arthur's champion takes on a series of bandit knights and overcomes them all. *Guinevere* is a more difficult book, nearer to the heart of the story of Arthur, and to the moral crux of Tennyson's reading of the legend. At the opening of the book, Guinevere sits between Enid and Vivien, the 'best' and 'the wiliest and the worst' of her ladies, while Mordred, like the serpent, looks over the wall (l. 29). Lancelot's ejection of him from his place precipitates the final discovery of Lancelot and Guinevere's adultery, and the Queen's flight to the nunnery at Amesbury.

Tennyson places the blame upon Guinevere: 'Mine is the shame, for I was wife, and thou/Unwedded', she tells Lancelot (118–19). The judgement is confirmed by the words of the novice about the 'wicked Queen' (l. 207), and by Arthur's own speech to his fallen wife, a passage which Tennyson loved to read aloud. Significantly, Tennyson altered the episode from Malory's version to make Arthur, not Lancelot, the visitor to Amesbury. If Tennyson's picture of Arthur's court depicts its decline and fall rather than its zenith, this pattern is repeated in the work of his contemporaries. William Morris's Arthurian poem, 'The 'Defence of Guenevere' of 1858, and Dante Gabriel Rossetti's dramatic water-colour, *Arthur's Tomb* (British Museum), are both forceful works about the aftermath of disaster. Like them, and like Swinburne in his *Tristram of Lyonesse*, Tennyson was drawn to the treatment of adultery in the Arthurian legends. Unlike Morris and Rossetti, with their awkward and even rough technical effects, he fails to convey the sexual passion of the lovers.

Tennyson's anxiety about female sexuality, underscored in the later books of his cycle, does not entirely darken the *Idylls*. In many ways these first poems reflect the cult of beauty of the Prinsep circle. In the past, aestheticism was usually associated with the 1870s and 80s, but many of the elements of art for art's sake can be traced to the 1860s. In the fine and decorative arts, this was a period when literary and genre paintings and high gothic design began to give way to a broader, and less specific, eclecticism. In painting, a new sensuousness is evident in the work of artists like Rossetti, James McNeill

Whistler and Frederic Leighton. This is frequently expressed through the representation of beautiful young women in sumptuous costumes, and in careful arrangements of colour and form, created through the use of fabrics, flowers and ceramics. Painting became more decorative and less morally assertive. New subject-matter, drawn from classical and medieval sources, represented a movement towards the abstract and decorative, as story-telling elements became subservient to the creation of mood and atmosphere.

The *Idylls*, of course, do have a narrative form, and they put forward a strong moral code. In other ways, however, these first four books reflect changing cultural patterns. They are some of the most decorative of Tennyson's poems, and, with their extended epic similes drawn with accuracy from the natural world, they are often reminiscent of Virgil. Visual effects predominate, and the lengthy descriptions of dress can be related to aestheticism.

Part of the problem of the *Idylls* results from an air of detachment. Elizabeth Browning wrote that the 'colour, the temperature, the very music, left me cold. Here are exquisite things, but the whole did not affect me as a whole from Tennyson's hands'.[18] Something of this may result from the preoccupation with surface decoration. Enid's dress 'All branch'd and flower'd with gold' (*The Marriage of Geraint*, 31), is comparable with Rossetti's paintings of beautiful women in fine fabrics. A painter, however, does not need to tell a story, he or she can concentrate upon the surface, the painterly effect.

Tennyson seems to have drifted away from Little Holland House in the later 1860s, when he started staying elsewhere on his visits to London. A simple man in many ways, Tennyson may have found the atmosphere of adulation overwhelming, although those unfriendly to him hinted that there was no limit to his power to absorb praise. There was certainly no personal rift of any kind. Tennyson persuaded Watts to buy a plot of land at Freshwater, and in 1873, following the sale of Little Holland House, a home for the painter and the Prinseps, The Briary, was built there by the aesthetic architect, Philip Webb.

8

The 1860s

With the publication of the 1859 *Idylls*, Tennyson's position as a 'popular' poet was fully established. After a first printing of 40 000 copies at 7s. each, a reprint was in preparation within six months. Royalties were soon bringing in £2000 a year from the *Idylls* alone, and Tennyson could begin to relax. The reviews were generally excellent. In the *National Review*, however, Walter Bagehot made the penetrating comment that Tennyson's days as the voice and inspiration of radical youth were over.

Politically, Tennyson was moving to the right, although he could still support the Poles when they rose against the Russians, or entertain the hero of the Italian Risorgimento, Garibaldi, at Farringford. His hostility to Napoleon III became increasingly shrill. One friend reported: 'Napoleon haunts his thoughts. He believes him about to attack England. Will America help us? he cries – we are but 500,000 against 600,000' (Letters, II, 236). Tennyson's contribution to the cause was a poem, written during the earlier invasion panic, and now reworked as 'Riflemen Form!', a call for a volunteer rifle force, published in *The Times* of 9 May 1859.

Like many of his contemporaries, Tennyson had a horror of mobs, especially dark-skinned mobs. Reports of the Indian Mutiny 'stirred him to the depths' (*Memoir*, I, 432), and he seriously entertained Woolner's suggestion that he write an epic on the subject. It took two decades to materialise, a whole-heartedly nationalistic poem on the 'Defence of Lucknow'.

Memories of the uprising probably stimulated Tennyson's most notorious political act, his contribution to the fund in support of Governor Edward Eyre, who had fired on rioters in Jamaica in 1865 and then exacted savage reprisals. Tennyson believed that Eyre's prompt actions had prevented further loss of British lives, and he opposed the call to try Eyre for murder. When Gladstone put the case for the other side, Tennyson 'did not argue. He kept asserting various prejudices and convictions. "We are too tender to savages; we are more tender to a black than to ourselves". "Niggers are tigers;

niggers are tigers"'.[1] Like the Dreyfus case in France, the Eyre case became a *cause célèbre*, dividing society on ideological lines. Tennyson allied himself with Thomas Carlyle, Charles Kingsley and John Ruskin, against John Stuart Mill, Thomas Henry Huxley and Herbert Spencer.

The abolition of slavery had been a central article of belief for the young Tennyson, but he responded with 'horror' to the American Civil War. 'He had always looked forward anxiously to the total abolition of slavery: but he hoped that it might have been accomplished gradually and peacefully,' wrote his son. (*Memoir*, I, 490) Many of Tennyson's American friends were Southerners, and he supported them in thinking the dispossession of slave-owners unjust: 'Altogether I am disappointed nay disgusted with the Northerners ever yelling and mouthing against their old European mother – who is now at least – the most unaggressive power in the Universe. I suppose it is the overproportion of the Celtic blood among them.' (*Letters*, II, 318–19)

In political terms, Tennyson's attitudes were unexceptional. A great poet, he was alarmingly ordinary in other matters, a prey to anxious fears, and easily impressed by what he read in the papers. Moves towards a universal franchise alarmed him, although he supported the principle: 'I think a state in which every man would have a vote is the ideal. I always thought it might be realised in England, if anywhere, with our constitutional history. But how to do it?'[2] This was Tennyson's challenge to Gladstone, when discussing reform bill proposals prepared by the Liberal party. Talking to the Queen in 1867, he again stressed his fear that 'Universal Suffrage and vote by ballot would be the ruin of us'.[3] In spite of his doubts, he still voted Liberal in the 1868 general election.

Although political attitudes find little direct expression in Tennyson's poetry, his critics deduced them from the poems themselves. The *Idylls*, for example, stress the advantages of a strong ruler and an ordered state. The dedication of the 1862 edition to the memory of the Prince Consort served to underline the 'establishment' nature of the poem. Unable to write an elegy immediately after the Prince's death, and recalling the Prince's admiration for the *Idylls*, Tennyson hit upon this way of expressing his sympathy for the widowed Queen Victoria. In his own lifetime, the Consort had been distrusted as a foreigner and an outsider, and the draft dedication referred to the 'fume and babble of a petulant hour' (Ricks, III,

264), a line which Tennyson was advised to omit, lest it should distress the Queen. He insisted on retaining a related passage:

> We have lost him: he is gone:
> We know him now: all narrow jealousies
> Are silent.

('Dedication', 14–16)

Victoria was delighted with the dedication, meetings followed, and the relationship became warm and close. The Queen enjoyed almost all of the 'laureate' pieces written for royal occasions.

The circumstances of the dedication are quite straightforward, but have always created misunderstanding. Readers immediately identified the Prince Consort with King Arthur, and this confusion has never been entirely dispelled. Swinburne called the poem the 'Morte d'Albert', and, for many years, the *Idylls* suffered from the association.

Few poets retain their lyric gifts beyond early middle age, and, after he reached fifty, Tennyson's poetry tended towards narrative or exposition. Not that the lyric impulse was entirely dead. Tennyson continued to write marvellous short poems until the end, often drawn from him by grief or recollection. His return to Cauterets on a family holiday, 31 years after his visit with Arthur Hallam, inspired a short lyric of almost oriental tautness and force, 'All along the valley'. Characteristically, the poem combines precise natural observation, that mountain streams are fuller at night when they carry the melted snow of the day, with an almost mystical sense of oneness with the dead friend. Cauterets, the 'paradise' of 1830, had become a 'rather odious watering place', as Tennyson ruefully put it (*Memoir*, I, 492), but, away from the noisy streets and the tourists, as he climbed up to Pont d'Espagne and the Lac de Gaube, the magic still worked:

> All along the valley, stream that flashest white,
> Deepening thy voice with the deepening of the night,
> All along the valley, where thy waters flow,
> I walk'd with one I loved two and thirty years ago.
> All along the valley, while I walk'd today,
> The two and thirty years were a mist that rolls away;

For all along the valley, down thy rocky bed,
Thy living voice to me was as the voice of the dead,
And all along the valley, by rock and cave and tree,
The voice of the dead was a living voice to me.

('In the Valley of Cauteretz')

Such impulses were rare, and they became rarer. Tennyson was now often at a loss for a subject, and Emily would ask friends to supply ideas: 'I wish you would give Alfred something to do. He is pretty well but for want of this',[4] she told Thomas Woolner, and it was the latter who provided the original stories for *Enoch Arden* and 'Aylmer's Field'. Unlike Wordsworth, whose *magnum opus* remained unwritten, Tennyson continued to experiment almost to the end, and the achievement of his later years is remarkably varied. If he did not match Yeats in forging a new lyric style for his old age, he certainly did not atrophy into sameness.

Emily's management did not stop at soliciting subjects for her husband's poetry. Knowing that it was important to ward off the threat of boredom in remote Farringford, she invited a stream of guests. Most persistent were the Farringford 'young men', a group of admirers a generation or so younger than the poet. It is significant that Tennyson increasingly shied away from the company of his contemporaries and equals, and basked in the admiration of newer friends. The distance between Farringford and London was only one reason for the gradual loosening of old bonds. Edward Fitzgerald, who did not bother to conceal his disparaging view of Tennyson's later poetry, was shunned. He received annual letters from Emily, but neither saw nor heard from Tennyson himself. Had he been prepared to come to Farringford, things might have been different. As it was, he remained in Suffolk, translating *Omar Khayyām*, writing some of the finest letters of the century, and rarely coinciding with Tennyson on his fleeting visits to London.

Fitzgerald was probably reacting against the intrusion of Emily. He continued to have a deep feeling for Tennyson himself, even when he complained of neglect. For Edward Lear, another contemporary of Tennyson, the position was exactly reversed. Of Lear's admiration for the poetry, with the exception of the *Idylls*, there can be no doubt. Down to his death he was still working on a series of drawings illustrating the landscapes of Tennyson's poems. But, by the 1860s, Lear's affection was largely directed at Emily, whom he regarded as an ideal wife, altogether too good for her husband. In his diary for 1864, he wrote in savage terms of the domestic Tennyson: 'the anomaly of high souled & philosophical writings combined with slovenliness, selfishness & morbid folly'.[5]

The attitude of the 'young men' was very different. They included the Irish poet William Allingham, the critic and poet Francis Palgrave, the sculptor Thomas Woolner and the Oxford don, Benjamin Jowett. All were in their thirties, unmarried, and, with the exception of Jowett, creative artists. Allingham was the customs officer at Lymington in Hampshire from 1863, and so within easy reach of Farringford.

The role of the young friends in the Tennyson household soon became established. Each would accompany Tennyson on his walks, and talk with him in his upstairs study. The poet forbade his friends to record his conversation, but Allingham clearly did so. His diary is one of the chief sources of biographical information about Tennyson in the 1860s. Tennyson could be repetitive as a conversationalist and the same comments and stories sometimes turn up in accounts by different people. The 'young men', often Christmas guests, would perform another useful function, by playing with and amusing the boys. Emily fought off the threat of school for as long as she could, eventually handing over her role as teacher to a succession of tutors. They too, and particularly the first, Graham Dakyns, were received as part of the family.

It has been argued, most destructively by Harold Nicolson, that 'the sweet incense' of domestic adulation 'had a rather narcotic effect upon his [Tennyson's] sterner faculties'.[6] The young friends, who had their position in life still to make, inevitably looked up to him with admiration, and were, in varying ways, dependent upon him for support, whether in gaining commissions or introductions. The most independent of the group was Jowett, who actually dared to use the word 'incense' to Tennyson himself, and got away with it. But, in the early 1860s, Jowett was in danger of expulsion from his Oxford fellowship for contributing a radical essay to the controversial volume, *Essays and Reviews*. The Tennysons, who enjoyed reading Jowett's Bible commentaries in the evenings, supported his position, and followed events with keen interest. After the dismissal of the case, Jowett went on to become Master of Balliol and the most distinguished of all Victorian academics.

Jowett and Woolner both formed close friendships with Emily Tennyson, corresponding with her over a number of years. Because of Tennyson's own virtual embargo on letter-writing, Emily became his link with the outside world. It was she who regularly sent him off on holiday with Francis Palgrave, to Scotland, the Peak District, Dartmoor and, most adventurously, to Portugal. All his life, Tennyson longed to see the tropics, but whenever he experienced a Mediterranean climate, he found the 'heat and the flies and the fleas and one thing or another' overwhelming and so turned back (*Memoir*, I, 441). The hill-town of Cintra, with its Byronic associations, reminded him of the Bois de Boulogne.

The best documented of his journeys is that to the West Country in 1860, when he explored scenes associated with King Arthur in Cornwall and the Scilly Isles. Woolner, Holman Hunt and another painter, Val Prinsep, son of the hostess of Little Holland House, made up the party. Tennyson drew on the experience when describing the infant King Arthur carried on the ninth wave to the cove beneath Tintagel. Hunt noticed the precision of Tennyson's observation, recalling how, at Kynance Cove, the poet climbed out onto a rock where Hunt and Prinsep were painting. Hunt remembered that: 'we had to find an abutting crag over which he could lean and survey the scene. In the original sense of the word, he was truly nervous, but looked steadily and scrutinisingly'. 'I could have stayed there all day,' Tennyson told Hunt.[7]

It was from this vantage point that Hunt painted one of his most jewelled watercolours, *Asparagus Island* (private collection). Another Hunt sketch 'of a rocky cave seen across a wooded valley', made Tennyson ask the artist whether the brilliant colour was a result of artistic licence or whether Hunt really believed that this was what he saw. Hunt replied (as he had just replied to Palgrave's identical question) that, to his eye, 'the two exactly matched'.[8] Tennyson and Palgrave concluded that Hunt's sight was quite unlike their own.

Hunt and Palgrave give very different accounts of the expedition. According to Palgrave, they made up a jolly, cheerful, party, and Woolner, when writing to Emily Tennyson about the poet's improving health and hearty appetite, told the same story. Tempers became frayed, however, once Woolner had departed for London. Tennyson hurt his leg (or possibly had an attack of gout), which meant travelling by coach with Palgrave while Prinsep and Hunt walked and sketched. This comparative inactivity seems to have added to his irritability. In a letter to Emily, Palgrave tartly noted that 'we were sorry not to have more of Hunt's company, but as he preferred his Art to our honourable society, what could be done?'[9]

During the evenings, they talked over pipes and port, often about the anthology of lyrics which Palgrave was planning. Hunt remembered Palgrave's accusing Tennyson of 'always' losing his temper, and of being offended 'with the most inadequate cause ever since our start'.[10] Palgrave had promised Emily Tennyson not to let the poet out of his sight, particularly on the cliffs. When Tennyson contrived give him the slip, Palgrave's only resource was to call out the poet's name. Fearful of being mobbed by the public, Tennyson had insisted on anonymity and was outraged by such publicity. He was no better pleased when, reverting to incognito, Palgrave referred to him as 'the old gentleman'. Many years later, Hunt remembered Palgrave telling Tennyson: 'You think no one has any notion in his head but the question, "Where is Alfred Tennyson, Poet Laureate?" whereas not one in a hundred we meet has ever heard your name.'[10]

Hunt's story has the ring of truth, even though it conflicts with the 'unfailing considerateness to me'[11] which Palgrave himself recalled. The mingled difficulties and delights of the relationship supply the background for Palgrave's intriguing account of Tennyson's way of looking at a view, a house or a painting. Tennyson insisted upon being left alone while he looked on in silence, sometimes for half an hour, and often smoking his pipe. He would, however, expect his companion to remain at a respectful distance, to be called upon when the silent contemplation was over. Palgrave had a special interest in both landscape painting and poetry, and his memoirs are scattered with literary and pictorial comparisons. Like many others, he noticed that Tennyson's short sight made him particularly aware of tiny details and that 'the scenery presented itself in its larger masses of light & shade, without the flicker of small disturbing spots of sunbeam or colour: – with the broad effects, in short, which we find in the great masters of Nature largely & practically conceived; the manner that marks the background scenery in the best Italian art, or the absolute landscape of Claude, Gainsborough, or Wilson'.[12]

It was Palgrave who observed that, as the poet grew older, 'he would renew earlier familiarity with the great poets of all time' (*Memoir*, II, 499). Tennyson increasingly saw himself as part of a tradition which included English and European poets of successive generations. His pantheon of greats was reflected in the devices put up on the mantelpiece of his new home at Aldworth, representing Chaucer, Dante, Milton, Shakespeare, Wordsworth and Goethe. He often quoted from Chaucer's 'Knight's Tale', and from Shakespeare's

sonnets, which he liked more than the plays. It was Goethe's short
poems like 'Kennst du das Land?' from *Wilhelm Meister* or 'Edel sei
der Mensch' (Das Göttliche) which moved him most. Predictably, he
preferred Dante's *Paradiso* to the harrowing *Inferno*, rating Milton
'for sound . . . often finer than Dante'. 'What . . . can be more
monotonous than the first lines of the "Inferno" with their "a-s"?', he
asked his son. (*Memoir*, II, 215) Looking at two busts of Dante and
Goethe in a shop-window in company with Fitzgerald, Tennyson
responded to his friend's question, 'What is wanting to make Goethe's
as fine as the other's?' with the crisp reply, 'The Divine'.[13]

Tennyson's preoccupation with the poetry of the past may reflect
an insecurity in the face of change. Although he made no assessment
of the role of poetry in the nineteenth-century to match Browning's
Essay on Shelley or Sydney Dobell's 'Lecture on the "Nature of
Poetry"', he must have sensed that poetry occupied a less central
place in the culture of his own time than it had in the romantic
period. His reaction to this was to see himself both as a link in a
chain, and as a creative writer reaching out to the widest possible
audience, 'a poet of the people'.

A good index to Tennyson's literary tastes is provided by *The
Golden Treasury*, a volume of lyrics selected by Palgrave, planned on
the Cornish holiday and published in 1861. The dedication to
Tennyson was justly deserved, for the poet had both encouraged the
project and played an active part in the process of selection. Few
tasks can have given him greater pleasure. Kathleen Tillotson has
shown that Tennyson's decisions on what should or should not go
into the book were often decisive.[14] He insisted on the inclusion of
several of the Elizabethan and Jacobean lyrics, like Thomas Nash's
'Spring, the sweet Spring', Lyly's 'Cupid and my Campaspe' and
Dekker's 'Art thou poor, yet hast thou golden slumbers?', against
the wishes of Palgrave's other advisers, Woolner and George Miller.
'He would not hear of the book' without Gray's 'Elegy' and Milton's
'Lycidas', 'L'Allegro' and 'Il Penseroso'. Other works in the volume
were favourites of his, the patriotic poems by Thomas Campbell and
Charles Wolfe which he loved to recite to his sons; 'The Battle of
Baltic', 'The Soldier's Dream', 'Hohenlinden' and 'The Burial of Sir
John Moore'. Sir Walter Scott's 'Maid of Neidpath', which tells of a
girl rendered so ill by her lover's exile that, on his return, he does not
recognise her, Tennyson thought 'almost more pathetic than a man
has the right to be' (*Memoir*, II, 502). Cowper's 'To Mary Unwin'
(presumably 'The twentieth year is well-nigh past') was another

poem which he could hardly read aloud without breaking down. Given the continued popularity of *The Golden Treasury* into the twentieth-century, Tennyson's taste may be said to have influenced generations of readers.

Tennyson's taste in poetry went back to writers far earlier than Dante and Chaucer. Palgrave records that on the Cornish trip he often sat down to read his pocket copy of Homer 'as we wandered over a wild rock-island in the Scillies. We took Homer, however, so much for granted, that I do not recall many discussions in honour of *Iliad* and *Odyssey*. It would have been like praising "Monte Rosa".' (*Memoir*, II, 499)

This was a period when many Victorians were obsessed with Homer. Suggestions by German scholars that he was not a single individual but represented a group of poets, or doubts about the historical context of the narratives, whipped up a *furor* among educated circles in England. Part of the anxiety was derived from the parallel with biblical studies. If Homer went down, it was felt, then the authenticity of the Bible might go with him.

Later in the century, the development of archaeology stimulated further controversy. Events and places, well known from classical literature, were suddenly given a startling immediacy. In 1877, the discoverer of Troy, Heinrich Schliemann, was lionised in London, but Tennyson was not impressed when Schliemann told him that ancient Troy was 'no bigger than the courtyard of Burlington House'. 'I can never believe that', the poet bluntly replied (*Memoir*, II, 217). Years later, he told Agnata Butler that he had 'no faith' in Schliemann: 'How could a great city have been built on a little ridge like that (meaning Hissarlik)? Where would have been the room for Priam's fifty sons and fifty daughters?'[15]

As a boy, Tennyson had first read Homer in Alexander Pope's translation before tackling the original Greek text. Homer had inspired some of his finest early poems, including 'Ulysses' and 'The Lotus Eaters'. His renewal of interest may have been provoked by the lectures on Homeric translation given by Matthew Arnold in 1861. Arnold had declared that Tennyson's blank verse would be an inappropriate medium for rendering Homer into English. In giving the lectures, Arnold was entering a field of heated scholarly debate. Five years earlier, Francis Newman, a brother of John Henry, had published a translation of the *Iliad*, using a ballad metre dismissed by his most severe critics as that of 'Yankee Doodle'. In arguing that a simple rhythm and a 'quaint, flowing, garrulous' vocabulary were appropriate for a poem of an early primitive age, Newman was implicitly accepting the argument that the *Iliad* was a composite and orally transmitted work.[16] In reply, Arnold took up a conventional Victorian standpoint, arguing that Homer's poem was intended for an élite audience. He envisaged Homer as a noble and liberally minded man, akin to himself.

In the early 1860s, Tennyson became absorbed with the problem of translating the *Iliad*. William Allingham reported that his conversation was 'all upon Classic Metres, of which he is full at present'. Allingham, no classical scholar himself, derived amusement from seeing Tennyson 'setting . . . right' the headmasters of both Harrow and Marlborough, Henry Montagu Butler and George Granville Bradley.[17] Like a child excited with a new toy, Tennyson complained to Gladstone (a leading Homer scholar) that Allingham wanted to scan his 'beastly bad' trial hexameters, 'couldn't see they had quantity'.[18] To illustrate the virtues of blank verse, Tennyson published in the *Cornhill* a translation of 22 lines taken from Book 8 of the *Iliad*, a passage which Arnold had partially rendered into hexameters, a form which Tennyson thought 'barbarous'. ('On Translations of Homer', 6) Tennyson's version is far livelier than Arnold's, broadly faithful to the original, but with a compelling vigour. It was one of several experiments, which included parallel prose and blank verse translations for a passage from Book 6.

Tennyson's dismissal of Allingham's wish to 'scan' and his demand that his friend recognise 'quantity' is an indication of his approach to a keenly-fought contemporary argument about classical scansion. When analysing the work of other poets, Tennyson was particularly concerned with questions of metre, and would pounce on any fault in metric structure, redrafting the line in correct form. The basis of his method derived from his own classical education. For him, metre was to be valued by quantity rather than accent, in terms of time like music, rather than numerically, by beat. When Tennyson read aloud, his care over timing produced what seems to us a 'sing-song' unnatural manner.

In writing his own poetry, Tennyson displayed a technical virtuosity unsurpassed in English and only matched (if at all) by Swinburne. As a young man, Tennyson had recited ballads to his friends, and some of his early poems, like 'The Sisters', echo vernacular ballad rhythms. In this he is comparable to Gerard Manley Hopkins, another poet with a passionate interest in scansion. Hopkins goes far beyond Tennyson in his use of multiple unstressed accents and alliteration, based upon the forms of old and middle English poetry, but Tennyson's translation of 'The Battle of Brunanburh', written in the 1870s, shows that he too was experimenting with such effects.

Tennyson's excursions into classical metre and subject matter, together with his keen interest in philological research, represent the scholarly side of his art. He remained equally determined to reach the general reader, and to widen the range of his poetry. In an age in which the novel was the predominant form of literature, Tennyson increasingly turned to story-telling and dramatic narrative, often within a domestic framework. In 1861, he embarked upon a new experiment, a poem in dialect, based upon an anecdote related to him by his great-uncle. 'Northern Farmer: Old Style' is the monologue of an old man who, near to death, refuses to give up his glass of ale, or to accept the paternity of an illegitimate child. Either way, he explains, he has supported the boy. His thoughts turn on a task nearly completed, the reclamation of a patch of waste land:

> Dubbut looök at the waäste: theer warn't not feeäd for a cow;
> Nowt at all but bracken an' fuzz, an' looök at it now–
> Warnt worth nowt a haäcre, an' now theer's lots of feeäd,
> Fourscoor yows upon it an' some on it down i' seeäd.

> (37–40)

The poem, like its successor, 'Northern Farmer: New Style' takes an honest, if quizzical, look at some of the hard facts behind the pastoral idyll. 'Proputty, proputty, proputty' rings in the ears of the 'new-style' farmer, as he forbids his son to marry the penniless vicar's daughter. (l.2)

The urban world is largely absent from Tennyson's poetry. He sets one poem in a children's hospital, and begins another, 'Sea Dreams', in the 'giant-factoried city-gloom', but he had almost no experience of industry or slum dwelling. (l. 5) Passing through Leeds, 'a city at that time almost sinfully dirty', with Palgrave in 1862, Tennyson startled his companion by announcing that 'if, as in the fairy stories, my choice were no London, or, all London, – all London I should have to decide for'.[19] It was, of course, a choice which he never had to make.

The most extended, and most successful, of Tennyson's poems of humble life is *Enoch Arden*, a version of the folk-myth of the sailor who returns to find his wife or sweetheart married to another. Comparable versions of the story were George Crabbe's *The Parting Hour* of 1812, and Elizabeth Gaskell's novel, *Sylvia's Lovers*, published after *Enoch Arden* was completed in 1863. Tennyson's immediate source was a story supplied by Woolner, who had related the tale on returning from Australia, and then, in response to a request, had written out a draft.

Bigamy was a popular issue in mid-nineteenth-century literature. *Aurora Floyd* and *Lady Audley's Secret*, the two best-known sensation novels of Mary Braddon, both deal with a woman's remarriage while her first husband lives. Tennyson is known to have read her work with avidity. *Lady Audley* later became a successful play, but bigamy was not a new subject in the Victorian theatre, where it had already furnished the plots for several other melodramas.

Tennyson's poem begins with games of 'keeping house', played by three children, Enoch, Annie and Philip. (l. 24) Later, Enoch, the fisherman's son, wins Annie as his wife, while Philip, the better-off miller's son, is left in despair. It is when Enoch's trade as a fishmonger declines that he decides to make a long and hazardous voyage abroad, leaving his wife and their three children at home. Annie begs him not to go, but, after setting her up in a shop, Enoch leaves, drawn by the idea of making a better life for his children. When, having been wrecked on a desert island, he fails to return, Annie eventually marries Philip, who has supported the family during Enoch's absence.

As a narrative, the poem is closely plotted. The number three recurs throughout, there are three children at the opening. Enoch and Annie have three children, of whom one dies, to be replaced by the child of Philip and Annie. Enoch saves three men from drowning, and is himself washed up onto the island with two others. Events repeat themselves, the boys' games of sharing Annie in marriage prefigure their adult life. At the end of the poem, Enoch greets the coming of death with the cry of 'A sail! A sail!/I am saved', as though he were still marooned on the island (907–8).

Tennyson clearly relished describing the tropical scene, writing in language which recalls 'The Lotus Eaters', and drawing on impressions of the botanical gardens in Lisbon and of the greenhouses at Chatsworth. Walter Bagehot thought the passage a piece of word-painting, not properly integrated into the narrative, but many modern critics regard it as a *tour de force*.[20] More precisely pictorial is the episode when, rescued at last, Enoch returns to England, and, looking through the framing window of his own house, sees within a family scene from which he, the voyeur, is excluded.

That *Enoch Arden* has more than a touch of the theatrical is clear in Richard Strauss's 'melodrama for the piano', a recitation written in 1898 for the director of the Munich opera. Such is Strauss's virtuosity that he succeeds in conveying the fateful doom of the piece, giving it the sense of inevitability of a Greek tragedy. When Enoch prays that his family may be rescued from poverty, whatever may befall him, or when Annie looks into the Bible to discover her husband's fate and, though finding the truth there, misinterprets it, these are moments when the story moves away from the confines of domestic realism and touches upon the supernatural and providential.

The poem was published in a new volume, *Enoch Arden etc.* in August 1864. The original idea for the title, 'Idyls of the Hearth' was more revealing, marking a return to the subject matter of the 'English Idyls' of the 1840s. The book was an immediate success, with 60 000 copies sold before the end of the year. Many reviewers were enthusiastic, but some questioned the poem's morality. Annie's remarriage (however innocently undertaken) *was* bigamous, and it also offended those who objected to second marriages in the first place, especially for women. Walter Bagehot, with a chilling awareness of class distinctions, complained that a real fishmonger and sailor would have been neither interesting nor noble. In the cause of making Enoch heroic, the poet made no use of dialect here, as he had in 'The Northern Farmer'.

This idealised presentation of working people is particularly striking in the illustrations made by Arthur Hughes for the 1866 edition. Hughes, a Pre-Raphaelite associate, was predominantly a painter, but he worked as an illustrator to support himself. Like the other members of the Pre-Raphaelite circle, he admired Tennyson's poetry. At least five of his paintings illustrate subjects from Tennyson, often quoted either on the frame or in the catalogue.

The theme of the disturbing return of those presumed dead recurs in Tennyson, and is associated by Christopher Ricks with the unexpected recovery of his own father from illness. Tennyson also had some direct experience of the effects of loss at sea. A Lincolnshire neighbour, Algernon Massingberd of Gunby Hall, disappeared in 1855 and was eventually presumed dead. At the time of his early acquaintance with Emily Sellwood, Tennyson had met her uncle, the famous explorer, John Franklin. In 1845, Franklin set out on a major naval expedition in search of a north-west passage, a quick route to the east, which had baffled explorers since the sixteenth-century. By 1848 serious alarm began to be felt about Franklin's fate, and a number of search expeditions were launched by both the Admiralty and the explorer's widow. Over the course of the next fifteen years, the search for Franklin became headline news and a topic of sensational interest to the British public.

The Tennysons followed these events with understandable interest. Emily's brother-in-law, Charles Weld, had helped with the planning of the expedition, and, in the 1850s, they all saw a good deal of Lady Franklin. 'Painful tidings of the Arctic Expedition', Emily wrote in her journal, when the first relics of the Franklin expedition were found and with them the first evidence of how the company had perished. (ET, *Journal*, p. 39) An outburst of horror greeted suggestions that, after Franklin's death, the survivors in their final extremity had practised cannibalism. Much later, in the 1870s, Tennyson wrote an epitaph for the memorial in Westminster Abbey.

> Not here! the white North has thy bones; and thou,
> 　　Heroic sailor-soul,
> Art passing on thine happier voyage now
> 　　Toward no earthly pole.

> ('Sir John Franklin')

Enoch Arden struck close to the hearts of contemporary readers, absorbed by this latest rendering of the old story of how the well-intentioned can bring disaster or shame upon themselves. Like Sophocles, in *Oedipus Rex*, Tennyson raises a taboo issue, and closes his narrative with recognition and discovery, although he does not describe the moment when Annie learns the truth. Instead, he places the whole weight of remorse upon the much-decried last lines:

> So past the strong heroic soul away.
> And when they buried him the little port
> Had seldom seen a costlier funeral.

> (909–11)

Robert Browning felt that Tennyson should have resisted such a conclusion, believing that a truly heroic Enoch would have spared Annie a knowledge of her bigamy. For readers dismayed by the apparent materialism of 'costlier', Browning's would have been a stronger ending. Tennyson, however, stood by his decision, declaring that 'The costly funeral is all that poor Annie could do for him after he was gone. This is entirely introduced for her sake, and, in my opinion, quite necessary to the perfection of the Poem and the simplicity of the narrative.'

Lady Audley's Secret has been interpreted as a novel of woman's struggle for autonomy in a male-dominated world. *Enoch Arden* lays itself open to quite another interpretation. The pivot of the narrative, Enoch's departure from his family, has been seen by Marion Shaw, not as Tennyson's contemporaries might have viewed it, as an act of commendable 'self help', but as 'perverse', 'excessive' and 'disproportionate', the result of a 'destructive urge'. Enoch's decision at his death to send a lock of their dead baby's hair to Annie, as proof of identity, becomes in this reading a 'final and terrible revenge upon the family and community he transgressed so many years before . . . Annie's new baby is illegitimized, her marriage to Philip made bigamous'.[21]

This interpretation suggests why the poem seems to have two levels of meaning, an outer conventional one, and another, far more disturbing meaning, which lies behind. The impeccably liberal sentiments of *Enoch Arden* will not stand up to close scrutiny. The poem, quite as much as *The Idylls of the King*, expresses the growing division in Tennyson between an idealising, perfecting tendency and (what had always been there) an inner understanding of disturbance, loss and discordance. Without this, perhaps, *Enoch Arden* would not have captured the public as it did. The Victorians could read any number of bland accounts of virtuous behaviour, but it was the extra elements of *Enoch Arden* which intrigued them. For the Laureate's serious critics, however, it was another sign of his progress downhill.

In a very different vein from *Enoch Arden*, was the poem Tennyson wrote a year later, 'Lucretius', an account of the destruction of a man's reason by uncontrolled sexuality. Alfred Austin detected a sexual element in the earlier *Idylls*, and believed that the public was determined to ignore it: 'The man who wrote "Vivien", and the parting scene between Guinevere and Lancelot, has not invariably been a moral milkman'.[22] 'Lucretius', a poem which many found uncomfortable, largely consists of a monologue by the Roman writer and philosopher, famous for his long unfinished poem, *De Rerum Natura*, and for his belief in the material nature of the universe.

In December 1857, Alfred and Emily Tennyson read together from Lucretius, at that time an almost forgotten author. Then, in 1864,

Hugh Munro brought out a new edition, with a translation, re-establishing Lucretius as a major writer. Palgrave took a copy to Farringford for Christmas, and Tennyson seems to have purloined it. This was the major source for the poem, although Tennyson apparently took his account of the wife's actions from St Jerome. The poem begins with an account of the distress of Lucretius's wife, Lucilia, at her husband's coldness and her decision to give him a love potion. After 25 lines, the form becomes that of the dramatic monologue as Lucretius finds his mind overborne by madness and lust. The monologue ends with his suicide, and the poem concludes with eight lines describing his wife's horror at 'having fail'd in duty to him.' (l. 277)

One theme in the poem is the idea of the permanence of the work of literature. In one of his lucid moments, Lucretius declares that his writing will last until the complete destruction of the universe. Even more powerfully expressed is the threat posed to this permanence by the sexual passions, and perhaps by nature itself. Tennyson's treatment of Lucretius's succumbing to the body and losing control of the mind is remarkably powerful:

> But now it seems some unseen monster lays
> His vast and filthy hands upon my will,
> Wrenching its backward into his; and spoils
> My bliss in being.

> (219–22)

Tennyson promised the poem to *Macmillan's Magazine*, but delayed giving his consent for publication because of anxieties over the copyright implications. When it eventually appeared in May 1868, a passage describing Lucretius's fantasy of an oread was omitted because publisher, editor and poet concluded that it might offend British readers.[23] The lines did, however, appear in the version published by the American magazine, *Every Saturday*:

> And here an Oread – how the sun delights
> To glance and shift about her slippery sides,
> And rosy knees and supple roundnesses,
> And budded bosom-peaks.

> (188–91)

Marion Shaw, not surprisingly, sees 'Lucretius' as a statement that women 'represent and appeal to the lower half' of man, 'that which lies beneath and which threatens to disrupt the rationalist ethic that Tennyson, through Lucretius, seeks to protect'. Women are therefore excluded from 'all the higher operations of the mind'.[24]

In the eyes of the public, Tennyson's stature and reputation grew with the years. To younger poets, however, his work seemed increasingly out of date. There had been little direct challenge to his position in the 1850s, but in the 1860s the tide began to turn against him. Other names became common currency, and Tennyson's position as an active poet, if not as a public figure, began to decline. It has been said that his wife isolated him from criticism, but Tennyson was too aware of currents in contemporary poetry to miss the tenor of the controversy.

One of the first voices to be raised against Tennyson was that of Matthew Arnold. In 1853, Arnold prefaced his third volume of poems with a statement of his beliefs. Great poetry, he declared, must draw on mythic subjects of permanent value. Arnold's main target in his preface was the Spasmodic school, and its concentration on the disturbed individual psyche, but his strictures could be taken to include Tennyson's domestic idyls and even *In Memoriam*. Privately, Arnold described Tennyson's elegy as one of a type of poem 'which have no beginning, middle or end, but are holdings forth in verse, which, for anything in the nature of the composition itself, may perfectly well go on for ever'.[25]

Many of Arnold's criticisms were voiced in letters to his close friend, Arthur Hugh Clough. Tennyson, wrote Arnold, dawdled with the 'painted shell' of the universe. Arnold was even afraid that his own 'Sohrab and Rustum' might be Tennysonian in places, 'at any rate it is not good'.[26] Clough, who became friendly with Tennyson, was less critical of him. On his side, Tennyson spoke of the 'power' of Clough's muse, even though the younger poet's disillusioned stance was so different from his own.[27] Arnold believed, with some justification, that Clough's swingeing attack on the class system, The Bothie of *Tober-na-Vuolich*, had had an influence upon *Maud*.

Clough and Arnold were half a generation younger than Tennyson. Other poets who came to prominence in the 1860s were younger and more directly under the influence of Tennyson himself. Among them were three members of the Pre-Raphaelite group, Dante Gabriel Rossetti, William Morris and Algernon Swinburne. All three drew inspiration from Tennyson, writing poetry rich in image and symbol, and marked by an extensive use of alliteration and assonance. Morris's *Defence of Guenevere* appeared in 1858, its Arthurian title poem slightly in advance of Tennyson's first four *Idylls*. More popular still were Morris's two long narrative poems, *The Life and Death of Jason* (which Tennyson liked) and *The Earthly Paradise*. Rossetti's *Poems* of 1870 included early works and the first section of his sonnet sequence, *The House of Life*, some parts of which Tennyson thought 'very fine'.[28]

The most talented poet of the three was Swinburne, whose *Poems and Ballads* of 1866, with their overt treatment of the erotic and the masochistic, sent shock waves through the reading public. As early as 1862, Julia Margaret Cameron told Tennyson about 'the mad worship of Swinburne', reporting that some said that 'Swinburne was greater than Shelley or Tennyson or Wordsworth'.[29] This 'worship' (put about by the Pre-Raphaelite Mutual Admiration Society) was somewhat premature as Swinburne had yet to publish anything of note, but by the later 1860s the idea that Swinburne was the new poet of the age gained ground. Tennyson, impressed that Swinburne did not force his poetry upon him, found him 'a very modest and intelligent young fellow' when he called at Farringford in 1858. (*Memoir*, I, 425) Swinburne was bowled over by the experience: 'stayed till long after midnight in his glorious little room, but what he said is to be remembered not here but in my soul for ever'. (*Letters*, II, 194)

Tennyson modified his first impressions, particularly after Swinburne had been personally rude to him. He believed that Swinburne had exceptional metrical talent, high praise indeed from Tennyson. 'I am and always have been your admirer', he wrote when, in 1891, Swinburne congratulated him on his eightieth birthday. (*Letters*, III, 428) Technically this was true, but Tennyson's 'objections' to Swinburne's subject-matter were as 'deep as heaven and hell'. (*Letters*, II, 395) His preoccupation with the destructive power of sexuality in the late 1860s and early 1870s, was in part a reaction to reading Swinburne. At the end of his life, Tennyson was outspoken on the subject to his daughter-in-law:

> Swinburne has written a sonnet in praise of Mademoiselle de Maupin. It is a beastly improper book, Swinburne himself has written shocking things.
>
> More harm can be done through bad literature than through anything else. The terrible thing is that man being higher than the

beast can through the fact of his intellect make himself lower than the beast.[30]

A similar reaction provoked Robert Buchanan to write his 'Fleshly School of Poetry' article in the *Contemporary Review* of 1871. For Buchanan, a decorative and sensuous style was a sign of spiritual degeneration. The 'sub-Tennysonian school' of poets were to him like Rosencrantz and Guildenstern to Tennyson's Hamlet, obtruding 'their smaller idiosyncrasies in the front rank of leading performers'. If Buchanan saw parallels with them in the 'fleshliness' of *Vivien* and the 'hysteria' of *Maud*, he was insistent that Tennyson had 'the moral and intellectual quality to temper and control it'.[31] Two years later, Tennyson's close friend, James Knowles, writing in the same journal, echoed Buchanan's jibes against 'women-like men' to 'whose fleshly gospel Tennyson had opposed an Imitation of Christ'.[32]

If Swinburne was now the darling of the undergraduates, who chanted his 'Dolores' in the streets of Oxford, Robert Browning was taken up by the intellectuals. Once Browning returned to literary London on the death of his wife, the balance between the two poets began to change. In 1864, he published his *Dramatis Personae*, the first of his books to be generally successful. Then, in 1867, came his Roman murder story, *The Ring and the Book*. Browning had offered the subject (found in a book in a Florence market place) to both Trollope and Tennyson. When they turned it down, he wrote his own version, with ten monologues representing different views of the murder, framed by introductory and closing books. Tennyson thought that it would be too difficult and too long for the public, but attitudes had changed. Browning, in his fifties, was now regarded as the man with potential, appealing to educated readers, while Tennyson was the man of the past. In 1877, the Young Men's Christian Debating Society passed a motion that 'The Poems of Robert Browning are of a higher order than those of Alfred Tennyson'. Four years later the Browning Society was founded. Both poets, however, came in for a devastating attack in 1869, when a young poet, Alfred Austin, launched into them in *Temple Bar*, describing Tennyson as third rate and Browning as the darling of the literary coteries. Tennyson, who believed that the article was motivated by personal spite, described the author of a 'bully'. (*Letters*, II, 523) 23 years later, Austin succeeded him as Poet Laureate.

9

Aldworth and the Later *Idylls*

The Tennysons had barely settled at Farringford when guide books began to draw attention to their home. The results were predictable. As more visitors came to the Isle of Wight, Farringford, once so secluded, became the goal of celebrity-seekers. Tennyson's hatred for 'cockneys', his name for unwelcome visitors, was understandable, if excessive. There are stories of tourists cutting pieces of stone from his gate, or climbing the trees in his garden in order to listen to his conversation. Some even came boldly to the front door. Tennyson's appearance contributed to the problem. With his big hat and cape, he was immediately recognisable.

In the mid-1860s, the Tennysons began to migrate to the mainland for the summer, renting rooms in cottages and farmhouses in the Surrey countryside: 'to fly now and then for the sake of a drier air, and also it must be confessed to take refuge occasionally from cockneys or lion-hunters' (Letters, II, 431). Emily's father lived at Farnham, and she had long cherished an idea of living on the high heathland near him. Even when Henry Sellwood moved away, Surrey still drew her. 'My wife,' Tennyson wrote, 'has always had a fancy for the sandy soil and heather-scented air of this part of England and we are intending to buy a few acres and build a little house here – whither we can escape when the cockneys are running over my lawns at Freshwater' (Letters, II, 445).

Farringford undoubtedly lost its charm for Emily once Hallam and Lionel were sent to school in 1864, much against her wishes. They started together at a small establishment run by a former headmaster of Eton, Charles Kegan Paul, who later became Tennyson's publisher. Hallam went from there to Marlborough in 1865 and Lionel, who stammered badly, went to Eton after a spell with a speech therapist. The boys' departure coincided with the death of Tennyson's mother, at her home in Hampstead. The eccentric unmarried sister, Matilda, now settled at Farringford, an arrival which cannot have compensated Emily for the loss of her sons.

By June 1867, Tennyson had found a plot of land known as Blackhorse Copse, high on the side of Blackdown, a few miles from Haslemere. A wide view stretched away to the south downs, and, nearer at hand, to Leith Hill.

> Green Sussex fading into blue
> With one gray glimpse of sea,

> ('Prologue to General Hamley', 7–8)

was Tennyson's tribute to the prospect, and, as at Farringford, the view decided the matter, and the land was bought.

Arriving at Haslemere station to look at his purchase, Tennyson was greeted by a young architect, James Knowles. Six years before, Knowles had been permitted to dedicate his popular version of Malory's *Morte Darthur* to Tennyson. A copy was dispatched to Farringford, where Emily read it aloud to the children. When Knowles called, Tennyson told him: 'I am so short sighted that I shall not know you if I meet you unless you speak to me.' This Knowles duly did, first offering Tennyson a lift, and then 'having been told A's errand [he] said I am an architect. A. replied, you had better build me a house, & Mr Knowles said "On one condition that you take my services freely only paying the journeys."' (ET, *Journal*, p. 263)

At 36, Knowles had considerable architectual experience, most notably from working with his father on the Grosvenor Hotel at Victoria Station. The Tennyson project helped to make his name, bringing him into contact with many famous men of the day. The new house was named Aldworth, after the village in Berkshire from which the Sellwoods came. Where a more opinionated designer would have insisted upon following his own scheme, Knowles allowed Tennyson his head, and Aldworth became as much Tennyson's creation as his own.

At the outset, the Tennysons planned to build a country retreat. They ended, probably encouraged by Knowles, with a substantial summer residence. Like the extensions to Somersby Rectory and to Farringford, Aldworth is Gothic in style, but this was the Gothicism of the High Victorians, not the early neo-Gothicism of the romantic period. It is contemporary with Gilbert Scott's St Pancras Hotel and with Street's London Law Courts. Between the ground and first floors runs a narrow stone band carved with leaves, flowers and small animals. On one side is a biblical passage chosen by Emily

Tennyson: 'GLORIA IN EXCELSIS DEO ET IN TERRA'. Above the crocketed dormer windows are shields on which the arms of the poet's ancestors and those of his wife were set. One remained uncarved, and Tennyson decided to leave it blank. 'Aldworth was bookish, typographical, says Priscilla Metcalf, comparing it to the Houses of Parliament.[1] There Sir Charles Barry overlaid a classical carcass with Gothic and Tudor decoration. At Aldworth, too, the building's layout is essentially Georgian in conception, with extensive medieval decoration, much of it inspired by motifs in Westminster Abbey. The steep roofs are in another style, French of the second Empire, and comparable to those at the Grosvenor Hotel.

Aldworth was built to suit Tennyson's own needs. His first-floor study looked out over the weald of Sussex, with his bedroom and that of Emily on either side. From the long south front the sitting-rooms and dining-room opened to the same prospect. A hall corridor ran across the middle of the house, allowing the poet a place for exercise on wet days as the colonnade had done at Farringford. His first bathroom gave him such joy that he began by bathing several times a day, throwing the water over the newly seeded lawns.

The Aldworth garden, like that at Farringford, was laid out with seclusion in mind. Trees and shrubs grew close to the house, and lawns were concealed within them. One summer house was protected against the west wind, the other against the east. Along the southern side, taking advantage of the view, there still runs a stone terrace, where the Tennysons planted red roses, hollyhocks and cypresses.

Aldworth was more accessible than Farringford, and, as the years went by, many of the Tennysons' friends visited them there. They made new acquaintances in the neighbourhood. One was James Henry Mangles, a horticulturist, who lived at Valewood a quarter of a mile away. Mangles' diary is a remarkable source for information on Tennyson's life and conversation in 1870 and 1871. Nearer Haslemere was Brookbank cottage, Shottermill, where Tennyson would call and talk with George Eliot and her companion, George Henry Lewes. Tennyson, who deeply admired her early novels, never guessed that George Eliot was the author of the hostile *Westminster* review of *Maud*. Nor can he have realised the effect he made upon the Leweses: 'Tennyson, who is one of the "hill folk" about here, has found us out, so that we have lost the utmost perfection of our solitude – the impossibility of a caller'.[2] Visits between the two households continued for several years. Not everybody was prepared to call upon an unmarried couple, and it says something for Emily Tennyson's strength of character that she ignored convention.

Building Aldworth drew Knowles into close association with Tennyson. He was outraged when the poet, talking too expansively at dinner, implied that he had paid Knowles for his work. Such traumas apart, the relationship ran smoothly. On visits to London, Tennyson began to stay with the Knowleses at the Hollies, beside Clapham Common, instead of with the Palgraves or the Woolners, both of whom lived near Regent's Park. In their different ways, all of Tennyson's younger friends helped to keep him amused. Woolner's and Palgrave's considerable knowledge of the fine arts provided a common point of interest. None, however, could readily be described as an intellectual. Nor indeed could Tennyson himself.

It was Knowles who was able to exploit Tennyson's diverse interests, both for the poet's benefit and for his own. One of Tennyson's friends in the Isle of Wight was Charles Pritchard, the astronomer, with whom he often talked about the relation of religion and science. In 1868 Knowles, Pritchard and Tennyson had a long discussion on metaphysics. According to Knowles, Tennyson then expressed a wish to talk regularly on such subjects with 'capable men in the manner & with the machinery of the learned Societies. "Modern Science" he said "ought surely to have taught us how to separate light from heat – & men ought to be able now-a-days to keep their tempers – even while they discuss theology."'[3] Knowles replied that, if Pritchard and Tennyson would join him, he was prepared to organise such a society.

The society, as first conceived, was to include Christians of all denominations, but non-Christians were admitted, and the society was dubbed metaphysical, rather than theological. Sixty distinguished Victorians were eventually given membership and an opportunity to meet once a month, from November to July, between 1869 and 1880. Tennyson, who did not enjoy debating, only attended twice, but he sent a poem written two years before, 'The Higher Pantheism', to be read by Knowles at the inaugural meeting on 2 June 1869.

The founding of the Metaphysical Society, a forum for discussion of questions and beliefs of all kinds, reflects some of Tennyson's own uncertainties. Charles Darwin's *Origin of Species by Means of Natural Selection*, published in 1859, had provoked a fierce debate between evolutionists and Biblical fundamentalists. Tennyson read *Origin of Species* with interest soon after its publication. In April 1861, Emily and he replaced their usual reading with an evening's talk of Darwin. Emily, predictably, disliked Darwin's ideas, but Tennyson was able to read the book as a work of natural history, and to find no threat in its theories of evolution: 'That makes no difference to me, even if the Darwinians did not, as they do, exaggerate Darwinism. To God all is present. He sees present, past, and future as one.'[4] He told one friend that it was 'a great truth', but 'only one side of a truth that had two sides'.[5] Tennyson continued to believe, as he had when writing the later parts of *In Memoriam*, that the most meaningful evolution was that in the spiritual life of man, for which he refused to account in material terms: 'no evolutionist is able to explain the mind of Man or how any possible physiological change of tissue can produce conscious thought'.[6]

'The Higher Pantheism', like other poems published in 1869, explores the relation of God and creation, putting forward the argument that the world is God's dream, and that material being, like the body of man, is a barrier to the union of man with God. On a smaller scale, and more teasingly, Tennyson states in 'Flower in the crannied wall' that, if the flower could be understood, so could God and man.

Knowles was endlessly useful to Tennyson. He hunted up books, handled money matters, and found London lodgings. Tennyson passed several winter visits in Albert Mansions, Victoria Street, a row designed by Knowles, and it was presumably through him that Tennyson bought the freehold of 27 houses on an estate designed by Knowles in Battersea. Knowles saw his poems through the press, probably persuaded him to finally complete 'The Lover's Tale', and even negotiated with Tennyson's publishers, a task from which most friends would have shrunk. He was deeply involved in Tennyson's change of publisher in 1869.

Tennyson had long wanted to make cheap editions of his work available and the popularity of *Enoch Arden* stiffened his resolve to issue sixpenny selections. Bertrand Payne, the manager of Moxons', disagreed with him, and brought out a five shilling volume as the first of a new series, *Moxon's Miniature Poets*. The second, a Browning, was dedicated, with a glowing tribute, to his predecessor.

Tennyson was not satisfied with the compromise. His wish to speak to a wider audience probably resulted in a decision to abandon his normal practice and publish a number of individual poems in periodicals in Britain and America. Emily Tennyson disapproved, voicing a commonly held prejudice against allowing magazines to print new poems. She felt that piecemeal publication impoverished later volumes, and that the selection of one magazine rather than another was disturbingly arbitrary. Tennyson's change of policy may have reflected his growing irritation with Moxon's and his dislike of Payne. Possibly it was an oblique move in the search for a new publisher. As it turned out, two of the magazines to which he contributed were owned by men who later took on that role. Like many people engaged in the book trade, both were Scots, Alexander Strahan and Alexander Macmillan.

Strahan founded a number of serious and successful magazines, including *Good Words*, known for the high quality of its illustrations and for its attempt to reach a broad readership. In 1868, two Tennyson poems appeared there, 'The Victim' and '1865–1866'. The £700 fee for 'The Victim' must have encouraged Tennyson to take Strahan seriously. The high prices paid by periodicals helped to build Aldworth. When Moxon's advertised a standard edition of his poems, to which he had not agreed, Tennyson felt able to go into the market. While Macmillan offered £3000 a year for the right to publish existing poems, the energetic Strahan made his way to Farringford offering £5000. This munificence disturbed Tennyson, and he was slow to decide. When he did so, he took only £4000 for the publication rights, and insisted upon Strahan taking 5 per cent of profits when new poems were printed.

Another of Strahan's magazines was *The Contemporary Review*, a liberal paper with intelligent articles for the serious-minded. Knowles published a rather amateurish essay on art and science there in February 1869, perhaps accepted by Strahan as part of his bid to capture Tennyson. When the editor of the magazine, Henry Alford, Dean of Canterbury, retired in 1870, Strahan claimed that Tennyson had asked him to employ Knowles on the paper. His initial task was to attract livelier contributors, which, through contacts given to him by Tennyson, Knowles was able to do.

Nearly a decade had passed since the publication of the first four *Idylls*, and many friends, including Knowles, had tried to persuade Tennyson to complete an Arthurian cycle. Ample financial rewards were offered, but Tennyson was nervous about interpreting the quest for the Holy Grail, a story he had abandoned years before. 'I doubt whether such a subject could be handled in these days,' he said, 'without incurring a charge of irreverence. It would be too much like playing with sacred things. The old writers *believed* in the Sangraal.' (Letters, II, 244). Emily Tennyson was particularly committed to the idea, believing this to be a truly noble subject for her husband to undertake.

When he began writing in September 1868, Tennyson had found a solution to his problem. By describing the vision of the grail through the words of Sir Percivale, he was able to evade any personal statement, and completed the book in under three weeks. Emily wrote in her journal: 'I doubt whether the "San Graal" would have been written but for my endeavour' (ET, *Journal*, pp. 292–3). Following his usual practice, Tennyson read the work aloud to family and friends, and then corrected a trial edition, set up a year before publication. Having overcome his initial misgivings, he then launched into three further books.

'Pelleas and Ettare', taken from Malory's story of the simple but brave young man who comes to Arthur's court, and falls in love with the worthless Ettarde, is, in Tennyson's words, 'almost the saddest of the Idylls'. Pelleas is first spurned by Ettare, and then deceived by Gawaine, a sign of the corruption spreading through Arthur's court after the Grail quest.

'The Coming of Arthur' takes up issues familiar to most thinking Victorians, as the poet probes Arthur's parentage and his qualifications for the throne. Here, as at other points in the *Idylls*, Christian parallels are apparent. Merlin, like Gerontius, recognises Arthur as the heir, and the doubting Leodogran is finally convinced through the agency of a dream. The balancing book, 'The Passing of Arthur', was largely made up of the old 1833 'Morte d'Arthur', set within the context of a monologue by the surviving knight of the round table, Sir Bedivere. The original version had also been framed in another story, but the light-hearted contemporary dialogue of 'The Epic', published in 1842, would have been entirely inappropriate here. The final book begins with an account of the battle in the west fought in a wasteland landscape:

> A land of old upheaven from the abyss
> By fire, to sink into the abyss again;
> Where fragments of forgotten peoples dwelt,
> And the long mountains ended in a coast
> Of ever-shifting sand, and far away
> The phantom circle of a moaning sea.

> (82–7)

The context of the *Idylls* is the fall of Camelot, but it also reflects the poet's foreboding of discordance and decadence in the society of his own time. His horror of sexual promiscuity, fuelled by reading the novels of Emile Zola, lies behind some of the themes of his Arthurian poem. Tennyson insisted that he was not writing an 'Epic of King Arthur. I should be crazed to attempt such a thing in the heart of the 19th Century' (*Letters*, II, 212). He could not, however, resist the temptation to give his poem the traditional twelve-book shape of an epic.

By the end of 1870, Tennyson had written another book, 'The Last Tournament'. Knowles was now sufficiently intimate to persuade Tennyson to publish it in *The Contemporary* for a payment of £500. The alternative was to bring it out in a booklet for copyright reasons. Knowles achieved this coup with many protestations that he only wanted Tennyson to act as he pleased, and against 'the exceeding might' of 'Mrs Tennyson's opinion to the contrary'.[7] When he had the temerity to beg the manuscript as a gift, Tennyson gave it to him.

The last tournament of Camelot is fought in defiance of the laws of chivalry. Anxious that Arthur may have discovered his adultery with Guinevere, Lancelot fights without energy, and the joust is won by Sir Tristram. Defying the custom of presenting the prize to a lady of the court, he returns to Isolt and is murdered by her husband, King Mark. Interwoven with this theme is the story of Arthur's challenge to Sir Pelleas, now the outlawed Red Knight. Pelleas blames Arthur for the corruption of his court, and dies in shame, overwhelmed by a rioting mob.

The last *Idylls* appeared piecemeal. *Gareth and Lynette*, was published in 1872. In 1873, *Enid* was divided into two books, eventually given the titles *The Marriage of Geraint* and *Geraint and Enid*. The final book, *Balin and Balan* appeared in 1885, having been written a decade before.

In their eventual arrangement, the 12 books have a closely worked structure and shape. Between the opening and closing *Idylls* the pattern is one of gradual disintegration and darkness. *Gareth and Lynette* and the two *Geraint* stories all deal with the dangers of pride and with the resultant misprizing of true love, but, at this stage in the cycle, these dangers can be overcome. In *Balin* and *Balan*, however, and in *Merlin and Vivien*, attempts at goodness are subverted through human weakness and the guile of Vivien. In *Lancelot and Elaine* a totally innocent girl is sacrificed to the sins of Lancelot and Guinevere, the canker which will, in Tennyson's version of the story, destroy Arthur's Camelot. Even in the *Holy Grail*, the spotless Galahad has to withdraw from the city, and, in doing so, bring about its downfall. In

Pelleas and Ettare and *The Last Tournament* infidelity and lack of faith conquer in a darkened world. A change is evident in the eleventh book as Guinevere seeks asylum in a convent, and begs forgiveness of her husband. *The Passing of Arthur* charts the ruin of the round table, but suggests the possibility of a second coming. Lancelot, who has struggled in mental turmoil throughout the cycle, dies redeemed.

It is hard to judge Tennyson's achievement. He aimed at far more than the Pre-Raphaelite poets who used this subject, and challenged the highest standards. The *Idylls of the King* are Virgilian in scope, and, like Virgil, Tennyson indirectly considers the fate of contemporary men and women. As narratives the books are often gripping, and there is much incidental excellence in the poetry, but the final effect of the cycle must be rated as disappointing.

The *Idylls* were generally well received and proved extremely popular. This was evidenced by the enormous quantity of popular imagery they inspired, including illustrations by Gustave Doré, a set of photographs by Julia Margaret Cameron, and innumerable tiles, plates, paintings, tapestries and sculpture.

Not everyone admired the *Idylls*. William Morris, who knew Malory well, described it as 'the transfusion of modern sentiment into an ancient story',[8] and Bulwer Lytton, who had published his own twelve-book *King Arthur* in 1848, told a friend that he could 'scarcely understand how any *man* could reconcile himself to dwarf such mythical characters as Arthur, Lancelot and Merlin, into a whimpering old gentleman, a frenchified household traitor and a drivelling dotard'.[9] In this century more discerning critics have explored the overall structure and image patterns of the cycle, revealing a greater unity than had before been thought.

Tennyson's anxiety about the late nineteenth-century world was exacerbated in the 1870s by a series of financial and publishing problems. One of the most striking of these episodes occurred in 1870 when Arthur Sullivan wanted to publish their collaborative song-cycle, 'The Window' or 'The Song of the Wrens'. Tennyson was usually as unenthusiastic about musical settings of his work as he was about illustrations; in the early 1860s, Sterndale Bennett had found him uncompromising in his insistence that the 'Ode Sung at the Opening of the International Exhibition' should be exactly as he had written it. Only Emily Tennyson and Edward Lear, who both subordinated the music to the text, satisfied Tennyson's demands. The poet always insisted that he was quite unmusical, but he enjoyed romantic ballads, and had some favourite works by

Beethoven, whose *An die Ferne Geliebte* was one inspiration for 'The Window'.

Tennyson wanted Millais to illustrate the song-cycle, but only one drawing, a charming sketch of a girl at a window, was completed. Deciding that his 'Wren' songs were 'silly'[10] and 'light' (*Letters*, II, 698), and would diminish his reputation, Tennyson resisted publication. Finding it unavoidable, he wrote a preface distancing himself from the whole undertaking, and regretting that the poems should appear, at Sullivan's insistence, at the time of the Franco-Prussian War.

Even more unpleasant was Tennyson's treatment of Charles Dodgson (Lewis Carroll) who had come into possession of an unauthorised copy of 'The Window'. When the scrupulous Dodgson wrote asking for permission to read it, Emily accused him of angering her husband. Tennyson interpreted Dodgson's failure to reply as defiance and wrote an insulting letter. In the end, the poet grudgingly retracted his accusations, but his irritability was clearly getting out of hand. He had become obsessed with privacy, both for his work and himself, and was tormented by the fear of losing money through pirated editions.

In 1873, Strahan's business failed, but Tennyson decided to stay with his partner, Henry S. King who offered him £5000 a year to publish the existing works with 5 per cent commission on new ones. Unfortunately, King fell ill in 1877 and died in the following year. Unlike several other Strahan authors, Tennyson remained with King's manager, Charles Kegan Paul, the Tennyson boys' former schoolmaster. Paul was a talented publisher, but he began to stir up all Tennyson's old anxieties. He put forward a plan, vetoed by the poet, to annotate the 1874 Cabinet edition, illustrating it with relevant photographs and prints. Defeated here, Paul brought out several new editions of the works and published Tennyson's first new volume for six years, *Ballads and Other Poems*, which included popular favourites like 'Rizpah', the story of a woman who gathers up the bones of her hanged son, and 'The Revenge'.

The sensible and energetic Knowles was able to shoulder some burdens for Tennyson, as he laboured to promote his best interests. The early 1870s represented the zenith of Knowles' influence in Tennyson's life, but hostile forces were already gathering. Knowles's biographer finds it hard to decide what Emily Tennyson really felt about Knowles. It was generally believed that Knowles was planning to be a second Boswell and to write Tennyson's biography.

After the poet's death, he published material which Emily deemed private, and she then spoke of the 'defects' in Knowles's character. 'He is the cleverest man we any of us have known – with that sort of cleverness which can adapt itself to the moods of men or work upon them in differing moods.'[11] Tennyson himself was well aware that Knowles could be very persuasive, and may have come to resent it. Seen from one viewpoint, the poet, whose simplicity was proverbial, was exploited by the shrewd Knowles. Unlike Tolstoy's friend, Vladimir Chertkov, Knowles was no disciple, but he did regard himself as a privileged interpreter of Tennyson, and so, like Chertkov, he fell foul of the poet's immediate family. Hallam Tennyson undoubtedly broke Knowles's power after 1875, and became, for Knowles, 'the greediest and most jealous of small-minded men . . . [he] was always miserably jealous of his great Father's affection for me'.[12] Tennyson continued to see Knowles, to send him poems for publication in the *Contemporary* and in Knowles's later journal, the *Nineteenth Century*, and even to stay in Clapham. But nothing was ever quite the same again.

10

History and Drama

In August 1874, Tennyson set out for the Pyrenees once more. The whole family spent a week in Paris, before leaving Lionel and Emily in Tours. It was thought that travel would benefit Emily's poor health, and Lionel had instructions from his father to read George Sand's *Consuelo* aloud to her. Meanwhile, the others went on into the mountains. Tennyson, entranced by the vision of the Pic du Midi d'Ossau, declared it more Homeric than anything in the Alps. Now 65, he was delighted when their guide complimented him on his energy, and climbed up the Cirque de Gavarnie before first light to sketch the sunrise. The climax of the holiday came with the now familiar walks to Cauterets and Pont d'Espagne, where Tennyson quoted favourite lines from Byron and Shelley.

The family were home in time for Hallam and Lionel to return to Cambridge, where both were undergraduates at Trinity. After their departure, Farringford felt particularly empty. Tennyson, ever optimistic about his wife's health, believed that the journey had done her good, but it seems to have been the last straw. She took to her sofa in a state of collapse, unable to manage the household or to act as secretary. Emily's illness may have been psychosomatic, and it has been suggested that she was depressive, her exhaustion fuelled by her mental state. Whatever caused it, she was now believed to be in a dangerous condition, and Tennyson, alarmed, pinned his hopes on a phosphorus treatment.

He recognised that 'overwork and over-letterwriting' had played a part in Emily's collapse, but excused himself, anxious that correspondents should not think him unfeeling, by remembering that *she* had insisted upon relying to his letters.[1] So neurotic was he about this chore, that he resented having to do it, even now that Emily was incapacitated. His refusal must have sprung from something deeper than mere inertia or fear of time-wasting. Possibly, letters, like Cockneys, represented an invasion. In the Christmas vacation, Hallam took on the unpalatable task, beginning the annual letter to Fitzgerald with 'I have become the family-secretary' (Letters, III, 92).

Tennyson's behaviour in bringing Hallam home from Cambridge was inexcusable. For the rest of his father's life, Hallam became his agent and letter-writer. It is easy to understand how this happened, but less easy to excuse it. It was Tennyson who had originally urged Hallam to study at Cambridge, and he now fobbed him off with vague promises of a return. Coming down without a degree was less of an issue than it would be today, but the implication was that Hallam no longer had a life of his own.

The best that can be said for Tennyson was that he was trying to protect Emily. On her side Emily was determined to save her husband's feelings at the expense of her son. If the idea of a secretary was mooted, Tennyson presumably shot it down, either on grounds of expense or of loss of privacy. Hallam, one of life's facilitators, slipped into a role often played by the daughters of great men. He accepted the sacrifice, but not without regret. Over the years, perceptive onlookers like Mary Gladstone, meeting him with his father at Hawarden in 1876, saw him as a disciple: 'nice and very light in hand and quickly interested: worships his Father and sits adoring'.[2] Next day, Tennyson read *Harold* aloud, sometimes referring to Hallam for a word or a passage, readily supplied by a son who knew the work by heart.

During this period, Tennyson was devoting himself to the study and re-creation of English history. Before the end of the decade, he had completed three plays and a number of poems all concerned with well-known historical events between the time of the Roman invasion of Britain and the end of the sixteenth-century. Reading historical works was one of Emily Tennyson's pleasures, and it may have been she who stimulated her husband's interest. In the 1850s and 60s they had read several historical texts together, among them John Lothrop Motley's *Rise of the Dutch Republic*, Carlyle's *Frederick the Great* and *French Revolution*, Thomas Hughes's life of *Alfred the Great*, William Lecky's *History of European Morals* and Sharon Turner's *England in the Middle Ages*. Two major histories of England were also on their list, those of Thomas Babington Macaulay and of James Anthony Froude. The scale of the interest is clear from Tennyson's surviving library which contains more than fifty works on British and European history before the French Revolution, the majority of them published between the later 1860s and the 1880s.

Part of Tennyson's historical reading was undertaken to provide background for *The Idylls of the King*. Nor was his research confined to books. In the autumn of 1864, the Tennysons took a family holiday in Brittany, hoping to discover more Arthurian material, but 'the people we found very uncommunicative, and, as far as we could discover, totally ignorant of the past history of their country, and of the Arthur legends' (*Memoir*, II, 5).

This was part of a tour of Paris and Northern France which took in numerous churches, cathedrals, palaces and castles, all rich in historical association. In Bayeux, Emily found the famous tapestry 'extremely interesting. It gives one a feeling of perfect truthfulness . . . The object of the piece seemed to us the justification of William. A good wife's deed. The Cathedral very fine – A. is, I hope, glad to have been here'. In Caen, the family enjoyed the music in the Abbaye des Hommes, founded by William I. An 'enormous' beadle took them to see the Conqueror's portrait and tomb, but Emily's pleasure was marred by her aversion to catholicism. 'The Nuns asked of the boys . . . with a longing tone are they Catholics? & I seemed to see a shudder come over them when I said "No."' (ET, *Journal*, 213) The visit was to bear fruit more than a decade later in Tennyson's play, *Harold*.

The Tennysons' interest in English history corresponded to the rising popularity of the discipline, among both the academic community and the general public. Macaulay and Froude enjoyed huge sales, and, later in the century, they were succeeded by a group of distinguished Oxford historians. Like so much else in the Victorian age, this was part of an attempted definition of identity, a search for roots. For a generation who still believed in progress towards a better world, the past contained clues to the present and to the future, and the study of national history and literature began to take the place formerly occupied by classical learning.

A phenomenon of the late nineteenth and early twentieth-centuries has been designated as 'Englishness', the creation of a sense of English identity. By implication, the Celtic countries were excluded, although the boundaries were never clearly drawn. Englishness has been variously associated with the public schools, the old universities, the southern rural counties, and the establishment of institutions like the National Portrait Gallery, the *Dictionary of National Biography* and the *Oxford English Dictionary*. It was exportable, and, as a source of 'enlightenment', was carried to the Empire. A basic element in this new form of nationalism was the study of English history, and to this Tennyson's history poems made an important and lingering contribution.

Tennyson was a poet first, a historian second. For his play, *Queen*

Mary, he drafted an introductory sonnet, putting forward the claims of art over fact:

> no man can send his mind
> Into man's past so well, that he can form
> A perfect likeness of long-vanished souls.
> . . .
> You see the past dilated through the fog
> Of ages. Do your best, for that remains.

> (Ricks, III, 15)

An historical dramatist cannot simply recount events, he must

> confuse
> This date with that and make a living scene.
> I do command the voices that I use,
> And am not Froude or Freeman, Hook or Green.

> (Ricks, III, 15)

All four were historians represented in Tennyson's library. Froude and Walter Hook, author of *The Lives of the Archbishops of Canterbury*, were well established, but the other two names show Tennyson's awareness of the state of contemporary historical research. Edward Augustus Freeman was best known for his *History of the Norman Conquest* (1869–76), a major source for *Harold*, and John Richard Green's *Short History of the English People* was one of the most influential books of the nineteenth-century, opening up the early history of the country to the general reader. When Tennyson met Green in 1877, they talked together of Thomas Becket, subject of Tennyson's third play.

Tennyson's 'historical' period lasted until 1881, the year of *The Foresters*, his play about Robin Hood. Like Sir Walter Scott and later historical novelists, he was attracted by points of change, when nations and cultures were forged in the aftermath of conflict. In the mid-1870s, Tennyson made a translation of the old English 'Battle of Brunanburh', which celebrated the victory of Athelstan of Wessex and his allies over an army of invaders. His interest in Brunanburh is typical of his impulse to explore the decisive moments of the national past.

The Tennysons were reading about another such event, the defeat of the Spanish Armada, in 1856, and they knew Froude's essay on three Elizabethan sailors, 'England's Forgotten Worthies'. The essay inspired Charles Kingsley's novel, *Westward Ho!*, John Millais' painting. *The Boyhood of Raleigh* (Tate Gallery), and was an important source for Tennyson's poem on Grenville, 'The Revenge', written early in 1877. Tennyson pursued historical accuracy as he did biological precision, reading reprints of the original documents and consulting the secretary of the Hakluyt Society. At the time, he was engrossed in Tudor history, and the poem followed closely on the production of *Queen Mary*. Here too, Spanish and English, Catholic and Protestant, are in conflict. Once again, Tennyson drew heavily upon Froude, this time consulting his history of the reigns of Queen Mary and Queen Elizabeth.

Tennyson's interest in English history was one factor in his venture into the theatre. He may also, like Henry James in the 1890s, have wanted to appeal to a wider audience. Hallam Tennyson refers to his father's love of the theatre, but there is little to suggest that Tennyson was more than an occasional attender in the second half of his life. Victorian Sardou's *La Tosca* he disliked for its 'hideous realism and unreality' (*Memoir*, II, 174), and when, in 1872, he saw *Bobil and Bijou* by two successful dramatists, Dion Boucicault and J. R. Planché, he was unimpressed. To Emily he wrote: 'I . . . was ashamed of my countrymen flocking to such a wretched nonentity, miserable stagey-toned, unmeaning dialogue: only one thing made amends, a young damsel whose dancing was music and poetry' (*Memoir*, II, 116).

In the 1870s, the theatre, popular throughout the century, was at the beginning of a radical change, as the programme of mixed entertainments gave way to the performance of a single play. When Tennyson first began writing for the stage, the 'spectaculars' with their huge casts and expensive sets were still at the height of their popularity, but the underlying trend was towards small-scale domestic drama. Tennyson had some familiarity with the writers of this movement. Hallam and Lionel were part of an amateur group performing in Freshwater under the direction of Julia Margaret Cameron. W. S. Gilbert, Thomas Robertson and Tom Taylor were all in their repertory, and Tennyson was 'seldom absent . . . he was a careful critic and never missed a point' (*Memoir*, II, 85).

With one disastrous exception, Tennyson selected historical subjects for his plays, following the romantic poets down the dangerous path of Shakespearean influence. Tennyson saw himself as continuing the historical cycle where Shakespeare had left off, with the birth of Elizabeth at the end of *Henry VIII*. These were the years of Tennyson's correspondence with Frederick Furnivall about the establishment of a Shakespeare canon. He helped Furnivall to sift through disputed plays, suggesting that *Henry VIII*, known to him from boyhood, might be collaborative. *Pericles, Two Noble Kinsmen* and *Edward III* were also scrutinised, and certain passages identified as by Shakespeare. The method of attribution was instinctual, but the approach was far from amateur. Tennyson's ear for rhythm and nuance was of the finest.

For the subject of his first play, Tennyson rejected William the Silent and Lady Jane Grey, and chose Mary Tudor. He rated Victor Hugo's drama on the subject as 'a mere travesty', and set out to tell the whole story of Mary's reign in five acts (*Memoir*, II, 422). He thought of *Queen Mary* as a chronicle play, and, to that extent, it looks ahead to the 'epic' dramas of the twentieth-century like Shaw's *Saint Joan* and Brecht's *Mother Courage*. All three plays follow in the episodic tradition of Shakespeare's history plays, but Tennyson was equally affected by the historical dramas of the Victorian period. In the 1830s and 1840s, William Macready (for whom Tennyson wrote a laudatory farewell sonnet) was Browning's Strafford and Bulwer Lytton's Richelieu at Covent Garden and Drury Lane. Contemporary with Tennyson's own entry into the theatre were productions of W. G. Wills' *Charles I* and of Tom Taylor's *Jeanne d'Arc*, plays which suited the large stages of the 'spectacular' theatres.

The story of Tennyson's life in the theatre is closely entwined with that of Henry Irving, the greatest actor of the day. Twenty years younger than Tennyson, Irving had come to the Lyceum Theatre in 1871. Tennyson first saw him there playing Richelieu, in 1873, and told Irving how he should tackle the part of Hamlet. When he saw Irving play the role in 1875, and again in 1879, Tennyson was gratified to think that his advice had been taken to heart.

Irving did not become manager of the Lyceum until 1878. Before that date the theatre was under the control of H. L. Bateman, and later of his widow, Sidney Frances Bateman. Irving's successes in *Hamlet* and in Lewis's melodrama, *The Bells*, gave him some leeway in negotiating to perform new plays, but, as a shrewd man of the theatre, he realised that *Queen Mary*, as Tennyson published it in 1875, was unperformable. Sidney Bateman told Tennyson that 'the exigencies of the stage demand that the play be reduced in length and that it may not be longer than Hamlet – and it ought to be half an hour shorter – and not fuller of characters, Hamlet being well known to be the *fullest play on the stage'* (Letters, III, 116).

Tennyson was prepared to distinguish between what he called 'a full Historical Drama' (Letters, III, 107) and an acting version, but the arguments about the cuts went on for months. Eventually, major alterations were made, reducing the play by about half, excluding some of the characters, and concentrating the drama on the queen herself. In Tennyson's opinion, Mrs Bateman, thinking only of her profits, wanted to strip the play of its richness as an historical drama. She even insisted on cutting most of the music by Charles Villiers Stanford, a friend of Tennyson's sons, refusing to let the dramatist pay the expenses himself.

Tennyson was absent from the London first night on 18 April 1876, but he saw the production in early May, enjoying the acting of the two principles, Kate Bateman as Mary and Irving as Philip of Spain. Some of the papers were enthusiastic, but audiences were poor, and the production closed on 13 May.

By this time, Tennyson had completed a second play, *Harold*. He had learnt some lessons from *Queen Mary*, and produced a work with more drama and fewer characters. When he read it aloud to the Gladstone family, it took him two and a half hours, about half the length of the uncut *Queen Mary*. Irving, however, refused *Harold* for the Lyceum, and it was never performed in Tennyson's lifetime. The subject was the Norman Conquest of 1066. As in *Queen Mary*, the words 'England' or 'English' are insisted upon. Harold and the Saxons are identified with England and the Normans are presented as cruel invaders, supported by the alien power of the papacy. Something of Tennyson's fear of invasion from France finds its way into *Harold*, together with his dislike of catholicism. Harold is the perfect Englishman, unimpressed by the coming of the comet or by the dreams and visions of the inactive Edward the Confessor.

As he had for *Queen Mary*, Tennyson read widely, listing among his sources Edward Bulwer Lytton's novel of 1848, *Harold, or the Last of the Saxons*, the main outlines of which he followed. By 1876, Bulwer was dead, and, in deciding to dedicate the play to Bulwer's son, Tennyson was perhaps laying the ghost of their animosity.

Your father dedicated his *Harold* to my father's brother; allow me to dedicate my 'Harold' to yourself. (*Memoir*, II, 216)

Harold is not an exciting play, and Irving probably did well to turn it down. With all its flaws, *Queen Mary* is a more vigorous work.

Becket, the third part of Tennyson's historical trilogy, was ultimately the most successful of his plays in the theatre, providing Irving with one of his greatest roles, but not until after Tennyson's death. In the 1870s, Irving rejected it as too long and undramatic.

In *Becket*, king, barons and church battle for control of England. The son of a London merchant, Becket is the new man, initially triumphing over the old Norman aristocracy, but eventually destroyed by it. Tennyson is careful to remind his audience that Henry II was a reformer as well as an autocrat, but his Henry is not an admirable character. He has tricked Rosamund Clifford into a mock marriage (by which means Tennyson rendered her respectable) and his mood fluctuates between sentiment and ruthlessness. Tennyson makes Eleanor of Aquitaine into a word-shaper or poet, and, through Becket's unhistorical rescue of Rosamund, he even clears her of murder.

Becket, like *Queen Mary*, covers a considerable span of time and space, one of its many inheritances from Shakespeare. Like Shakespeare, Tennyson brings in lower-class characters, beggars and country-people, to comment on the doings of the great, directing our sympathy towards those who are unjustly abused by the court and the barons. Becket himself is presented as a champion of the underprivileged, his life paralleled with that of Christ, whose redeeming death is echoed in Becket's martyrdom. Following the contemporary taste for biblical typology, Tennyson gives Becket some of Christ's attributes, so that, from the first scene, in which Becket's mother is reported as having seen visions before his birth, this biblical parallel runs through the play. The crucifixion is visually recalled in two crosses, one Queen Eleanor's present to Henry II, which he gives to Rosamund, and the other Becket's cross of state, carried before him when he defies Henry at Northampton in Act I, Scene III, and later present in the murder scene. The worldly meaning of Becket's cross is secondary to its symbolism. When the Archbishop of York warns that the king may tear out his eyes, Becket replies:

> So be it. He begins at top with me:
> They crucified St. Peter downward,

and, later in the scene, the chorus chant:

> Blessed is he that cometh in the name of the Lord!

> (Act I, Scene III)

Tennyson's use of Christian symbolism is predictable in a drama about a saint and martyr. Elsewhere, however, he seems to be approaching T. S. Eliot's position and questioning Becket's motivation in stage-managing his own martyrdom, and meeting his murderers in a place chosen by himself. Here, as in *The Holy Grail*, Tennyson is inclined to put forward an explanation which takes account of human psychology. As a staunch anti-catholic, he was critical of Becket's loyalty to the papacy, a topic of some contemporary relevance. In 1870, the Pope had declared the doctrine of infallibility. As Tennyson put it in 'The Christ of Ammergau':

> They made the old Pope God –
> Which God, if He will, may pardon.

(Ricks, III, 2)

Tennyson did not give up the theatre, even after the disappointments of the trilogy. His one-act play from Boccaccio, *The Falcon*, was performed by William and Madge Kendal at the St James's Theatre in 1879. Far more impressive was *The Cup*, produced at the Lyceum in 1881. Irving, now manager of the theatre, was working in partnership with Ellen Terry. When delaying performance of *Becket*, Irving suggested that Tennyson write a shorter play. *The Cup*, which takes its subject from Plutarch, was the result. It was performed as the first part of a double bill with a nineteenth-century classic, Dion Boucicault's *Corsican Brothers*.

Plutarch tells the story of a Galatian woman, Camma. Her husband, Sinnatus, is killed by order of Synorix, who has fallen in love with her. Camma takes refuge in the temple of Artemis, but then agrees to marry her persecutor. At the ceremony, she poisons him when they drink together from a sacred cup. With Irving as Synorix, Ellen Terry as Camma and William Terriss as Sinnatus, the play had the benefit of some of the best acting in London. Tennyson thought that Irving had made Synorix 'a villain, not an epicurean' (*Memoir*, II, 385), but he was widely agreed to have given an impressive performance.

This was a production in the style of the late nineteenth-century classical and aesthetic movements. The sets were by Hawes Craven (who had been involved with *Queen Mary*), and some of the designs (perhaps including the cup itself) were by E. W. Godwin. The temple was the work of Knowles, and was built, like the other sets, with archaeological accuracy. The critic of the *Illustrated London News* was typical in finding it 'a triumph of scenic art'.[3] *The Cup* was Tennyson's greatest lifetime success in the theatre, but most of the praise was for the production, not the play.

Tennyson wrote two more plays. His Robin Hood drama, *The Foresters*, was requested by Irving, who turned it down. *The Promise of May*, written to please an insistent woman friend, Sabine Greville, was a 'modern village tragedy' in three acts (*Memoir*, II, 267). It was in prose, a departure from Tennyson's usual blank verse, and an approximation to the manner of Boucicault and Arthur Pinero. The heroines of the play are Dora and Eva Steer, the two daughters of a well-to-do farmer. Eva, betrayed by her lover, the radical and discontented Philip Edgar, is presumed dead, but she reappears just in time to save her sister, whom Edgar is courting under another name. Eva then dies, exhausted by her ordeal.

The Promise of May was first performed in 1882 under a new manager at the Globe Theatre, Mrs Bernard Beere, who took the part of Dora. There was a vogue for rural dramas, but *The Promise of May* was a disaster. The sets, costumes, programme and music were praised for their charm and freshness, and some critics defended the acting, but almost all dismissed the play with scorn. Too long for its subject matter, it was 'utterly undramatic' in construction and 'feeble' in dialogue. 'The Laureate cannot write a playable play', was *Punch*'s verdict. *The Falcon* and *The Cup* had been saved by fine acting, but '*The Promise of May* must be an utter frost'.[4]

The attacks centred on the character of Edgar who, it was said, 'inflicted on the audience the most extraordinary soliloquies touching communism, agnosticism, free-love, and other wholly undramatic topics'.[5] Charles Bradlaugh was attempting to take his seat as an MP without swearing the Parliamentary oath, and critics often compared Edgar to him. On the first night, a Saturday, rumours spread that the play was anti-socialist, and a hostile audience came to jeer and hoot. One reviewer advised Tennyson to stick to the more restrained Lyceum. To add a ridiculous touch to an already hopeless state of affairs, the Marquess of Queensberry (later to be the scourge of Oscar Wilde), outraged at Tennyson's presentation of a freethinker, stood up on the third night and protested loudly at this travesty of the truth. At home, Tennyson's rantings about the decadence of modern life were accepted without comment. On the stage of a public theatre, his sentiments sounded ridiculous and hopelessly out of date.

Hallam and Lionel Tennyson were present on the first night,

together with the Gladstones. They must have tried to keep the bad news from their father, but he clearly heard some part of it. Afterwards, he explained that he meant Edgar to be duplicitous and shallow, not a free-thinker, and that he was attempting to revive the drama: 'I had a feeling that I would at least strive to bring the true Drama of character and life back again', he told one correspondent, but the audience clearly preferred 'their melodramas, their sensationalisms, their burlesque . . . On the whole I think I am rather glad of the row for it shows that I have not drawn a bow at a venture' (Letters, III, 237). The débâcle brought Tennyson's experiments in the theatre to an end. If he still 'believed in the future of our modern English stage when education should have made the masses more literary', after *The Promise of May* he never wrote another play (*Memoir*, II, 174).

11

Turning Again Home

Among writers in English, only W. B. Yeats matches the quality and intensity of feeling in Tennyson's poems of friendship. In 'The Municipal Gallery Revisited' Yeats sets himself as a speaker in a public place, surrounded by portraits which give meaning to his life.

> Think where man's glory most begins and ends,
> And say my glory was I had such friends.[1]

Yeats was consciously creating his own mythic structure, attempting to discern a permanent truth within the fluidity of his existence. In Tennyson's 'In the Garden at Swainston', the poet stands outside Sir John Simeon's house on the day of his funeral, listening to the nightingales, whose song tells of 'a passion which lasts but a day' (l. 10). The poet, however, recalls passions which endure, as he walks with the 'shadows of three dead men' (l. 3), Simeon, Henry Lushington and Arthur Hallam.

> Two dead men have I loved
>   With a love that ever will be:
>   Three dead men have I loved and thou art last
>   of the three.

> (13–15)

For all their marked differences in tone and style, the two writers return to a common point. In the face of the passage of time and of mortality, memory, with all its limitations, survives. The two poems, like the portraits in the Municipal Gallery, represent two levels of memory, the more immediate one of being in the garden or the art gallery, and the more distant recollection of lost human intercourse and conversation. Tennyson had been a poet of memory from boyhood, and his late poems of association and recall look forward to the 'memory' writers of the early twentieth-century, Yeats, Marcel Proust and Alain Fournier.

186

Some of the best poems of Tennyson's later years mark the deaths of his friends. When Brookfield died in 1874, Tennyson wrote a sonnet recalling their Cambridge days, and drawing Brookfield's memory together with that of Arthur Hallam, 'the lost light of those dawn-golden times'. 'I cannot laud this life, it looks so dark,' the poet concludes, 'I shall join you in a day.' ('To the Rev. W. H. Brookfield', 7, 12 and 14)

When Edward Fitzgerald died in 1883, it brought to an end one of the longest and most complicated of all Tennyson's friendships. Fitzgerald had not spared his criticism, and, at some deep level, Tennyson probably feared that Fitzgerald might be right to prefer the early work. One of Fitzgerald's perennial regrets was that he very rarely saw his old friend. In September 1876, however, Tennyson and Hallam made a short tour in Norfolk, and proposed themselves for a visit to Fitzgerald in Suffolk on their way back. The two men fell easily into conversation as though there had been no break. Fitzgerald wondered whether such a sign of advanced age was altogether desirable. For two days they pursued the old arguments, and told the old stories. Fitzgerald was mortified that the meat was too tough for Tennyson to eat, but he liked Hallam for his simplicity and straightforwardness. He recalled Tennyson sitting in the sun on an iron seat, with the trees in leaf and with pigeons around him. In the poem which he wrote for Fitzgerald's birthday in 1883, Tennyson evokes the same scene:

> Whom yet I see as there you sit
> > Beneath your sheltering garden-tree,
> And while your doves about you flit,
> > And plant on shoulder, hand and knee
> Or on your head their rosy feet.

> ('To E. Fitzgerald', 5–9)

By then, another Cambridge friend, James Spedding, had died, knocked down in the street. It is presumably to him and to Brookfield that Tennyson refers when he writes of 'Two voices heard on earth no more'. 'But', he goes on, 'we old friends are still alive' (41–2). It is part of the irony of Tennyson's relationship with Fitzgerald that this poem, with its praise both of the man and of the translator, came too late. A few days after it was written, and before Fitzgerald could read it, he too was dead.

In the spring of 1879, Charles Tennyson Turner died in his early seventies. Alfred Tennyson wrote to his widow, Louisa, who survived her husband for only a short time: 'Keep your heart up, my dear. *He* is waiting for you yonder. I send you a brother's kiss' (Letters, III, 172). (Hating letter-writing as he did, Tennyson wrote several moving letters of condolence.) June was a particularly cold and wet month and his thoughts turned to his brother's body, lying in the sodden ground:

> But thou art silent underground,
> And o'er thee streams the rain,
> True poet, surely to be found
> When Truth is found again.

('Prefatory Poem to my Brother's Sonnets', 13–16)

Outwardly at least, life went on as usual. *The Falcon* was performed in the winter, and Tennyson was at work on *The Cup*. Early in the new year, the Tennysons took a house in Belgrave Street, and entertained a good deal. Among their guests was the young Thomas Hardy, whose *A Pair of Blue Eyes* Tennyson admired. Henry James and James Russell Lowell, the writer and American Minister to London, ate an uncomfortable lunch with the Tennysons, in an 'unpeopled waste' with 'places for possible when not assured guests'. Coming in late to an empty table, Tennyson growled: 'Do you know anything about *Lowell*?', whereupon, Emily in an 'anxious quaver' told him 'Why, my dear, this *is* Mr Lowell!'[2]

By June, Tennyson was near nervous collapse. He was worried by a request that he stand for the rectorship of Glasgow University. Finding that the contest was a political one, he hastily withdrew. According to his son, he suffered a liver attack and began to hear 'perpetual ghostly voices' (*Memoir*, II, 244). A change of scene was prescribed, and having failed to book berths to Canada, father and son decided upon Venice.

Before leaving, Hallam consulted a young Freshwater neighbour, Emily ('Pinkie') Ritchie, about the essential sights of Venice. A devoted Ruskinian, she advised them to read the master. There is no copy of *The Stones of Venice* in Tennyson's surviving library, and it is not clear whether the advice was taken. Following Pinkie's directions, the Tennysons made a special study of Tintoretto, a painter whom Ruskin had 'discovered'. Tennyson particularly admired *The*

Presentation of the Virgin in the Church of the Madonna del Orto, and the *Crucifixion* in the Scuolo of San Rocco. These works, with their striking sense of theatre, and bold contrasts of light and shade, seemed to him 'original, dramatic, and sublime in their treatment of subjects which had often been painted before' (*Memoir*, II, 246). On the whole he found the Venetian churches dark and the pictures dim, but he 'stood long' before a small *Virgin and Child* in the Church of the Redentore. (Then attributed to Bellini, it is now thought to be the work of Alvise Vivarini.)

Like many Victorian tourists, the Tennysons were staying, not in the city itself, but in a large new hotel on the Lido, the seaside resort of Venice. Here Tennyson found an unexpected solace in wandering by himself through the overgrown Jewish cemetery, crowded with graves. Shelley was often in his mind, as a reminder of youth, and he would go out in a gondola to watch the Venetian sunset. All in all, Venice disappointed him, as things long-anticipated usually did: 'having dreamt all his life of this city on the sea', he admired the Grand Canal, but not the more mundane, if vigorous, life of the side canals (*Memoir*, II, 246).

On the way home, he was delighted with Verona, and walked all day on the peninsula of Sirmione, stretching into Lake Garda. His mind was again engaged, as in the Jewish cemetery, with the time-lessness of human loss. Sirmione had been the subject of a poem of joyful homecoming by the Roman poet, Catullus. In the lyric which Tennyson wrote about his visit to the peninsula, he conflated this poem with another, where Catullus salutes the grave of his brother in Asia Minor with the words 'Frater ave atque vale'. This mingling of joy with sadness is the keynote of one of Tennyson's finest, and most technically accomplished, late poems:

Row us out from Desenzano, to your Sirmione row!
So they row'd, and there we landed – 'O venusta Sirmio!'
There to me thro' all the groves of olive in the summer glow,
There beneath the Roman ruin where the purple flowers grow,
Came that 'Ave atque Vale' of the Poet's hopeless woe,
Tenderest of Roman poets nineteen-hundred years ago,
'Frater Ave atque Vale' – as we wander'd to and fro
Gazing at the Lydian laughter of the Garda lake below
Sweet Catullus's all-but-island, olive-silvery Sirmio!

('Frater Ave Atque Vale')

Pinkie Ritchie was one of a group of girls who were often at Farringford. Hallam and Lionel had grown up with the Cameron children in Freshwater, where the young Prinseps, the two Thackeray daughters and their cousins, the Ritchies, were regular guests. As a result, the poet found himself a centre of attraction. Several of the girls record how they walked with him on the down, listening to his conversation and being taught to understand the natural world. Virginia Woolf naughtily parodies this aspect of Tennyson's later life in her spoof play, *Freshwater*. On one evening, Tennyson told his young female guests that he liked to see their hair long and flowing. 'Putting your hair up' was a rite of passage for Victorian women, and he was implicitly suggesting that they reverted to their girlhood. 'We all therefore sat round the dessert table with our hair down, and for the rest of the evening he approved of us very much, and said he wished the Empress Eugénie would set the fashion. What he especially disliked was seeing the whole ear, as "So few women have specially small, well-shaped ears to show".' (*Memoir*, II, 85)

On another occasion, Pinkie came back from a dance at two in the morning to find Tennyson sitting up for her: 'the invitation to come up to his den, where he was still smoking, took me aback'. Tennyson talked 'delightfully . . . What I chiefly remember was the way in which he told me "never to get spoilt by the world"' (*Memoir*, II, 86). Pinkie was among those who heard Tennyson read 'The Revenge' aloud in the spring of 1878. He seized her hand and 'squeezed it so hard that she gave a little cry, on which he stopped. "Did I hurt you?" She – "Oh never mind. Please go on." He – "I didn't know I was pinching you. Must hold on to something, but a table-leg will do just as well."'[3]

Tennyson may have thought that a table-leg would do as well, but Pinkie Ritchie was a trusted confidante for the rest of his life. One evening, over his port, he even talked to her of Arthur Hallam. 'How you would have loved him!', he concluded.[4] When Tennyson and Hallam stayed close to the Ritchies at Pontresina in the Engadine in 1873, Pinkie appeared in 'Swiss country costume – a striped blue skirt & a dark blue gown'. 'Walking like Diana,' said Tennyson. Pinkie took the Tennysons up to see 'most beautiful snow'. Hallam reported that his father looked 'very young & well' and 'in good spirits'. Reporting on the kindness of the Ritchies, Hallam told his mother: 'Papa says she [Pinkie] is really the flower of the flock'.[5]

The young Ritchies and Prinseps followed in the traditions of Little Holland House, where art and beauty carried all before them, and where Tennyson, like G. F. Watts, was an object of admiration. Among the other young women who hovered around was the fascinating Laura Tennant, whom he dubbed 'the little witch' (*Memoir*, II, 279). More uneasy with him was Gladstone's daughter, Mary, who came to Farringford in 1879 with her cousin, Margaret Cowell-Stepney. Mary was nervous about the 'near the wind things' which Tennyson occasionally said to her.[6] She tried never to be separated from her cousin, but Tennyson found opportunities to approach her: 'He suddenly began to stroke my nose, having discovered it was a "petit nez retroussé", and declared it meant all sorts of naughty things, and then found they were counteracted by my "strong jaw"'.[7] In the same vein, Tennyson said to her, two years later, 'Oh, you wild-eyed thing. I ought always to know you with yr. great wild eyes'.[8]

Mary Gladstone, like Pinkie Ritchie, was aware of a childlike innocence in Tennyson. He was no Ibsen, inspired by the youth of Emilie Bardach to write *The Master Builder*. The only later poems of Tennyson which deal with his feelings for a woman are addressed to Emily Tennyson and to Rosa Baring, the loves of his youth. For Emily, he wrote 'June Bracken and Heather' in 1891. This is a poem of deep and loving affection, but there is still, so many years on, more passion in 'The Roses on the Terrace', which associates memories of the terrace at Harrington Hall with that at Aldworth:

> Rose, on this terrace fifty years ago,
>   When I was in my June, you in your May,
> Two words, '*My* Rose' set all your face aglow,
>   And now that I am white, and you are gray,
> That blush of fifty years ago, my dear,
>   Blooms in the Past, but close to me to-day
> As this red rose, which on our terrace here
>   Glows in the blue of fifty miles away.

On 15 January 1884 Tennyson was gazetted as a Baron, the greatest public honour ever bestowed upon a British poet. Frederic Leighton's peerage, conferred 12 years later, was given as much for his public work on behalf of artists as for his painting. The elevation was hedged round with difficulties, many of them created by the poet. He had already refused a baronetcy on more than one occasion, proposing unsuccessfully that Hallam should receive the title in his stead. It has been suggested that he refused the baronetcy because he was holding out for a peerage, but it is doubtful whether the refusal represented more than a wish to remain plain Mr Tennyson, a sense that a true poet should be able to rise above such distinctions.

At the time of the barony offer, Gladstone was once again prime minister. Hallam, Tennyson and the Gladstones were cruising on the North Sea as guests of the MP for Perthshire, Sir Donald Currie. Gladstone approached Tennyson through Hallam, stressing that he intended to honour 'literature'. To Hallam, Tennyson 'said at once that he did not want the title, that it would do no good to literature but that many literary men would be jealous'.[9]

A further complication came when, following Tennyson's suggestion, the yacht sailed to Norway and Denmark. The party was welcomed to Copenhagen by the King and Queen and by their guests, the Czar and Czarina of Russia (with their son, later the Czar Nicholas II), the King and Queen of Greece, and the Princess of Wales with her children. It was on this occasion that Tennyson, prevailed upon to read 'The Grandmother' and 'The Bugle Song' aloud, patted the Czarina, whose identity he had mistaken, on the shoulder, saying 'My dear girl, that's very kind of you, very kind' (Letters, III, 259).

Queen Victoria was furious that Gladstone (whom she disliked) had gone abroad without her permission, but she nonetheless agreed to offer Tennyson a barony. Accepting, he decided to call himself Baron Tennyson-d'Eyncourt. Having grasped the peerage which had eluded his uncle, he may have felt the need to ram the point home. Fortunately, after problems with the Heralds, he took the simpler title of Baron Tennyson of Aldworth and Farringford. It has been suggested that Tennyson became a peer for Hallam's sake, as a way of assuaging his guilt for his exploitation of his son, and this may well have been the case.

As Tennyson had anticipated, some congratulated him, and others despised him for taking the honour, most believing that Emily and Hallam had forced his hand. Whatever the truth, the status conferred by the title did little for Tennyson's reputation. When he took his seat in March 1884, he did not ally himself with Gladstone or the Liberals, but sat with the independents on the cross benches, voting as his conscience dictated.

The last years of Tennyson's life are well documented. A stream of journalists and admirers descended upon the grand old man of literature, defying his dictates by recording his conversation. Their accounts agree upon one thing, Tennyson's preoccupation with the past. A man in his late seventies and eighties has a long memory, and Tennyson was proud of his, recounting tales of his youth as he tried to understand the patterns of his life. Unlike many poets, he did not lose his enthusiasm with advancing age. When the decade of drama was over, he produced three books of new poems, with a fourth coming out shortly after his death. All sold in enormous numbers. Browning was more prolific through his last two decades, but there was an increasing failure of inspiration in his work. Tennyson, as each new Browning volume arrived, delightfully expressed his amazement at his old friend's productivity: 'I have yet again to thank you and feel rather ashamed that I have nothing of my own to send you back; but your Muse is prolific as Hecuba and mine by the side of her, an old barren cow' (Letters, III, 60).

Tennyson's new poems, though less extended than Browning's, were in a variety of styles and modes, reflecting his vigour and inventiveness. By good fortune, he also changed his publisher for the last time in 1884, finding with Alexander Macmillan the stability that he had once enjoyed with Edward Moxon. Macmillan had known Tennyson for a quarter of a century, and had several times attempted to secure the contract, always finding that Tennyson 'wanted too much money'.[10] By the mid-1880s, however, Tennyson's long period in the theatre had seriously reduced his profits. The later plays never sold well, and things only began to pick up when Macmillan brought out a one-volume complete works for 7s. 6d, which sold 15 000–19 000 copies a year for the rest of the decade.

Some of Tennyson's late poems suggest that he had reached a final position of 'acceptance'. 'Mystic' works, like 'The Ancient Sage' and 'Vastness', express a positive sense of the deity's presence in all things, countering the prevailing scepticism of the late Victorian world. In 'The Ancient Sage', a 'venerable master' tells his young and disillusioned follower of the Nameless, whose voice can be heard within oneself, but whose being exists beyond all limits of knowledge, time and space. 'The Ancient Sage', like similar poems of this period, projects a personality which should not be uncritically associated with the poet's own, even though certain passages, like those about 'The Passion of the Past', are clearly autobiographical (l. 219).

A totally different poem, 'Locksley Hall Sixty Years After', underlines the pitfalls of assuming a close identification between the poet and the poem. Here, an old man returns to the scene of his early love, and tells his grandson what he thinks of the modern world. Like 'The Ancient Sage', this is a poem where youth is instructed by age, but the dominant theme is one of disillusionment and of hostility to change:

Gone the cry of 'Forward, Forward,' lost within a growing gloom;
Lost, or only heard in silence from the silence of a tomb.

Half the marvels of my morning, triumphs over time and space,
Staled by frequence, shrunk by usage into commonest commonplace!

(73–6)

As with *Maud*, Tennyson denied that these were his own sentiments, but undoubtedly some of his ideas are expressed, including his loathing of 'the troughs of Zolaism' (l. 145), and his fear that democracy could lead to demagogery. Like Kipling in 'Recessional', he attacks the complacency of 1887, Jubilee year:

Hope the best, but hold the Present fatal daughter of the Past,
Shape your heart to front the hour, but dream not that the hour
  will last.

(105–6)

In conclusion, 'Locksley Hall Sixty Years After', becomes a poem of reconciliation, as Amy's husband, scorned in 'Locksley Hall', is lamented: 'Worthier soul was he than I am, sound and honest, rustic Squire'. (l. 239)

In 1886, Tennyson began work on a new poem which became 'Demeter and Persephone'. Hallam Tennyson suggested the subject 'because I knew that my father considered Demeter one of the most beautiful types of womanhood.' For the original source, Tennyson went even further back into his past, to the time when as a boy, he had translated Claudian's *Proserpine* into English. The Demeter myth, which inspired some of the most mysterious and intense religious practices of antiquity, can be related to several strands of late nineteenth-century thought. Tennyson was a friend of Max Müller, famous in his day for conceiving of myth as a symptom of decaying language, and for relating mythic structures to aspects of sun worship. Tennyson describes Persephone's spell in the underworld, and her return to the light, as alternations of sun and darkness. Ceres calls upon her fellow gods:

To send the noon into the night and break
The sunless halls of Hades into Heaven?

(133–4)

The subject of Persephone, in her dual role as goddess of sunlight
or of Hades, appealed to other Victorians. Walter Pater lectured on
the darker side of the myth in 1875, and Dante Gabriel Rossetti and
Frederic Leighton both produced their own versions. In a series of
paintings and sketches, Rossetti shows the goddess in Pluto's palace
(1882 version, Birmingham City Museum and Art Gallery), while,
for Leighton, as for Tennyson, the myth is conceived in terms of light
breaking into darkness, or of the love of a mother for her child. (1891,
Leeds City Art Gallery) Tennyson's poem incorporates the idea of
Christianity, as Ceres foresees the coming of 'younger kindlier Gods',
a conclusion reminiscent of Keats's 'Hyperion'. (l. 129)

For some commentators, Persephone may represent the imagination, existing both in the darkness of the creative unconscious and in
the light of the everyday world. But Tennyson does not, like Pater
and Swinburne, imply that Hades is creative. For him, growth belongs on earth, to which fertility only returns when Ceres is reunited
with her daughter. Tennyson's use of the myth has also been interpreted in more directly personal terms, as a covert rebuke to
Swinburne who was well-known for his 'Hymn to Proserpine'. Coming closer still, 'Demeter and Persephone', with its dramatisation of
a parent's overwhelming loss, must relate to the death of Lionel
Tennyson.

Lionel had married Eleanor Locker, the daughter of Tennyson's
old friend, in 1878. They were a particularly attractive young couple,
and their three sons, Tennyson's first grandchildren, were a source
of delight to him. Rumour had it, however, that Lionel had never
settled down and that the marriage was unhappy. Lionel had been
working at the India Office since 1877, and, in 1885, he travelled to
India with his wife, on the advice of the Viceroy, Lord Dufferin.
While hunting, he contracted a fever, and, after three months of
critical illness, was sent home, only to die as the boat crossed the Red
Sea, his body being committed to the deep.

The strain of this long-drawn-out illness upon his parents must
have been acute. Tennyson's letters reveal little, but the bad news,
when it came, was devastating. If, as seems likely, the difficult Lionel
was not as deeply loved as the pliant Hallam, this can only have

added to the grief. Hallam had devoted himself to his father, but Lionel's determination to escape from the demands of home marked him out as his father's son.

Tennyson's poem, 'To the Marquis of Dufferin and Ava', is an elegy in the verse form of *In Memoriam*. Stanzas X and XI briefly, but tragically, describe the bereaved father's dreams, his involuntary guilt at having been absent:

> And now the Was, the Might-have-been,
> And those lone rites I have not seen,
> And one drear sound I have not heard,
> Are dreams that scarce will let me be,
> Not there to bid my boy farewell,
> When That within the coffin fell,
> Fell – and flashed into the Red Sea.
>
> (38–44)

Once again, Tennyson had to endure a death abroad, the sense of an unspoken farewell, with not even the consolation for 'fools of habit' of knowing that Lionel rested

> beneath the clover sod,
> That takes the sunshine and the rains.
>
> (*In Memoriam*, X, 13–4)

Tennyson's health remained good until near the end of his life. One of his few concessions to age was to agree to take his walk before rather than after lunch. At the end of 1888, however, he became ill, with what his son describes as 'a bad attack of rheumatic gout . . . brought on chiefly by walking in the rain and storm, and getting drenched'. The old man's thoughts and dreams (as recorded by Hallam) were in keeping with his late poems. Looking down over the weald of Sussex 'he had wonderful thoughts about God and the Universe, and felt as if looking into the other world' (*Memoir*, II, 347–8). His death was expected, and Benjamin Jowett wrote to Hallam regretting that he would see him no more. But Tennyson slowly recovered, escaping the paralysis which his doctors had feared, though seriously weakened by his long illness: 'it has left a good deal that is very trying to me, body and mind' (*Letters*, III, 396).

In August came his 80th birthday, with a flood of letters and attention. Browning's affectionate words gave him particular pleasure, coming as they did in the wake of an unhappy episode. The publication of Edward Fitzgerald's letters earlier in the year had revealed Fitzgerald's apparent pleasure on the death of Elizabeth Barrett Browning in 1861. Browning, outraged, was inclined (without justification) to incriminate Tennyson. Emily wrote to clear the air, but Tennyson, who had kept aloof, now felt able to reply to Browning with heartfelt pleasure: 'To be loved and appreciated by so great and powerful a nature as yours will be a solace to me, and lighten my dark hours during the short time of life that is left to me.' (*Memoir*, II, 360) In fact, it was Browning who died first, a few months later.

On his 82nd birthday, in 1891, Tennyson received a more unexpected tribute, a birthday ode from Swinburne. The gracious reply shows how deeply it was valued: 'I am and always have been your admirer, and in your Birthday Song I find metre and diction as lovely as ever; but the touch of kindliness toward myself – implied in your praise or overpraise of what I may have accomplished in literature – moves the heart of the old Poet more, I think than even the melody of the verse.' (*Letters*, III, 428)

After his illness, Tennyson's thoughts turned all the more insistently to death and to the need to understand his own life. 'Merlin and the Gleam', one of the most autobiographical of his poems, tells of his pursuit of the 'gleam' of imagination. The poem returns once more to the loss of Arthur Hallam and to the savage reviews of Tennyson's youth, before considering his present position:

> Last limit I came –
> And can no longer,
> But die rejoicing.

> (110–12)

In October 1889, Tennyson wrote the lyric which, by his wish, closes all editions of his poetry, 'Crossing the Bar'. As in several of these latest poems, the surrounding sea is the poet's bourne. Like Ulysses he is to sail out beyond the stars.

Each year, Tennyson and Hallam took a sea voyage. In 1892, they went to the Channel Islands, where Tennyson, as always, delighted in rocky shores. Frederick Tennyson had lived on Jersey since 1859, and, at his home, St Ewold's, high above the town, the brothers recalled their youth. Frederick refused an invitation to the Isle of Wight and the brothers parted, well aware that they would not meet again.

Tennyson was still writing. 'The Death of Oenone', a sequel to the poem written in the 1830s, tells how Oenone, having refused to save her former love, Paris, is consumed on his funeral pyre. The other major poem of the last two years, 'Akbar's Dream', specifically rejects the idea of 'suttee', the immolation of the widow, as the Mogul emperor encourages religious toleration in his empire. The poem, like 'The Ancient Sage', calls for a universal understanding of the oneness of God.

During the summer of 1892, Tennyson was aware of growing weakness. He left Farringford for Aldworth with regret, but in Surrey he continued walking and driving. In London in July, he found the crowds at the Royal Academy exhibition oppressive, but enjoyed the prehistoric sections of the Natural History Museum. Tennyson's 83rd birthday came on 9 August. Tired and unwell, he continued to see friends and family. Hallam had married Audrey Boyle in 1884, and she was often her father-in-law's companion.

By the end of September, Tennyson's doctor, Sir Andrew Clark, had been sent for, and through the next days the poet's condition gradually worsened. Tennyson himself did not expect to recover, although he was saddened to realise that he would never see Irving's production of *Becket*, now definitely scheduled for the next year. He was gratified that another of his rejected plays, *The Foresters*, had achieved success at Daly's theatre in New York, with Ada Rehan as Maid Marian. 'O, that Press will get hold of me now!' was one of Tennyson's last statements, two days before his death (*Memoir*, II, 426). He had a horror of biography, particularly after the publication of Froude's life of Carlyle, which he regarded as unjust and intrusive.

On Wednesday 5 October, Tennyson asked to be given his Shakespeare, opening it at his favourite lines from *Cymbeline*. After bidding farewell to Emily and Hallam, he lay motionless, holding Audrey's hand. In the early hours of Thursday, he died with the full moon shining onto the bed.

Westminster Abbey was chosen over Farringford, where Emily would eventually lie, and the coffin left Aldworth on a wagonette, covered in flowers. The funeral service on 12 October was a national event. Some of Tennyson's surviving friends were pall-bearers: The

Duke of Argyll, James Anthony Froude, William Lecky and Benjamin Jowett. In the nave were representatives of regiments and organisations associated with him: the Light Brigade, the Rifle Volunteers and the Gordon Boys' Home. Emily was not present, but the choir sang her setting of 'Silent Voices'.

If he were in Poet's Corner today, Tennyson might be surprised at some of the memorials around him. Edward Lear and Lewis Carroll are there, and a poet of whom he had probably never heard, Gerard Manley Hopkins. Henry James and Thomas Hardy are nearby. Of some things, however, he would have been assured. His predecessors as Poet Laureate, and Wordsworth in particular, are in their places, and beside him is Browning, the other great, if sharply constrasting, poet of the Victorian age.

Notes

1   A LINCOLNSHIRE BOYHOOD

1. J. O. Hoge, ed., 'Emily Tennyson's Narrative for her Sons', *Texas Studies in Literature and Language* XIV (1972), 96.
2. H. D. Rawnsley, *Memories of the Tennysons* (1900), p. 225.
3. See C. Tennyson and C. Ricks, 'Tennyson's "Mablethorpe"', *Tennyson Research Bulletin* II, iii (1974), 121–3 [hereafter *TRB*].
4. A. Pollard, 'Three Horace Translations by Tennyson', *TRB* IV, i (1982), 16.
5. H. D. Paden, *Tennyson in Egypt* (1942), p. 103.
6. C. Tennyson and C. Ricks, 'Tennyson's "Mablethorpe"', p. 121.
7. This painting is still at Farringford. I am grateful to Dr Christopher Brown, Chief Curator of the National Gallery, for the attribution.
8. A. G. Weld, *Glimpses of Tennyson* (1903), p. 12.
9. J. Kolb, ed., *The Letters of A. H. Hallam* (1981), p. 457.
10. R. B. Martin, *Tennyson: The Unquiet Heart* (1980), p. 48.
11. E. A. Knies, ed., *Tennyson at Aldworth: The Diary of J. H. Mangles*, (1984), p. 122.

2   CAMBRIDGE

1. C. Tennyson, *Alfred Tennyson* (1949), p. 55.
2. E. A. Knies, ed., *Tennyson at Aldworth: The Diary of J. H. Mangles*, p. 97.
3. S. T. Coleridge, *Aids to Reflection*, ed. D. Coleridge (7th edn, London, 1854), p. 155.
4. Arthur Hallam visited Coleridge at Highgate, but Tennyson, although invited, never went. Coleridge's rude remarks on Tennyson's handling of metre would not have encouraged him.
5. *Shelley's Adonais: A Critical Edition*, ed. A. D. Knerr (New York, 1984), pp. 445–6.
6. H. B. Bryant, 'The African Genesis of Tennyson's "Timbuctoo"', *TRB*, III v (1981), 200.
7. J. Kolb, ed., *Letters of A. H. Hallam* (1981), p. 319.
8. H. Hallam, ed., *Remains in Verse and Prose of A. H. Hallam*, (1863 edn), p. 24.
9. H. Allingham and D. Radford, eds, *William Allingham: A Diary* (1907), p. 295.
10. Kolb, *Letters of A. H. Hallam*, p. 245.
11. P. J. A. Clark, *Henry Hallam* (Boston, 1982), p. 23.
12. Kolb, *Letters of A. H. Hallam*, p. 261.
13. Ibid, pp. 243 and 249.
14. Ibid, p. 257.

15. Hallam, *Remains of A. H. Hallam*, p. 78.
16. Several of Tennyson's friends asked for an explanation of the final line of this passage, and, recognising the difficulty, Tennyson explained that Michaelangelo, like Hallam, had 'a broad bar of frontal bone' over his eyes.
17. Kolb, *Letters of A. H. Hallam*, p. 343.
18. Ibid, p. 538.
19. Ibid, p. 365.
20. 'Alfred Tennyson's *Bildungsgang*: Notes on his early reading', *Philological Quarterly*, LVII (1978), 93–5.
21. I. Armstrong, *Victorian Scrutinies* (1972), p. 71.
22. Ibid, p. 109.
23. Ibid.
24. H. Tennyson, *Materials for a Life of A. T.* (privately printed), II, 69.
25. H. D. Rawnsley, *Memories of the Tennysons*, p. 101; Allingham and Radford, *William Allingham: A Diary*, pp. 293–5; C. Tennyson, *Alfred Tennyson*, p. 451.
26. Armstrong, *Victorian Scrutinies* p. 85.
27. Ibid, p. 122.
28. F. Brookfield, *The Cambridge 'Apostles'* (London, 1906), p. 8.

3   ARTHUR HALLAM

1. A. Sinfield, *Alfred Tennyson* (1986), p. 32.
2. J. Kolb, ed., *Letters of A. H. Hallam* (1981), p. 401.
3. Ibid, p. 780.
4. Ibid, p. 375.
5. J. C. Hixon, 'Cauteretz Revisited', *TRB*, II, iv (1975), p. 146.
6. Although Tennyson imples that he lay under the waterfall, he must have done this from a considerable distance, as the area at the base of the fall is both very wet and rock-strewn.
7. Kolb, *Letters of A. H. Hallam*, p. 375.
8. Ibid, p. 377.
9. Ibid, p. 379.
10. Ibid, p. 613.
11. Ibid, pp. 613–14.
12. Ibid, p. 616.
13. Ibid, p. 770.
14. Ibid, p. 616.
15. F. Brookfield, *The Cambridge 'Apostles'* (1906), p. 268.
16. Kolb, *Letters of A. H. Hallam* p. 618.
17. *TRB* I, i (1967), 12.
18. C. Tennyson and H. Dyson, *The Tennysons: Background to Genius* (1974), p. 81.
19. Kolb, *Letters of A. H. Hallam* p. 482.
20. Ibid, p. 508.
21. Ibid, pp. 601–2.

22. Ibid, pp. 509 and 537.
23. A. D. Culler, *The Poetry of Tennyson* (1977), p. 72.
24. Kolb, *Letters of A. H. Hallam* p. 697.
25. E. F. Shannon Jr, *Tennyson and the Reviewers* (1952), pp. 18–19.
26. J. D. Jump, *Tennyson: The Critical Heritage* (1967), p. 66.
27. Ibid, p. 74.
28. H. Tennyson, Manuscript materials for memoir, I, 143, Tennyson Research Centre, Lincoln [hereafter TRC].
29. Jump, *Tennyson: The Critical Heritage*, p. 86.
30. Ibid, p. 93.
31. Ibid, p. 95.
32. Kolb, *Letters of A. H. Hallam* pp. 748 and 746.
33. *Tennyson: Interviews and Recollections*, ed. N. Page (1983), p. 125.
34. Kolb, *Letters of A. H. Hallam* p. 768.
35. Ibid, p. 767.
36. Ibid, p. 785.
37. J. O. Hoge, ed., *Letters of Emily Tennyson*, (1974), p. 249.
38. E. A. Knies, ed., *Tennyson at Aldworth: The Diary of J. H. Mangles*, (1984), p. 83.
39. R. W. Rader, *Tennyson's Maud: The Biographical Genesis* (1963), pp. 11–19.
40. A. M. Terhune and A. B. Terhune, eds, *The Letters of Edward Fitzgerald*, (1980), I, 140.
41. 'Tithon' was later extended and published as 'Tithonus'.

4 THE UNSETTLED YEARS

1. W. Wordsworth, 'Preface to Lyrical Ballads', *Wordsworth's Literary Criticism*, ed. W. J. B. Owen (London, 1974), p. 81.
2. H. Hallam, ed., *Remains in Verse and Prose of A. H. Hallam* (1863 edn), p. 215.
3. N. A. Rupke, *The Great Chain of Being* (1983), p. 193.
4. Ibid, p. 227.
5. Ibid, pp. 225–30.
6. See R. W. Radar, *Tennyson's Maud: The Biographical Genesis* (1963).
7. H. D. Rawnsley, *Memories of the Tennysons* (1900), p. 68.
8. C. Ricks, *Tennyson* (1972, rev. edn 1989), p. 137.
9. R. B. Martin, *Tennyson: The Unquiet Heart* (1980), p. 219.
10. M. B. Raymond and M. R. Sullivan, eds. *The Letters of Elizabeth Barrett Browning to Mary Russell Mitford*, (1983), III, 214.
11. Martin, *Tennyson*, p. 219.
12. The first line quoted here was not included when Tennyson published the poem in 1885.
13. Raymond and Sullivan, *E. B. Browning to M. R. Mitford*, III, 220.
14. A. Sinfield, *Alfred Tennyson* (1986), p. 131.
15. J. Kolb, ed., *Letters of A. H. Hallam* (1981), p. 600.
16. M. Timko, '"The Central Wish"; Human Passion and Cosmic Love in Tennyson's Idyls', *Victorian Poetry* XVI (1978), 3–4.

17. W. E. Fredeman, '"The Sphere of Common Duties": The Domestic Solution in Tennyson's Poetry', *Bulletin of the John Rylands Library* LIV (1972), 365.
18. J. D. Jump, *Tennyson: The Critical Heritage* (1967), p. 268.
19. John Spedding, *Mirehouse* (Norwich, 1988), p. 7.
20. *Tennyson's Maud*, ed. S. Shatto (1986), p. 19.
21. W. F. Pollock, *Personal Reminiscences* (1887), I, 113.
22. Terhune and Terhune, *Letters of Edward Fitzgerald* (1980), I, 211.
23. T. Wemyss Reid, *The Life, Letters and Friendships of Richard Monckton Milnes* (London, 1890), I, 221.
24. Sinfield, *Alfred Tennyson*, pp. 11–56.
25. H. Tennyson, ed., *Tennyson and his Friends*, (1911), p. 131.
26. C. R. Sanders, 'Carlyle and Tennyson', *Proceedings of the Modern Language Association of America* LXXVI (1961), 84 [hereafter *PMLA*].
27. Ibid, p. 88.

5 THE POET OF THE AGE

1. H. Tennyson, ed., *Tennyson and his Friends*, (1911), p. 408.
2. A. M. Terhune and A. B. Terhune, *The Letters of Edward Fitzgerald* (1980), I, 258.
3. H. Tennyson, *Tennyson and his Friends*, p. 408.
4. Terhune and Terhune, *Letters of Edward Fitzgerald* I, 408.
5. H. Tennyson, *Tennyson and his Friends*, p. 143.
6. W. F. Pollock, *Personal Reminiscences* (1887), I, 186.
7. J. O. Waller, *A Circle of Friends* (1986), pp. 99 and 108.
8. J. O. Hoge, ed., 'Emily Tennyson's Narrative for her Sons', *Texas Studies in Literature and Language* XIV (1972), 101.
9. Terhune and Terhune, *Letters of Edward Fitzgerald* I, 239.
10. M. House, G. Storey and K. Tillotson, *Letters of Charles Dickens*, Pilgrim Edition, (Oxford, 1974), III, 213.
11. P. Kelley and R. Hudson, *The Brownings' Correspondence*, (1986), IV, 408.
12. Ibid, IV, 385.
13. C. Ricks, *Tennyson* (1972; rev. edn 1989), p. 147.
14. Terhune and Terhune, *Letters of Edward Fitzgerald* I, 312 and 315.
15. Ibid, I, 327.
16. J. D. Jump, *Tennyson: The Critical Heritage* (1967), pp. 113–14.
17. E. J. Shannon, *Tennyson and the Reviewers* (1952), p. 77.
18. Jump, *Tennyson: The Critical Heritage*, p. 136.
19. I. Armstrong, *Victorian Scrutinies* (1972), p. 145.
20. M. Raymond and M. R. Sullivan, *The Letters of E. B. Browning to M. R. Mitford* (1983), I, 415.
21. House, Storey and Tillotson, *Letters of Charles Dickens*, III, 306.
22. B. R. Clark, 'Tennyson across the Atlantic', *TRB*, V, i (1987), 3.
23. Kelley and Hudson, *The Brownings' Correspondence*, VI (1988), 32.
24. Terhune and Terhune, *Letters of Edward Fitzgerald*, I, 315.
25. C. A. Marchand, ed., *Byron's Letters and Journals*, (1976), V, 100.

26. K. Tillotson, ed., *The Letters of Charles Dickens*, Pilgrim Edition, (Oxford, 1977), IV, 610.
27. C. R. Sanders, 'Carlyle and Tennyson', *PMLA* LXXVI (1961), 86.
28. C. E. Norton, ed., *Correspondence of Carlyle and Emerson*, (1883), II, 158–9.
29. W. Ward, *Aubrey de Vere* (1904), p. 87.
30. D. Patmore, *Coventry Patmore* (1949), p. 91.
31. Ward, *Aubrey de Vere*, pp. 73–4.
32. C. B. Stevenson, 'Tennyson on Women's Rights', *TRB*, III, no 1 (1977), 25.
33. Ibid, p. 23.
34. Raymond and Sullivan, *E. B. Browning to M. R. Mitford*, III, 240.
35. Jump, *Tennyson: The Critical Heritage*, p. 167.
36. Ibid, p. 168.
37. Ibid, p. 113.
38. S. T. Coleridge, *Miscellaneous Criticism*, ed. T. M. Raysor, (London, 1936), p. 430.
39. A. G. Weld, *Glimpses of Tennyson* (1903), p. 51.
40. J. Woolford, *Browning the Revisionary* (London, 1988), p. 89.
41. T. S. Eliot, 'In Memoriam', *Essays Ancient and Modern* (London, 1936), p. 187.
42. H. Allingham and D. Radford, eds, *William Allingham: A Diary* (1907), p. 55.
43. A. Lang, *Alfred Tennyson* (Edinburgh and London, 1901), p. 80.
44. J. Dixon Hunt, ed., *In Memoriam: A Casebook* (London, 1970), p. 100.
45. Shannon, *Tennyson and the Reviewers*, p. 142.

6   MARRIAGE AND FARRINGFORD

1. C. R. Sanders, 'Carlyle and Tennyson', *PMLA* LXXVI (1961), 87.
2. W. Ward, *Aubrey de Vere* (1904), p. 87.
3. F. Hill, 'The Cracroft Diary', *TRB*, III, i (1977), 27–8.
4. H. D. Rawnsley, *Memories of the Tennysons* (1900), p. 71.
5. J. O. Hoge, *Letters of Emily Tennyson* (1974), p. 44.
6. R. B. Martin, *Tennyson: The Unquiet Heart* (1980), p. 332.
7. J. O. Hoge, *Letters of Emily Tennyson*, p. 46.
8. T. Bliss, ed., *Thomas Carlyle: Letters to his Wife* (1953), p. 271.
9. J. O. Hoge, *Letters of Emily Tennyson*, p. 46.
10. J. Knowles, 'Aspects of Tennyson: II', *Nineteenth Century* XXXIII (1893), 167.
11. J. O. Hoge, *Letters of Emily Tennyson*, p. 54.
12. F. D. Maurice, *Theological Essays* (Cambridge, 1853), p.v.
13. J. D. Jump, *Tennyson: The Critical Heritage* (1967), pp. 184–5.
14. F. W. Robertson, *Lectures, Addresses etc.* (1876), pp. 314–5.
15. A. M. Terhune and A. B. Terhune, *Letters of Edward Fitzgerald* (1980), II, 83.
16. E. F. Shannon, 'Tennyson's "Ode on the Death of the Duke of Wellington"', *Studies in Bibliography*, XIII (1960), 152.

17. C. Y. Lang, *Tennyson's Arthurian Psycho-Drama*, Tennyson Society Occasional Paper (Lincoln, 1983).
18. H. Tennyson, *Materials for a Life of A. T.* (privately printed), II, 367.
19. F. T. Palgrave, Tours with Alfred Tennyson, manuscript, TRC.
20. P. Waddington, *Tennyson and Russia*, Tennyson Society Monograph (Lincoln, 1987).
21. J. Knowles, 'Aspects of Tennyson: II', p. 182.
22. W. H. Russell, *Despatches from the Crimea: 1854–56*, ed. N. Bentley (London, 1966), p. 31.
23. Ibid, p. 155.
24. *The Times*, 13 November 1854, p. 6.
25. *The Times*, 15 November 1854, p. 7.
26. T. Pinney, ed., *Essays of George Eliot* (London, 1963), pp. 190–1.
27. Ibid, pp. 193 and 197.
28. Quoted in J. Woolford, *Browning the Revisionary* (London, 1988), p. 84.
29. J. D. Jump, *Tennyson: The Critical Heritage*, p. 246.
30. Letter of 29 December 1855, TRC.
31. See D. Culler, 'Monodrama and the Dramatic Monologue', *PMLA*, XC (1975), 366–85.
32. O. Doughty and J. R. Wahl, *Letters of D. G. Rossetti*, (Oxford, 1965), I, 281.
33. C. Tennyson, *Alfred Tennyson* (1949), p. 289.

7 TENNYSON AND THE ARTS

1. W. Ward, *Aubrey de Vere* (1904), p. 227.
2. W. M. Rossetti, *The PRB Journal*, ed. W. E. Fredeman (Oxford, 1975), p. 72.
3. M. Lutyens, ed., 'Letters from John Everett Millais', *Walpole Society*, XLIV (1972–4), 15.
4. W. H. Hunt, *Pre-Raphaelitism and the Pre-Raphaelite Brotherhood* (London, 1905–6), II, 124–5.
5. O. Doughty and J. R. Wahl, *Letters of D. G. Rossetti* (Oxford, 1965), I, 239.
6. E. Tennyson, incomplete letter, no date [1857], Bodleian Library f. 146.
7. J. O. Hoge, ed., *Letters of Emily Tennyson* (1974), p. 120.
8. H. Tennyson, ed., *Tennyson and his Friends* (1911), p. 292.
9. Letter of 27 October 1860, TRC.
10. See L. Ormond, *Tennyson and Thomas Woolner*, Tennyson Society Monograph (1981).
11. M. N. Cohen, ed., *Letters of Lewis Carroll*, (London, 1979), I, 34.
12. D. Du Maurier and D. P. Whiteley, eds, *The Young George Du Maurier*, (London, 1951), p. 112.
13. L. Ormond, 'George Frederic Watts: The Portraits of Tennyson', *TRB*, IV, ii (1983), 48.
14. Ibid, p. 49.
15. Ibid, p. 50.
16. A. Rose, ed., *The Germ*, (Birmingham, 1984), p. xxvii.

17. W. H. Hunt, *Pre-Raphaelitism and the Pre-Raphaelite Brotherhood* II, 172.
18. H. Allingham and E. B. Williams, *Letters to William Allingham*, (London, 1911), p. 104.

8 THE 1860s

1. H. F. Brown, *Letters and Papers of John Addington Symonds*, (London, 1923), p. 2.
2. Ibid, pp. 3–4.
3. H. Dyson and C. Tennyson, *Dear and Honoured Lady* (1969), p. 85.
4. L. Ormond, *Tennyson and Thomas Woolner* (1981), p. 24.
5. V. Noakes, *Edward Lear* (London, 1968, rev. edn 1985), p. 198.
6. H. Nicolson, *Tennyson* (1923), p. 200.
7. W. H. Hunt, *Pre-Raphaelitism and the Pre-Raphaelite Brotherhood* (London, 1905–6), II, 211–12.
8. Palgrave, Tours with Alfred Tennyson, TRC.
9. F. T. Palgrave to Emily Tennyson, 2 October 1860, TRC; see J. Bronkhurst, 'Asparagus Island', *The Pre-Raphaelites*, Tate Gallery Exhibition Catalogue (London, 1984), p. 292. The 'wooded landscape' is unidentified.
10. W. H. Hunt, *Pre-Raphaelitism and the Pre-Raphaelite Brotherhood* II, 212 and 206.
11. G. Palgrave, *F. T. Palgrave* (1899), p. 63.
12. Palgrave, Tours with Tennyson, TRC.
13. H. Tennyson, *Tennyson and his Friends* (1911), p. 146.
14. K. Tillotson, 'Palgrave's *Golden Treasury* and Tennyson: Another Source', *TRB*, V, ii (1988), 49–54.
15. N. Page, *Tennyson: Interviews and Recollections* (1983), p. 46.
16. R. M. Ogilvie, *Latin and Greek* (London, 1964), p. 156.
17. H. Allingham and D. Radford, eds, *William Allingham: A Diary* (1907), pp. 93 and 94.
18. H. F. Brown, ed., *Letters and Papers of J. A. Symonds* (1923), p. 9.
19. H. Tennyson, *Materials for a Life of A. T.* (privately printed), II, 369.
20. W. Bagehot, 'Wordsworth, Tennyson and Browning', *National Review*, New Series I (1864), 27–66.
21. M. Shaw, *Alfred Lord Tennyson* (1988), pp. 66–70.
22. J. Bristow, ed., *The Victorian Poet: Poetics and Persona* (1987), p. 166.
23. See E. F. Shannon, 'The Publication of Tennyson's "Lucretius"', *Studies in Bibliography*, XXXIV (1981), 146–86.
24. M. Shaw, *Alfred Lord Tennyson* p. 128.
25. K. Tillotson, 'Rugby 1850: Arnold, Clough, Walrond, and *In Memoriam*', *Review of English Studies*, IV, xiv (1953), pp. 122–40.
26. H. Lowry, ed., *Letters of M. Arnold to A. H. Clough*, (Oxford, 1932), pp. 63 and 145.
27. H. Tennyson, ed., *Tennyson and his Friends* (1911), p. 204.
28. R. Collins, ed., 'Recollections of Tennyson by Sir George Prothero', *Victorian Newsletter* no 66 (1984), 30.
29. *The Autobiography of Sir Henry Taylor* (London, 1885), II, 193–4.

30. A. Tennyson, 'Talks and Walks', manuscript. TRC.
31. J. Bristow, *The Victorian Poet: Poetics and Persona* pp. 140–1.
32. P. Metcalf, *James Knowles* (1980), p. 257.

9   ALDWORTH AND THE LATER IDYLLS

1. P. Metcalf, *James Knowles* (1980), p. 205.
2. G. S. Haight, ed., *The George Eliot Letters*, (New Haven, 1955), V, 169.
3. P. Metcalf, *James Knowles*, p. 213.
4. H. Tennyson, *Tennyson's Creed*, Tennyson Society (Lincoln, 1974), p. 7.
5. W. Knight, 'A Reminiscence of Tennyson', *Blackwood's Magazine*, CLXII (1897), 268.
6. H. Tennyson, *Tennyson's Creed*, p. 7.
7. P. Metcalf, *James Knowles*, p. 259.
8. J. W. Mackail, *William Morris* (1899; World's Classics edition, Oxford 1950), p. 308.
9. E. Lytton, *Life of Edward Bulwer, First Lord Lytton* (London, 1913), II, 431.
10. H. Allingham and D. Radford, *William Allingham: A Diary* (1907), 146.
11. P. Metcalf, James Knowles, p. 340.
12. Ibid, p. 341.

10   HISTORY AND DRAMA

1. H. Tennyson, *Materials for a Life of A. T.* (privately printed), III, 237.
2. L. Masterman, ed., *Mary Gladstone: Diaries and Letters* (1930), p. 111.
3. *Illustrated London News*, 8 January 1881, p. 31.
4. *Punch*, 25 November 1882, p. 244.
5. *Illustrated London News*, 18 November 1882, p. 514.

11   TURNING AGAIN HOME

1. W. B. Yeats, *Collected Poems* (London, 1955), p. 370.
2. F. W. Dupee, *Henry James: Autobiography*, (1956), pp. 588–9.
3. R. Collins, ed., 'Recollections of Tennyson by Sir George Prothero', *Victorian Newsletter* no. 66 (1984), p. 31.
4. N. Page, *Tennyson: Interviews and Recollections* (1983), p. 113.
5. H. Tennyson, letters to E. Tennyson, 22 and 26 August 1873, TRC.
6. L. Masterman, ed., *Mary Gladstone: Diaries and Letters*, p. 157.
7. Ibid, p. 158.
8. Ibid, p. 220.
9. H. Tennyson, *Materials for a Life of A. T.* (privately printed), IV, 73.
10. J. S. Hagen, *Tennyson and his Publishers* (1979), p. 161.

Bibliography

WORKS PRIMARILY CONCERNED WITH TENNYSON

Campbell, Nancie, (ed.), *Tennyson in Lincoln: A Catalogue of the Collections in the Research Centre*, 2 vols (Lincoln: Tennyson Society, 1971–3).

Colley, Ann, *Tennyson and Madness*, (Athens, Georgia, 1983).

Culler, A. Dwight, *The Poetry of Tennyson*, (New Haven, 1977).

Dean, Dennis, *Tennyson and Geology*, (Lincoln: Tennyson Society, 1985).

Gliserman, Susan, 'Early Victorian Science Writers and Tennyson's *In Memoriam*: A Study in Cultural Exchange', *Victorian Studies*, XVIII (1975) 277–308 and 437–59.

Hagen, June Steffenson, *Tennyson and his Publishers*, (London, 1979).

Hill, Francis, 'The Disinheritance Tradition Reconsidered', *TRB* III, ii (1973), 41–54.

Hoge, James, O., (ed.), *Lady Tennyson's Journal*, (Charlottesville, 1981).

_____, (ed.), *The Letters of Emily Lady Tennyson*, (University Park, 1974).

Jenkins, Elizabeth, *Tennyson and Dr. Gully*, (Lincoln: Tennyson Society, 1974).

Jordan, Elaine, *Alfred Tennyson*, (Cambridge, 1988).

Jump, John D., *Tennyson: the Critical Heritage*, (London, 1967).

Killham, John, *Tennyson and the Princess: Reflections of an Age*, (London, 1958).

Knies, Earl A., (ed.), *Tennyson at Aldworth: the Diary of James Henry Mangles*, (Athens, Georgia, 1984).

Knowles, James, 'A Personal Reminiscence', *Nineteenth Century*, XXXIII (1893), 164–88.

Lang, Cecil Y., *Tennyson's Arthurian Psycho-Drama*, (Lincoln: Tennyson Society, 1983).

Lang, Cecil Y. and Shannon, Edgar F. Jr (eds), *The Letters of Alfred Lord Tennyson*. 3 vols, (Oxford, 1981–1990).

Martin, Robert Bernard, *Tennyson: The Unquiet Heart*, (Oxford, 1980).

Mattes, Eleanor, *In Memoriam: The Way of a Soul*, (New York, 1951).

Millhauser, Milton, *Fire and Ice: The Influence of Science on Tennyson's Poetry*, (Lincoln: Tennyson Society, 1971).

_____, 'Tennyson's *Princess* and *Vestiges*', *PMLA*, LXI (1954), 337–43.

Ormond, Leonée, *Tennyson and the Old Masters*, (Lincoln: Tennyson Society, 1989).

_____, *Tennyson and Woolner*, (Lincoln: Tennyson Society, 1981).

Paden, W. D., *Tennyson in Egypt: A Study of the Imagery in his Earlier Work*, Lawrence, 1942).

Page, Norman, (ed.), *Tennyson: Interviews and Recollections*, (Totowa, 1983).

Palmer, D. J., (ed.), *Tennyson*. (Writers and their Background, London, 1973).

Peters, Robert, (ed.), *Letters to a Tutor: The Tennyson family letters to Henry Graham Dakyns: 1861–1911*, (Metuchen, 1988).

Pitt, Valerie, *Tennyson Laureate*, (London, 1962).

Rader, Ralph, *Tennyson's Maud: the Biographical Genesis*, (Berkeley, 1963).
Rawnsley, H. D., *Glimpses of the Tennysons*, (Glasgow, 1900).
Redpath, Theodore, 'Tennyson and the literature of Greece and Rome', in H. Tennyson, (ed.), *Studies in Tennyson*, (London, 1981).
Ricks, Christopher, *Tennyson*, (London, 1972; rev. edn 1989).
Sanders, C. R., 'Carlyle and Tennyson', *PMLA*, LXXVI (1961), 82–97.
Scott, P. G., '"Flowering in a lonely word": Tennyson and the Victorian Study of Language', *Victorian Poetry*, XVIII (1980–1), 371–81.
_____, *Tennyson's Enoch Arden: a Victorian Best-Seller*, (Lincoln: Tennyson Society, 1970).
Shatto, Susan, (ed.) *Tennyson's Maud: A Definitive Edition*, (London, 1986).
Shatto, Susan and Shaw, Marion, (eds), *Tennyson: In Memoriam*, (Oxford, 1982).
Shaw, Marion, *Alfred Lord Tennyson*, (Hemel Hempstead, 1988).
Shannon, Edgar J. Jr, *Tennyson and the Reviewers*, (Cambridge, Mass., 1952).
Sinfield, Alan, *Alfred Tennyson*, (Oxford, 1986).
_____, *The Language of Tennyson's In Memoriam*, (Oxford, 1971).
Tennyson, Charles, *Alfred Tennyson*, (London, 1949).
Tennyson, Charles and Dyson, Hope (eds), *Dear and Honoured Lady: The Correspondence of Queen Victoria and Alfred Tennyson*, (London, 1969).
Tennyson, Charles and Dyson, Hope, *The Tennysons: Background to Genius*, (London, 1974).
Tennyson, Hallam, *Materials for a life of Alfred Tennyson*. 4 vols, (privately printed).
_____, *Tennyson: A Memoir*, 2 vols, (London, 1897).
_____, (ed.), *Tennyson and his friends*, (London, 1911).
Tennyson Research Bulletin, (Lincoln: Tennyson Society, 1967–).
Timko, Michael, *Carlyle and Tennyson*, (London, 1988).
Waddington, Patrick, *Tennyson and Russia*, (Lincoln: Tennyson Society, 1987).
Waller, John O., *A Circle of Friends: The Tennysons and the Lushingtons*, (Columbus, 1986).
Weld, A. G., *Glimpses of Tennyson*, (London, 1903).
Wheatcroft, Andrew, *The Tennyson Album*, (London, 1980).
Wickens, G. Glen, 'Two Sides of Early Victorian Science and the Unity of *The Princess*', *Victorian Studies*, XXIII (1980), 369–88.

BACKGROUND WORKS

Allen, Peter, *The Cambridge Apostles: the Early Years*, (Cambridge, 1978).
Allingham, Helen and Radford, D., (eds) *William Allingham: A Diary: 1824–1889*, (London, 1907).
Armstrong, Isobel, *Victorian Scrutinies: Reviews of Poetry: 1830–1870*, (London, 1972).
Attridge, Derek, *The Rhythms of English Poetry*, (London, 1982).
Bristow, Joseph, *The Victorian Poet: Poetics and Persona*, (London, 1987).
Chadwick, Owen, *The Victorian Church*. Part One 1829–1859, Part Two 1860–1901, (London, 1967 and 1970).

Hallam, Henry, (ed.) *Remains in Verse and Prose of Arthur Henry Hallam*, (London, 1863).

_____, *Writings*, ed. T. H. V. Motter, (Modern Language Association of America, New York, 1943).

Houghton, Walter, *The Victorian Frame of Mind*, (New Haven, 1957).

Kelley, Philip and Hudson, Ronald, (eds), *The Brownings' Correspondence*, (Winfield, 1984–)

Knight, David, *The Age of Science: the Scientific World View in the Nineteenth Century*, (Oxford, 1985).

Kolb, Jack, (ed.), *The Letters of Arthur Henry Hallam* (Columbus, 1981).

Metcalf, Priscilla, *James Knowles*, (Oxford, 1980).

Palgrave, G. F., *F. T. Palgrave*, (London, 1899).

Raymond, M. and Sullivan, M. R. (eds), *The Letters of Elizabeth Barrett Browning to Mary Russell Mitford*, 3 vols (Waco, 1983).

Rupke, Nicholas, *The Great Chain of Being: William Buckland and the English School of Geology: 1814–1849*, (Oxford, 1983).

Simpson, Roger, *Camelot Regained* (Cambridge, 1990).

Srebrnik, Patricia, *Alexander Strahan*, (Ann Arbor, 1986).

Terhune, A. K. and A. B., *The Letters of Edward Fitzgerald*, 4 vols (Princeton, 1980)

Turner, Frank, *The Greek Heritage in Victorian Britain*, (New Haven, 1981).

Index